A Star-Crossed
Golden Age

A Star-Crossed Golden Age

Myth and the Spanish *Comedia*

Edited by
Frederick A. de Armas

Lewisburg
Bucknell University Press
London: Associated University Presses

Associated University Presses
440 Forsgate Drive
Cranbury, NJ 08512

Associated University Presses
16 Barter Street
London WC1A 2AH, England

Associated University Presses
P.O. Box 338, Port Credit
Mississauga, Ontario
Canada L5G 4L8

The paper used in this publication meets the requirements of the American National Standard for Permanence of Paper for Printed Library Materials Z39.48–1984.

Library of Congress Cataloging-in-Publication Data

A star-crossed Golden Age : myth and the Spanish comedia / edited by Frederick A. de Armas.
    p. cm.
Includes bibliographical references and index.
ISBN 0-8387-5376-0 (alk. paper)
    1. Spanish drama—Classical period, 1500–1700—History and criticism. 2. Mythology in literature. I. De Armas, Frederick Alfred.
PQ6106.S73   1998
862'.309—dc21   97-39644
                                         CIP

Contents

Preface

THIS volume grew out of an NEH Institute held at Penn State University in June and July of 1994. The faculty, the director, and a number of the participants expressed the desire to record and further the discussions and insights of that summer. This institute offered an introduction to one of the least known "Golden Ages" of the theater (Spanish drama from 1580 to 1680), in the context of its Italian Renaissance models and of its successors in other European literatures. The Institute (and consequently this book) have been entitled "A Star-Crossed Golden Age" to reflect the tension between the artistic and political situations of the period: the *comedia* gained prominence at a time when the Spanish empire was beginning to decline. Playwrights such as Calderón de la Barca and Lope de Vega mirror both the dream of empire and the threat of its fall through the use of mythology. This book seeks to develop the link between mythology and the *comedia* through a number of approaches. These include the use of astrology, cartomancy, pre-Socratic elemental cosmology, iconography, hagiography, metamorphoses, Jungian principles, Lacanian psychoanalysis, the philosophy of Schopenhauer, Santayana's poetics, syncretism, gender studies, and Vedic theories. Indeed, the title of the collection also reflects the relationship between the heavens and the sublunary world as encountered both in the ancient ptolemaic system and the *comedia*.

For centuries, the presence of the pagan gods in the *comedia* was regarded as mere adornment, and the proliferation of mythological spectacle plays performed at the Spanish court was seen as a trivial exercise in praise of a monarch. Both of these critical attitudes have been set aside during the past twenty years as mythological plays have undergone intense scrutiny and the mythological substructure of many other *comedias* has been foregrounded. This volume is particularly concerned with the second question, the mythological structure of Golden Age theater, although some mythological spectacle plays as well as sacramental plays based on mythology are also discussed. As Charles Ganelin has stated, myth is the stuff of which the *comedia* is made. But why would these plays rely so heavily on classical mythology? To what texts did the playwrights turn in order to bring the gods into their *comedias?* How are these models used? How are we to find mythological structures in plays where classical allusions are a commonplace? And finally what is the function of mythological characters and allusions in the *comedia?* Do they serve to discuss matters of power, gender, or ideology? Do they reflect Renaissance syncretism or medieval allegorizing? Some of these questions will be broached in this volume, which is intended as an introduction to the topic. It is hoped that future studies will continue to address these and other questions.

The pagan gods survived the Christian Middle Ages and flourished in the Renaissance in a number of guises and disguises. The well-known studies of Jean Seznec, Edgar Wind, and Leonard Barkan have given us a comprehensive view of these transformations. Many if not all of these metamorphoses can be located in the Golden Age theater. Starting in late classical antiquity, the stories of the gods and heroes of Greece and Rome came to be regarded as allegories. Christian writers sought to make classical literature palatable to pious prelates and their followers through a series of allegorizations that rendered them as examples of Christian ideas or showed how the tales hid through fiction important moral truths or physical phenomena. The latter would tie in with Medieval and Renaissance acceptance of the ancients in matters of science and philosophy. But, during the Renaissance, myths were believed to contain veiled truths, truths that pointed to the Christian God as the originator of these fables. While these Neoplatonic syncretic interpretations proliferated, there was also a movement directed towards origins, towards the representation of the pagan gods in their classical guise. Realizing the vast gap between the ancient world and the Renaissance, poets strove through humanistic learning (including archeology and the study of ancient languages and cultures) to approach the great ancient authorities such as Homer and Virgil for the epic, Sophocles and Seneca for tragedy, and Ovid and Heliodorus for tales and stratagems of love and desire. Indeed, Ovid's myriad metamorphoses became, according to Leonard Barkan, the focus for the continuation of the counterreligion of paganism. His metamorphoses became not only ways to show inner conflict and transformation, but they could lead to two extreme views: Pythagorean metempsychosis and pessimistic mutability. The magical and numinous universe of the ancients along with their satirical and materialistic/atomistic view of the cosmos was replicated by many a Renaissance writer. While some strove for syncretism, the joining of classical and Christian ideals, others decried the continued intrusion of the pagan within the Christian. And yet, there was little that could be done to erase remnants of ancient belief and traces of the classical pantheon: the zodiac, the planets, and even the days of the week were named after the pagan gods. Classical literature and philosophy carried with it almost unsurpassed authority while at European courts monarchs strove to compare themselves to ancient gods and heroes.

Translations of the classical writers into Spanish (from Gonzalo Pérez's translation of Homer's *Odyssey* [1556] to Jorge de Bustamante's popular version of Ovid's *Metamorphoses* [1543?]) did much to inspire the poets and playwrights of the Golden Age. But so did manuals of mythology such as those by Juan Pérez de Moya and Baltasar de Vitoria which were replete with Medieval allegories and Renaissance visions of ancient deities. While Lope de Vega sought to reject classical principles in his *Arte nuevo de hacer comedias* (*New Art of Writing Plays*), he did so with a thorough knowledge of these principles and with ample quotations from ancient writers and Renaissance commentators. Although Lope may have been guilty of what Thomas Greene labels as "Leonardo's heresy"—a resistance to imitate the ancients, countering it with a desire to follow "nature"—his works are filled with classical minutiae. As for Calderón, his many plays based on classical mythology reflect the court's desire to emulate the ancients. Juan de Pineda's syncretism will be echoed by Calderón in his later *autos* (sacramental plays). It should thus come as no surprise that even the representation of Christian saints in the *comedia* was "tainted" with paganism. Spanish playwrights would use mythology to deepen, embellish, exalt, and even authorize saintly deeds, mighty rulers, heroic actions, and the power of love. Indeed, mythology was often viewed as veiling truths that ought to be "revealed" again and again.

A Star-Crossed Golden Age is divided into four sections. The first takes up the "physical tradition," which, according to Jean Seznec, connects astral bodies with the ancient gods. But, as will be shown in this volume, this physical tradition goes well beyond astrology to connect the pagan deities with the four elements out of which the world was thought to be composed. These gods will also be connected to different forms of magic and divination including cartomancy. In the first article, Lope de Rueda's famous interlude *Las aceitunas* (*The Olives*) is examined from the perspective of the pre-Socratic elemental theories, showing how each of

the four key objects at the beginning of the interlude stands for
one of the four elements. Then this elemental weave is linked
with the contest between two goddesses, Juno and Minerva, in
order to show how each represents a different view of woman in
society. While Juno stands for traditional marital roles, Minerva
expresses the belief that woman can go beyond her place as a
homemaker and become active in the economy of the household
and even in the creation of artistic works. Francisco J. Martín also
foregrounds the link between elemental theory and myth in his
study of *El burlador de Sevilla* (*The Trickster of Seville*). He explains
that without *burladas* (deceived/dishonored women)—either willing participants or not—there would be no *burlador* (trickster).
Through an insightful analysis of the elemental makeup of the
four female characters Tisbea (water), doña Ana (air), Isabela
(fire), and Aminta (earth), Martín traces don Juan's transforma-
tion/metamorphosis from a "hombre sin nombre" (man without
a name) to the "burlador de Sevilla" (trickster of Seville). Turning
to cartomancy as another way to contact the ancient gods or
demons, Ron Friis explores the concept of life through death as
Hermetic *pharmakon* in Cervantes's *La Numancia*. Through an
analysis of the archetypal images of the Tarot he shows how the
fate of the city is inscribed in a reading of these cards. The last
essay in this section is an example of the more commonly accepted interpretation of the physical tradition. Here, Carolyn Nadeau explores the astrological and mythological underpinnings
of the García-Lucrecia-Jacinta love triangle in Alarcón's *La verdad
sospechosa* (*Suspect Truth*) in order to evince the importance of both
Diana/Luna and Sol/Apollo in the dynamics of desire within
the play.
   The second section is entitled "The Metamorphic Tradition,"
thus following Leonard Barkan's use of this phenomenon as met-
onym for the classical world. The first article in this section serves
as a bridge since it includes elements from the physical tradition.
In this essay, Nancy Mayberry uncovers four metamorphic myths
(Apollo-Daphne, Chloris-Flora, Venus-Adonis, Venus-Mars) in
Blas Fernández de Mesa's *La fundadora de la Santa Concepción* (*The
Founder of the Holy Conception*). She also explores the role of the
two horoscopes in the play and analyzes the color and flower
symbology that decorate Beatriz's transformation into the
founder of the order of the Santa Concepción. This is one of two
essays that foregrounds the astonishing mixture of hagiography
and myth in the *comedia*. Christopher Weimer's essay includes
one of the metamorphic myths found in Mayberry's piece. In-

stead of focusing on the much treated theme of *privanza* in Tirso de Molina's *Privar contra su gusto* (*The Reluctant Royal Favorite*), Weimer's study explores Tirso's imitation (and rewriting) of Ovid's *Metamorphoses*. He describes King Fadrique's pursuit of Leonora de Cardona in terms of Daphne's flight from Apollo and Juan and Isabel's romance in terms of the Diana-Acteon story in order to analyze questions of power, desire, and gender. Weimer also shows how metamorphoses served to represent the characters' "psychological and emotional evolution." Questions of gender, which had been broached by Weimer, become the focus of Anita Stoll's survey of the myth of Achilles in the *comedia*. Gender confusion in Tirso de Molina's *El Aquiles* (*Achilles*), Cristóbal de Monroy's *El caballero dama* (*The Gentleman as Lady*) and *Héctor y Aquiles* (*Hector and Achilles*) and Calderón's *El monstruo de los jardines* (*The Monster of the Gardens*) and *Las manos blancas no ofenden* (*White Hands do not Offend*) allow her to compare and contrast the treatment of man-woman relations in these plays and to show how gender differentiation is central to classical mythology and Golden Age theater. For the fourth and last chapter of this section, Thomas A. O'Connor has graciously made available his published essay on Calderón's *El monstruo de los jardines* which was a topic of discussion at the institute. His insights on Calderón's use of mythology have been utilized by several authors in this volume.

The third section of the book focuses on woman as pagan goddess in the plays of the Spanish Golden Age. Hayden Duncan-Irvin divides myth into categories and connects these with the threefold nature of the goddess Diana in Lope de Vega's *El perro del hortelano* (*The Dog in the Manger*). She also offers a Lacanian interpretation of Diana's function in the honor driven environment of Naples. The second essay by Gordon Sumner illuminates the relationship between Astraea, goddess of chastity, truth, and justice and Casilda in Lope's *Santa Casilda,* calling for a critical reappraisal of all the *comedias de santos* (saints plays). Indeed, this essay, like Mayberry's, foregrounds the curious connection between hagiography and mythology. The final essay in this section is by Darci Strother. She deals with the sources of the myth of the *serrana* (mountain woman) in Vélez de Guevara's *La serrana de la Vera* (*The Mountain Woman from Vera*). The article focuses on Gila's dual gender role and shows how she creates her own myth through her deeds.

The fourth and last section of the book is dedicated to Calderón de la Barca. The three articles discuss three different types of plays: mythological spectacle plays, courtly metaphysical drama and sacramental plays. María Esther C. de Moux delves into duality using Jung's theories and Hermetic principles. She explores astral myths and their presence in emblems as seen in Calderón's *La estatua de Prometeo* (*Prometheus's Statue*). Timothy Ambrose turns to ancient conceptions of theater to discover the nature of labyrinths in Borges and Calderón's *La vida es sueño* (*Life is a Dream*). He shows, for example, the relationship between the Minotaur's name (Asterion) and that of the goddess of the Golden Age (Astraea). By foregrounding a number of paradoxes within the mythological subtexts of the play, Ambrose is able to delve into questions of *maya* and infinity with the aid of Vedic principles and Schopenhauer's philosophy. The last essay by Daniel L. Heiple takes up the two versions of the Orpheus myth in Calderón's sacramental plays showing how they represent Christian "truth" in very different ways. In the earlier play, myth is not seen as intrinsically containing veiled truths. Allegory is simply used as metaphor for truth. The second *auto*, on the other hand, specifically argues for Renaissance syncretism, that is, the veiled presence of Christian revelations within the myth itself.

In conclusion, I would like to express my appreciation to all of those who made this volume possible. My thanks to Ron Friis for his editorial assistance. Without the support of the National Endowment for the Humanities, this project would not have been possible. I would like to recognize the assistance of those who helped me put together the Institute: the Department of Spanish, Italian, and Portuguese, headed by Leon Lyday, and the College of Liberal Arts (Dean Susan Welch and Baiba Briedis). I would also like to recognize the faculty of the Institute: Daniel L. Heiple, Amilcare A. Iannucci, Melveena McKendrick, Thomas A. O'Connor, Didier Souiller, and Henry Sullivan. Chapter seven has been previously published. I would like to thank University Press of America for permission to include a revised version of Thomas O'Connor's essay. Translations of cited passages are made by the authors of the individual articles, unless noted.

A Star-Crossed
Golden Age

Part 1
The Physical Tradition

Juno's Tempest and Minerva's Weave:
The Elemental Disquiet of Lope de Rueda's
Las aceitunas

Frederick A. de Armas

Although Lope de Rueda's interlude *Las aceitunas* (*The Olives*) has been generally regarded as a canonical text and has consistently been included in histories and anthologies of Golden Age theater, the amount of critical discourse on this *paso* is surprisingly sparse. Perhaps its apparently anecdotal and humorous nature has been a stumbling block for lengthy essays on the piece. As Angel Valbuena Prat once put it:

> El mundo cómico de Rueda carece de las complejidades ideológicas de un Gil Vicente o un Sebastián de Horozco. . . . El batihoja pensaba en un auditorio apartado de toda especulación intelectual . . . Por esto las situaciones de los pasos son simplemente motivos del pueblo para producir la risa, sin la menor complicación espiritual. (1. 829–30)

> [Rueda's comic world lacks the ideological complexity of a Gil Vicente or a Sebastián de Horozco . . . The goldsmith was writing for an audience far removed from any intellectual specualtions . . . Due to this fact, the situations presented in the interludes are driven simply from the author's desire to make people laugh without any spiritual complications whatsoever.]

Now that two new editions of Lope's *pasos* have appeared (Canet Vallés [1992], González Ollé and Tusón [1992]) as well as an English translation (Listerman), it may be time to take a careful look at this well-known text.

Questioning whether the interlude is simply part of the popular theater of the age or whether it contains erudite elements, José Luis Canet Vallés reminds us that "la risa tiene una estructura definida, perfectamente documentada en los manuales retóricos y poéticos" (laughter has a well-defined structure, clearly documented in manuals of rhetoric and poetics") (34). Furthermore, the *pasos* seem to have a direct connection with another well-known literary tradition. Oriental in origin, the tale is found in the *Calila e Dimna* in the seventh *exemplo* of *El conde Lucanor* and in Gil Vicente's *Auto de Mofina Mendes* (Valbuena Prat 1. 830). Noting that most critical studies of *Las aceitunas* indicate its debt to Don Juan Manuel, F. González Ollé turns to this and other instances of the plot claiming that the Oriental tale "de ningún modo puede entrar en la categoría de *fuente*" (can by no means be considered a source, per se) (45). Also discounting Italian sources, González Ollé concludes that the episodes and events of these interludes gather meaning from "determinados motivos del folklore literario universal" (certain motifs from universal literary folklore) (45), thus rejecting the importance of a literary or erudite tradition as key to the *paso.* Indeed, Valbuena Prat, although pointing to the literary tradition, claims that *Las aceitunas* is a "sencilla aportación al tema" (a simple contribution to the theme) (1. 830). Consequently there is a debate whether the *paso* contains learned or popular elements.

Attempting to explain the simultaneous rise of popular theaters in Spain and England, Walter Cohen sees the parallel phenomena as having a common root: "Spanish and English plays stand apart from all other European drama because they synthesize native popular and neoclassical learned traditions" (17). In this essay I would like to explore the intermingling of folkloric, mythological, and biblical traditions in order to show how the artful weaving of these different strands creates an interlude that is far from primitive, simple, and anecdotal. Rather, it is a piece of consummate artistry where the interweaving of elements provide an intricate design while the contrastive strands add a certain disquiet. Indeed, the elements of which it is composed can be linked to the theory of the four elements proposed by Empedocles, which is part of the accepted vision of sublunary matter during the Renaissance and Golden Age. Through the clash of elements the play foregrounds the disharmony and disquiet that pervades the world.

In spite of its brevity, Lope de Rueda's *Las aceitunas* can be clearly divided into three sections that recall the three act format of the later *comedia nueva:* (a) an introductory section where the conflict is represented, (b) the development of the central anecdote, and (c) a sudden conclusion. Although the interweaving of strands is most obvious in the main section of the text, some of its elements (including the four Empedoclean elements) are also found in the introduction. This initial section of the *paso* is of necessity very brief. For this reason, it must include a technique that will lend concision to the development of character, ideas, and plot, a method of adding complexity and emotion to what may appear to be a very simple conflict. In order to understand how Lope de Rueda was able to achieve his dramatic aims in the introduction with such few words, it will be useful to recall T. S. Eliot's controversial essay on the problems of *Hamlet*, where he claims that the protagonist "cannot objectify" his emotions, something that must happen if the play is to succeed:

> The only way of expressing emotion in the form of art is by finding an objective correlative, in other words, a set of objects, a situation, a chain of events which shall be the formula of that *particular* emotion (100).

In his attempt to elaborate upon the meaning of the "objective correlative,"[1] Eliseo Vivas cites from García Lorca's "Llanto por Ignacio Sánchez Mejías" ("Lament for Ignacio Sánchez Mejías") showing how the poem refers to "objects and situations directly involved in the death" as a means to arouse or express certain emotions. These include the shroud, the moon, the sand, the breeze, and the olive grove (13). These objects are not only meant to arouse emotion. They create a complex set of textual and contextual relationships that enrich *agon*, character, thought, and events. Lope de Rueda's *Las aceitunas* will also utilize a discrete number of objects to create in a very few pages a weave of great complexity. Four key elements or correlative objects will appear in the introduction to the *paso* and lead us, as in García Lorca's poem, to the olive grove.

As subsequent scholarship has discovered, Eliot did not actually coin the phrase "objective correlative." It actually derives from George Santayana,[2] whose statements are more in line with the focus of this essay: "The poet's art is to a great extent the art of intensifying emotions by assembling the scattered objects that naturally arouse them" (263).[3] Since for Santayana, "waking life is a dream controlled" where logical thoughts struggle to dominate, the poet must reverse this trend as she "dips into the chaos that underlines the rational shell of the world and brings up some superfluous image, some emotion dropped by the way, and reattaches it to the present object" (261). This bringing together of scattered objects with their lost significance serves to create "new structures, richer, finer, fitter to the primary tendencies of our nature" (263). Although Lope de Rueda's *paso* appears to be a short prose work that serves to arouse laughter, it actually follows Santayana's poetic road since the text searches for the primary in the forgotten gods of Greece and Rome and develops structures out of their elemental qualities.

The interlude begins with the arrival of Toruvio soaking wet from a storm. Like the breeze in García Lorca, the "tempestad" (storm) (177)[4] of Lope de Rueda becomes an object out of which emanates both meaning and emotion. It becomes an objective correlative for the emotional storm that will shortly be unleashed—the conflict between Toruvio and his wife Agueda. The cosmic nature of the conflict is made obvious from the start: "que no parecía sino que el cielo se quería hundir y las nuves venir abaxo!" (It seemed like the sky was sinking and the clouds were tumbling down!) (177).[5] Although the reader/spectator is thus told of the cosmic relevance of the conflict, the actual mythological level will not be revealed until the central section of the *paso*. Frustrated and angry, drenched and hungry, Toruvio turns from the heavenly tempest to his earthly desires—food. He asks: ¿qué os terná aparejado de comer la señora de mi muger?" (I wonder what that wife of mine has cooked up for supper?) (177). But this second element (food) appears to be elusive. It is missing and so is Toruvio's wife, thus increasing the husband's anger and frustration. To the inquiry as to Agueda's whereabouts, the daughter Mencigüela responds that she is at her neighbor's house where she has gone to "ayudar a coser unas madexillas" (helping with some sewing) (178). Here we find the third key object or element of the introduction. While a *madeja* is a skein of thread, it also means "a weak lazy person" or someone who is "confused" (Velázquez 437; Covarrubias 778). From proverbs and deeds derived from popular culture, the reader/spectator comes to perceive the Agueda as lazy and confused. Instead of preparing a meal for the husband according to the prescribed patriarchal ritual, she has gone to visit a friend. Upon returning, Agueda does not attempt to mollify her husband. Instead, she kindles the conflict between them by making fun of his hard work: "ya viene de hacer una negra carguilla de leña" (Here's our Patriarch, bringing a little bundle of wood on his back, so don't touch him) (178). As Ollé and Tusón explain, "negra" here has a "función despectiva o rebajadora" (a belittling or pejorative function) (141). Coupled with the diminutive used for the load the husband carries, the statement is nothing less than a challenge to his work. He naturally responds stressing the heaviness of the load. The "leña" or bundle of wood is the fourth key object of the introduction. It represents work, thus creating an opposition between the lazy Agueda and the hard-working Toruvio. Again through a popular proverb we gain a more complete perspective. According to Covarrubias, in specific contexts "leña" often refers to fights or beatings: "Cargar a uno de leña, darle muchos palos" (To load someone up with firewood, to beat someone up) (761). But the beating is a metaphorical one. It takes place through language.

These four objects are elemental in nature recalling earth, water, air, and fire. They also have numerous other contexts for the sixteenth-century spectator. As S. K. Heninger has asserted, "The pattern of the tetrad is omnipresent, providing a common origin for all natural systems in the world, and thereby interrelating them" (168)—the four seasons, the four humors, the four qualities, and the four ages of the human being are but some of the basic quaternities. It should come as no surprise, then, that there are four characters in Lope de Rueda's *paso*, two males and two females, each probably representing a different humor, a particular season, and the ages of a human being.[6] Although much more could be said of the tetrad in this interlude, my purpose in evoking this Empedoclean construction is to point to the richness acquired by objects and characters through this recuperation of an ancient structure. As noted above, this essay will concentrate on the elemental nature of the objects. The text begins with the tempest or water, continues with food or earth, proceeds with weaving which can represent air, and ends in the wood that is to be used for fire. But these elementals are in turmoil, either through excess, lack, misuse, or conflict. Cosmic disharmony is thus presented through a certain disquiet in human relations and emotions. Furthermore, M. J. Woods has argued that one way in which the elements portray chaos rather than order is through transelemental imagery.[7] When Toruvio once again demands his food, he explains that he is "drenched to the bone" (Listerman 67). The Spanish expression "hecho una sopa d'agua" (made into a soup of water) (179) fuses the first two objects "tempestad" and "comida," water and earth, while "sopa" is itself a mixture of earth (food) and its watery constitution. By utilizing this transelemental imagery, the text signals the beginnings of a verbal fight among husband and wife. The four elemental objects have served as "objective correlatives" arousing the emotions both in the characters and the spectators: "Tempestad" and "leña" reflect disharmony and verbal beating while the lack of food and the "madexillas" point to the character of Agueda and her relationship to her husband. Indeed, the first two objects can also reflect characterization, showing Toruvio as hardworking and determined.

As Carroll B. Johnson explains: "The antagonism between husband and wife is firmly established before the subject of the olives is ever broached. Agueda accuses Toruvio of having neglected to plant them" (7). The introduction has thus set up the conflict. Its object, the olives, seems a most unlikely topic of contention. In fact, Toruvio attempts to mollify his wife by telling her that he has indeed planted the olive tree. As Johnson explains: "Instead of being gratified, Agueda seems miffed by the fact that her husband has indeed remembered to plant the tree. She attacks in a new direction" (7), asking "Y adónde lo plantastes?" (And where did you plant it?) (179). Again Toruvio seeks to pacify his wife explaining that the planted the olive tree: "allí junto a la higuera breval, adonde, si se os acuerda, os di un beso" (Over by that new-bearing fig tree where I first kissed you) (179). These two trees, the olive and the fig become the correlative objects of the central part of the *paso*. There is no question that by bringing up the fig tree Toruvio is attempting to intensify the loving emotions of his wife, since this object is related in his and her mind to a location of love, the place where he kissed her. In his essay on "quickness" included in *Six Memos for the Next Millennium*, Italo Calvino asserts that: "the moment an object appears in a narrative, it is charged with a special force and becomes like the pole of a magnetic field, a knot in the network of invisible relationships. The symbolism of an object may be more or less explicit, but it is always there. We might even say that in a narrative any object is always magic" (33). Furthermore, these objects, when used to the fullest, can provide a quickness in the narrative by being able to convey so many things, so many meanings, so many feelings.

This is precisely what happens in *Las aceitunas*. The mercurial quickness of the dramatic interlude sacrifices nothing to the "concentration and craftsmanship" of Vulcan (Calvino 54). The richness of Rueda's *paso* is brought out through contextualization. It is through the infusion of classical deities and folkloric elements that these arboreal objects become laden with magical significance. Let us begin with the fig tree. In Agustín Moreto's *El desdén con el desdén*, the *gracioso* Polilla describes the relationship between his master Carlos and the haughty princess Diana in terms of a "una breva / en la cima de una higuera" (An early fig, on top of a fig tree) (404–5). Just as boys throw stones at this *breva*, or first fruit of the fig tree, in order to render it more mature and bring it down to consume it, Carlos works on Diana's emotions through the stones of "disdain applied by means of reason" (Exum 21), hoping that Diana/the fig will fall from the tree so that he can enjoy her. In her reexamination of this image, Frances Exum questions if the extended image of the falling fig represents, "the virtual annihilation (consumption) of one party by the other" (46). Her answer is that Polilla's vision "is belied by the conduct of his social superiors" (49). In *Las aceitunas*, like in Polilla's folkloric tale, Toruvio's kiss could represent the stones that make the fruit fall—that lead Agueda to fall for him. But it is clear that in Lope de Rueda's *paso*, like in Moreto's *comedia*, the woman refuses to be consumed by the man.

It is not surprising that Polilla uses the fig as an image of woman's fall.[8] In the Christian tradition, the fig has often been substituted for the biblical apple as the fruit that originated the fall from paradise.[9] Indeed, the fig tree appears over and over again in the Bible and the patristic tradition, as John Freccero has documented.[10] It stands for desire and in biblical terms "all desire is ultimately a desire for God, so all signs point to the Word" (Freccero 23). Toruvio's use of the word "higuera" could be a means to recapture a paradisiacal setting, a land infused by God's presence. The word carries with it both the desire that led to the fall and the attempt to recapture paradise after the fall: "higuera" refers to the remote paradisiacal past (the moment he kissed Agueda under the fig tree). It also points to a future where the fig and the olive can grow side by side—when Toruvio and his wife can again live in harmony. By using this "magical" word he hopes to rekindle the godlike bliss of beginnings in the future. Still, the consumption of the fruit and the objectification of a woman in a patriarchal society stand in the way of harmony. The couple must learn how to live together in peace, respecting each other's being in order to recapture a lost paradise. Freccero's notion that the fig tree as representative of desire is related to "apocalyptic time" (24) will be reflected at the end of the *paso* in the "descent" of a "god" into the world.

Toruvio's desire for perfection in marriage is also brought forth in the play through the association of the fig tree with a classical deity. The fig is sacred to Juno.[11] As goddess of marriage (Conti 128–34), she is "guardian of wedlock bonds" (Virgil, *Aeneid* IV. 59; vol. 1, 401), and thus Toruvio, in evoking the tree, is invoking the goddess and calling upon her protection. He must appeal to her since she has been far from propitious. Let us recall that the play begins with a storm, and Juno is associated with such

weather events—often directed at those who Venus favors. In the
Aeneid (I. 50–64; vol. 1, 245), for example, she persuades the wind
Aeolus to raise a storm against Aeneas (Venus's son) and the
Trojan fleet. But Juno can cause these storms on her own, according to Natale Conti: "tiene la capacidad de promover lluvias y
granizadas" (has the capacity to bring about rains and hail storms)
(132). This is made possible through her association with the element air. When Empedocles codified the four elements he associated each with a different deity[12] (Heninger 170). This linkage
has remained far from stable, different figures from the pagan
pantheon coming to represent specific elements at different times
(Heninger 174). However, Natale Conti, Pierre de La Primaudaye,
and George Sandys[13] are just some of the sixteenth- and
seventeenth-century writers who associate Juno with air. The
storm to which Toruvio refers combines both air and water:
"¡ . . . el cielo se quería hundir y las nuves venir abajo!" (It
seemed like the sky was sinking and the clouds were tumbling
down!) (177).[14] As Conti notes, Juno was raised by Oceanus and
Thetis since "el aire nace de las aguas" (air is born of water) (132).
Rather than Juno's tempest of air and water, Toruvio is hoping
for her blessing in matrimony and for a beneficent rain that will
lead to the growth of his crops. As Conti asserts: "Y cuando
Júpiter se ha inflamado de amor a Juno y la abraza, se multiplican
todo tipo de hierbas y frutos" (And when Jupiter flares with love
for Juno and embraces her, all manner of fruits and grasses
sprout) (132).

It may be Toruvio's wish, as an earthly Jupiter, to embrace his
beloved Agueda as he had once done under the fig tree. But Juno
is not looking upon him in a positive manner. As Alexander S.
Murray states: "Like the sudden and violent storms, however,
which in certain seasons break the peacefulness of the sky of
Greece, the meeting of this divine pair often resulted in temporary quarrels and wranglings, the blame of which was usually
traced to Hera [Juno]" (46). The storm in Lope de Rueda's *paso* is
but a prelude to a tempestuous scene between husband and wife.
It may be that Juno's destructive force—the storm directed at his
marriage—relates not only to Toruvio's actions but also to his
wife's desires. Perhaps, like Murray states, the blame can be
traced to the character who is supposed to mirror Juno. Agueda
does not mirror this goddess. She does not embody the qualities
that Juno expects in a wife. She seems more interested in the
olive than in Juno's tree. At first glance there seems to be no
opposition between these two arboreal figures. Calderón's *La*

humildad coronada de las plantas (*Humility Crowned Among the Plants*) provides the common identification of this tree with peace.[15] It also appears as such in Juan Rodríguez del Padrón's *Siervo libre de amor*.[16] In asking about the olive tree, Agueda could be thinking of peace in the home, just as Toruvio's recollection of the fig tree was a plea for harmony. Indeed, according to Spanish folklore the olive insures the fidelity of the husband (Leach 820). And if we are to pursue the parallel Toruvio/Jupiter, such a talisman would be of great import.[17] In accusing Toruvio of forgetting to plant the olive tree, Agueda may be questioning her husband's whereabouts that day and his fidelity. But Toruvio did plant the tree: "¿Pues en qué me he detenido sino en plantalle como me rogastes?" (Why would I be late if I wasn't planting it as you requested) (179).[18] This statement should bring about the hoped-for peace inherent in the olive and the matrimonial harmony evoked the fig tree. Furthermore, the planting of the olive could recall the olive leaf brought back by the dove, announcing the end of the flood for Noah.[19] This Christian icon could serve to attenuate the pagan tempest in the *paso*. But such is not the case.

It is at this point that Agueda describes her fantasy:

> Que aquel renuevo de azeitunas que plantastes hoy, que de aquí a seis o siete años, llevará cuatro o cinco hanegas de azeitunas. Y que, poniendo plantas acá y plantas acullá, de aquí a veinte y cinco o treinta años, ternéis un olivar hecho y derecho." (179–80)

> [In six or seven years we'll have seven or eight bushels of olives, and if we plant a shoot here and a shoot there, we'll have another entire grove in another twenty-five or thirty years.]

In Christian and biblical traditions, the olive represents prosperity (Smith 468). Agueda seems even more concerned than her husband with financial success. She insists that they sell the olives at "dos reales castellanos" (for two Castilian silver pieces) (180) while the husband is willing to take much less.[20] The couple engage in a brutal battle of words as to the worth of their future crop—the olive harvest to be collected in six or seven years. Their war of words is far from the images of harmony and peace evoked by the fig and the olive. In order to understand Juno's tempest, it must be recalled that the olive was the tree of a rival deity, Minerva.[21] Born from Jupiter's head, she sprung to life "out of the black tempest-cloud, and amidst the roar and crash of a storm" (Murray 89). Thus she is "at once fearful and powerful as a storm" (Murray 89). The play's initial tempest thus represents both Juno's anger and Minerva's birth. The first is angry at Agueda's allegiance, while the second is slowly shaping Agueda into an admirable figure, leading her to a rebirth.

Toruvio views his wife in terms of subservience—Agueda will answer to his every need on returning from the fields. She ought to be preparing dinner rather than wasting her time weaving with a neighbor. And yet, it is Athena/Minerva who "turns to the arts of peace and watches over spinning and weaving in the women's quarters and the pressing of olives in the fields" (Rowan 217). Far from being the lazy wife pictured by Toruvio, Agueda, like Minerva, expands and develops the fields of endeavor that are reserved for women. Her weave represents woman's abilities in the arts. She wishes to take part in the economic development of the household by counseling her husband to plant the olive and to charge more for it when taken to market. As Rowan states, Minerva represents "a balance between matriarchal and patriarchal values" (219). Toruvio, who does not perceive this equilibrium in his wife, rejects her authority in the fields of agriculture and economics, since they traditionally belong to the man. Conti argues that Minerva is a very distinct and unusual goddess since "la sabiduría es muy rara en las mujeres" (wisdom is very rare in women) (239). Toruvio thus resists his wife's counsel since he is supposed to be the wise one, not realizing that Agueda is being shaped by Minerva into becoming a new model for women, one that seeks to establish an equilibrium between patriarchy and matriarchy. Lope de Rueda's *paso* thus dramatizes the clash between a more traditional view of woman represented by Juno and Minerva's wisdom.

Born out of Jupiter's head, that is, out of the elemental fire, she, like Juno, represents air:

> Contaron los egipcios que ésta fue hija de Júpiter y siempre virgen, dado que el aire es de naturaleza incorruptible y ocupa el lugar más alto, por lo que se dice que nació de la cabeza de Júpiter." (Conti 239)

> [The Egyptians believed that she was the daughter of Jupiter and was always a virgin, given that air is pure in its nature and occupies the highest of places, from which it is said that she was born of Jupiter's head.]

The storm is thus a double one in the play. Since woman's wisdom is supposed to be inferior to man's, Toruvio resists Agueda's counsel. But her goddess is higher in the elemental realm than Toruvio's Juno. Both deities are synonymous with air,[22] thus they can both approve of Agueda's weaving. But while Juno's weave is a mere mechanical craft, Minerva's is a remarkable art of which she is the supreme knower. Arachne should have known better than to challenge her.[23] As the inventor of all the arts,[24] Minerva not only deals in the airy flows of thread, but must embody Jupiter's fiery intellect. It is this intellect that can propel her (and Agueda) into new fields. Juno, on the other hand, mixes air with a lower element, the water of the emotions. Two trees, two goddesses, and an elemental structure with its four correlative objects provide this *paso* with a richness and weave unsurpassed at this early moment in Spanish theater. Its mercurial quickness may fool an audience into believing that it lacks Vulcan's methodical craftsmanship. But *Las aceitunas*, as its title indicates, belongs to Minerva. When her sacred olive tree in Athens's Acropolis was thought to have been destroyed, "there sprang suddenly from the root which remained a new shoot, which, with wonderful quickness, grew to a length of three yards, and was looked on as an emblem of the regeneration of the city" (Murray 93). In similar fashion, Lope de Rueda's quickness is far from rustic. Like Vulcan, who helped to bring about the birth of Minerva,[25] the Spanish playwright forges a fiery interlude where a simple weave hides a consummate artistry and where the contest between two goddesses and the elemental disquiet it creates points to the problematics of gender and social interaction. A neighbor, Aloxa, has to intervene in the end to solve the conflict. As a deux ex machina he brings heavenly authority to bear upon the tempest of words. His command is clear: "Ora, andad, vezino; entráos allá adentro y tené paz con vuestra mujer" (And you, Toruvio, go on in and make peace with your wife) (183). Minerva's peace is triumphant,[26] pointing to a new future where the goddess will seek to balance the tensions within a society that has forgotten woman's artistry and wisdom.

Notes

1. "It should now be clear that Eliot hesitates between the following two propositions . . . I) Poetry arouses emotion in the reader; II) The poem expresses emotion" (Vivas 10).

2. Philip Blair Rice goes so far as to assert that Santayana's correlative objects "remind the reader who is versed in contemporary criticism of T. S. Eliot's rather

barbarous key phrase (which he may very well have adopted from Santayana's better one), the 'objective correlative' of an emotion" (271).

3. This statement is discussed in McElderry (179) and in Rice (268).

4. All references to *Las aceitunas* are from González Ollé and Vicente Tusón's edition.

5. Unless otherwise indicated, all translations are from Listerman. This particular translation is my own.

6. Toruvio, described as a "viejo" would be the *senectus* (old age/winter); his wife would represent *iuventus* (maturity/fall); and the daughter *adolescentia* (youth/summer). The neighbor who comes in at the end of the play could well stand for *pueritia* or childhood/spring since his resolution of the conflict brings about what Santayana has called "new structures . . . fitter to the primary tendencies of our nature" (263), that is, a new beginning. For the different theories on the ages of man/woman see Heninger (168–74) and Burrow (12–36).

7. Descriptions of catastrophes such as earthquakes usually make use of transelemental imagery as in Gabriel Bocángel who sees the tremor as waves on the earth. In this manner, "disturbed" imagery reflects disturbances in nature (119).

8. The negative image of woman as a fig to be consumed reaches its culmination in the anecdote of a wife who hung herself on a fig tree. Upon hearing this story, a man from Sicily asks the narrator to give him that tree so that he could plant it in his garden and be rid of his wife. Told by Cicero as a misogynistic joke (*De Oratore* II, lxix), it appears in Zabaleta's *Errores celebrados* where the Spanish writer attempts to temper the misogynistic and patriarchal tale by stating that "El imperio que tiene el marido sobre la mujer no es como el que tiene el dueño en la alhaja sino como el que tiene el alma en el cuerpo" (74). In spite of his protestations Zabaleta still perceives woman as inferior to the man—she is still part of his "imperial" (and material) domain. For other food images in Lope de Rueda, see Nadeau (in press).

9. "El padre Pineda en su libro primero de su Monarquía Eclesiástica, cap. 2, alega muchos autores que afirman el árbol vedado en que Adam pecó aver sido especie de higuera" (Covarrubias 688).

10. Relating how Augustine read of the biblical fig tree while sitting under the shade of one such tree, Freccero asserts: "Behind that fig tree stands a whole series of anterior images pointing backwards to Genesis; Augustine's reader is meant to prolong the trajectory by applying it to his own life and extending it proleptically toward the ending of time. . . . The fig tree, under the shade of which all this takes place, stands for a tradition of textual authority that extends backwards in time to the Logos and forward to the same Logos at time's ending when both desire and words are finally fulfilled" (24–25).

11. "Among the Romans it was sacred and the milk of the wild fig was sacrificed to Juno Caprotina" (Leach 377).

12. Diogenes Laertius reports Empedocles's divisions: "*Jupiter* is *Fire*, *Juno* the *Earth*; *Pluto* the *Air*; and *Nestis* the *Water*" (Heninger 170).

13. See Sandy's title page of his translation of Ovid's *Metamorphoses* (Oxford 1632).

14. Virgil describes a storm created by Juno in words somewhat reminiscent of Toruvio's exclamation. The goddess explains: "esparciré una negra nube mezclada de granizo y agitaré todo el cielo con truenos" (Conti 132; Virgil IV. 120–22; vol. 1, 404–5).

15. Vitoria calls this tree "símbolo de la paz" (symbol of peace) (259).

16. In this sentimental romance, there are three roads related to three trees and three parts of the human being: the heart, the will, and the understanding. The olive is related to the third road: "muy agra y angosta senda qu[e] el siervo entendimiento bien quisiera seguir" (66). The editor of the text thus relates the olive to the peace acquired through the reason and wisdom of Pallas Athena (66).

17. Speaking of the goddess Juno, Vitoria asserts: "Avia mucho de dezir de los celos que tuvo de su marido . . . Pero no fueron sin gran fundamento" (There is much to be said concerning the jealousy she felt towards her husband . . . But these [feelings] were not without foundation) (238).

18. This is my own translation.

19. For discussion of the dove, the olive, and the flood, see Vitoria, 255.

20. "Que basta pedir a catorze o quinze dineros por celemín" (180). In his translation of the *pasos*, Listerman explains the high value of the *real castellano*: "This particular *real* in the interlude, which bore the royal arms, was of silver and was worth thirty-four *maravedis*" (116).

21. Juno and Minerva are depicted as rival deities together with Venus in the judgement of Paris. For pictorial representations of *Minerva Pacifica* holding an olive branch see Wittkower 130–35.

22. Juno's Greek name Hera is an anagram for air in that language (Heninger 175).

23. On the contest between Minerva and Arachne, see Vitoria (249–53).

24. "Minerva había inventado todas las artes" (Conti 237).

25. "Fue el dios Vulcano con una hacha o segur, y abriendole la cabeça, salió la Diosa Minerva" (It was Vulcan who went with a hachet or axe and upon opening [Jupiter's] head, there emerged the Goddess Minerva) (Vitoria 242).

26. It will be up to the daughter, Mencigüela, to forge this new future. After all, Aloxa refers to her as "como un oro" (183). Out of the marital battle of opposites will emerge a new "golden" age where woman will no longer have act as Mencigüela, continually saying yes to those in authority.

The Presence of the Four Elements
in *El burlador de Sevilla*

Francisco J. Martín

There is overwhelming evidence of the importance of astrology, Pythagorean numerology, and the analogical form of knowledge that linked macrocosm to microcosm during the era in which *El burlador de Sevilla* was written. These concepts were of significance both inside and outside of Spain during this time, as were classical mythology and the supernatural—"the supernatural haunted Shakespeare's plays as it haunted the minds of his contemporaries" (Laroque 36–37). Astrology's influence on how man thought continued despite the hypotheses proposed in 1543 by the Polish astronomer Nicolaus Copernicus in his *De Revolutionibus Orbium Coelestium*, theories that would not be confirmed until 1609 by Johannes Kepler, and in 1610 by Galileo Galilei. And even despite these confirmations, the knowledge of the world gained by this new science of astronomy would still not come to form part of popular understanding for many years. In the early modern world, even medicine remained anchored in Galen's theories. According to this famous Greek physician, and faithful to the tradition begun by a treatise attributed to Polybus entitled *The Nature of Man*, there existed four humors, or fluids, in the human body, which corresponded to the four elements of which the world was composed. In fact, "the human microcosm could be understood only in reference to the macrocosm of all creation" (Laroque 101). The importance and far-reaching effect of these popular ideas is clear. As M. J. Woods stated, "The idea of the universe being built upon the basic structure of the four elements of earth, air, fire and water . . . is sufficiently commonplace for its currency in 17th-century Spain not to need much demonstration." Furthermore, "Apart from all else, the account of the creation in the Book of Genesis was sufficient to ensure that thinking in terms of the various elements came naturally to people" (114). Frederick A. de Armas concurs with this notion, and reminds us that "It should be recalled that Empedocles' assertion that man's habitat was composed of four elements or roots . . . was common-place in the epoch" (1982, 62). This critic continues by assuring us that "These concepts and correspondences were common-places in Medieval and Golden Age Spain" (63). Coexisting with this phenomenon was a vibrant atmosphere of literary renovation and experimentation, particularly manifest in the field of poetry. Luis de Góngora, for example, produces his revolutionary compositions *Polifemo* and *Las soledades* during this period, in which ideas like Saint Hildegard of Bingen's *homo quadratus*, "linked with countless fours in the cosmos, in astronomy, in meteorology, in the elements, in arithmetic, [and] in the New Testament" (Barkan 1975, 124), become the subjects of literary study. As Barkan notes, such ideas "can be extremely rich material for metaphor, especially in traditions that borrow heavily on Neoplatonism and mysticism" (1975, 124).

Keeping in mind the preponderance of these concepts in seventeenth-century Europe in general, and in seventeenth-century Spain in particular, it seems curious to me that, up to this point, there has not been more critical attention paid to the fact that in *El burlador de Sevilla*, a play of undeniable popularity and success, there are precisely *four* female characters with whom the protagonist Don Juan interacts. This fact is of special significance, when considering that the work was developed in an atmosphere immersed in the cosmogony that was so in vogue,[1] given the nature of the relationships between Don Juan and the four female characters, and keeping in mind the theological overtones of the work itself.[2] It is precisely in this light that I propose a reading of *El burlador de Sevilla*, which will serve as the object of the present study.

Before passing to the identification of the correspondences that exist between the work's four central female characters and the four elements, it is necessary to point out the pervasive nature of the aforementioned theme in *El burlador de Sevilla*, as evidenced by the following specific reference to the four elements given at the beginning of the work:

> Como es verdad que en los vientos
> hay aves, en el mar peces,
> que participan a veces
> de todos cuatro elementos,[3]

(346–49)

> [Just as it is true that in the wind
> there are birds, and in the sea there are fish,
> which sometimes share
> all four elements,]

Another direct mention is made later in the first act by Coridón, who, when speaking with Tisbea, expresses that he has no doubt about her suitors' tenacity in following her wishes through "el mar, . . . la tierra, / . . . el fuego y . . . el viento" (vv. 652–53: "The sea . . . the earth, . . . the fire and . . . the wind").

Having in mind the reigning conventions during the era regarding this subject, as have been mentioned, and the references cited above—this theme was obviously not far from the playwright's mind—it becomes possible not only to trace direct or indirect allusions to the aforementioned cosmogony in this work, but also to arrive at the conclusion that the entire play, *El burlador de Sevilla*, was designed within a framework which closely followed the classical system in question. This system, created by Empedocles, conceives of "un universo de cuatro 'raíces' y dos grandes fuerzas que lo estructuran" (Rico 14: "a universe [made up] of four roots and structured by two great forces"). These "four elements or roots," as de Armas puts it, "mingle and separate under the opposing impulses of Love and Strife to cause generation and decay in mortal things" (1982, 62). In my view, this is precisely the system that can be seen to operate in *El burlador de Sevilla*. In accordance with the tenets of this system, the play's four principal female characters come to correspond to the four elements. Don Juan comes to signify the previously mentioned forces of Love and Strife,[4] while, speaking in general terms, Isabela has a correspondence to fire, Tisbea primarily to water, Doña Ana to air, and Aminta, a *villana* (peasant woman), to earth. The order in which these four women appear, both on stage and in Don Juan's life, might at first glance seem unplanned or coincidental. However, apart from perfectly matching the system of balancing alternations by which the elements are presented in the sequence of light-heavy-light-heavy, the ordering of the play's four women obeys point for point, interestingly enough, the scheme of ideas through which Plato, using the proportional system, derived the concept of the four elements and their intrinsic values:

> Accordingly the god set water and air between fire and earth, and made them, so far as was possible, proportional to one another, so that as fire is to air, so is air to water, and as air is to water, so is water to earth, and thus he bound together the frame of a world visible and tangible. (Barkan 1975, 21)

It becomes clear, then, following this system, why Isabela must be the first of the four women to appear in the play, and why Aminta must be last.

Isabela is the character in this play who seems to be in possession of fire, or at least in a situation of being able to produce it: "Quiero sacar una luz" (v. 9: "Let me fetch a light"). Tisbea, the "hermosa pescadora" (v. 686: "beautiful fisher woman), represents water by definition, albeit fresh water, rather than the saltwater of the sea which would be viewed as having a negative connotation, "donde la muerte se fragua" (v. 523: "where death is forged"). Doña Ana, who "emerges from the barest sketch," as Ruth Lundelius has affirmed, and "is the most perfunctorily delineated of Don Juan's conquests," (10) would represent air, since her letter arrives to Don Juan "por la estafeta del viento" (v. 1301: "by the courier of the wind"). Aminta, destined to be the "esposa de un villano" (v. 1801: "wife of a peasant"), and inhabitant of the countryside where her betrothed woos her "Sobre esta alfombra florida" (v. 1688: "Upon this blossoming carpet") and where her wedding is scheduled to be celebrated, represents earth.

It becomes immediately apparent, however, that, especially in the case of Tisbea, the four elements are not represented in the four female characters at all times in their purest forms. Quite to the contrary, in each of the four women we discover multiple correspondences to all of the other three elements not specifically represented by the woman in question. This combination of the elements in the female characters serves as a perfect illustration of the phenomenon which Woods has termed "trans-elemental imagery" (118),[5] and is demonstrated in passages such as the following: "Como es verdad . . . / . . . / que *participan* a veces / de todos cuatro elementos" (vv. 346–49: "Just as it is true . . . that [they] sometimes share all four elements." Emphasis mine, here and in subsequent quotes). In Isabela's case, although she has been seen to represent fire, her world is also characterized by allusions to earth and water—"en sus márgenes te dio / *tierra* la espumosa orilla del *mar* de Italia" (vv. 87–88: "in its shores the foamy shore of the Italian sea gave you [dry] land")—as well as to air—"Sí atrevo, / que *alas*[6] en tu favor llevo" (vv. 106–07: "Yes, I do dare, since your favor gives me wings"); "Sí, / que el bien suena y el mal *vuela*" (vv. 328–29: "Yes, because good is heard of, while evil flyes"); "es verdad que en los *vientos* / hay *aves*, en el *mar peces*" (vv. 346–47: "it is true that in the wind there are birds, and in the sea there are fish"); and "¡Ay, *veleta*; ah, débil *caña*!" (v. 370: "O [fickle] weathervane! O feeble reed!").

Tisbea, "the most completely characterized and hence the most interesting woman in the play" according to Lundelius (9), operates within a framework in which the evocations of all four elements (rather than just *her* element—water), not only exist as has been seen in the case of Isabela, but are much more numerous and well defined:

> Yo, de cuantas el *mar*,
> pies de *jazmín* y *rosas*,
> en sus *riberas* besa
> con fugitivas *olas*,
> aquí, donde el *sol* pisa
> soñolientas las *ondas*,
> alegrando zafiros
> las que espantaba sombras,
> por la menuda *arena*,
> unas veces *aljófar*,
> y átomos otras veces
> del *sol* que así le adora,
> oyendo de las *aves*
> las quejas amorosas,
> y los combates dulces
> del *agua* entre las *rocas*,
> en pequeñuelo *esquife*,
> ya en compañía de otras,
> tal vez al *mar* le peino
> la cabeza *espumosa*.
> Ya con la sutil *caña*
> que el débil peso dobla
> del tierno *pececillo*
> que el *mar* salado azota,
> o ya con la *atarraya*
> que en sus moradas hondas
> prende en cuantos habitan
> aposentos de *conchas*[7] . . .

(376–403)

> [I, amidst all those [fisher women]
> whose feet of jasmine and rose
> in its shores the sea kisses
> with its fugitive waves,
> here [I am] (immune to love), where the sun meets
> the sleepy waves,
> joyfully turning into sapphires
> the shadows it dissipates [in its wake]
> over the fine sand,
> sometimes [turning it] into seed pearls,
> and other times into atoms

of sun[beams], paying the sun homage in this way,
[here I am,] listening to
the amorous warblings of the birds,
and to the sweet combat
of the water against the rocks,
[as I,] on my little skiff,
in the company of other fisher women,
may comb
the foamy surface of the sea.
Either with my nimble rod,
which is bent by the paltry weight
of the tender little fish
that the salty sea thrashes about;
or with my casting net,
which in its lodgings
catches all those who make their home
in conch shells . . .]

Additional references continue to be presented throughout Tisbea's appearances in the play, such as: "Quiero entregar la *caña* / al *viento* y a la boca / del *pececillo* [el] cebo" (vv. 480–82: "I wish to cast to the wind my rod, and to the little fish's mouth the bait"), etc. Certainly, of all of the references given, the most patent and complete by far is the one previously cited, in which all of the four elements appear explicitly mentioned: "el mar . . . la tierra, / . . . el fuego y . . . el viento" (vv. 652–53: "the sea . . . the earth, . . . the fire and . . . the wind"). In any case, despite the principal identification of this fisherwoman with water, it is evident that fire ends up playing a dominant role in her world. Although Tisbea throws herself into the water—"¡Al mar se arroja" (v. 1042: "She casts herself into the sea!")—at the conclusion of the primary episode in which she appears, her ultimate complaint is: "que se abrasa el alma" (v. 1045: "my soul is on fire!"). This is due to the dominant and vindictive presence of Love, to which she complains, and of which she had arrogantly proclaimed herself master, "porque en tirano imperio / vivo, de Amor señora" (vv. 456–57: "for I live in possession of a tirant's power, as the master of Love"). Tisbea is observed to be "como un Don Juan femenino, que también tiene un gusto sádico en hacer sufrir a los hombres como Don Juan hace sufrir a las mujeres" (Silverman, as quoted in *El mito* 215: "like a female Don Juan, who also sadistically enjoys making men suffer, just as Don Juan makes women suffer"); this of course serves as a foreshadowing of the eventual outcome that will befall the *burlador.* Fire will be

the element in which Don Juan will find death—"la muerte, con
la que el amor se identifica" (Miras 238: "death, with which love
identifies itself")—as is exemplified in his final cry of agony:
"Que me quemo, que me abraso. / Muerto soy" (vv. 2857–58: "Oh,
I am burning! Oh, I am consumed! I'm dead").

Despite Doña Ana's sketchy development, and the fact that she
is an ethereal character founded principally on the realm of the
voice (air), it is also possible to distinguish traces and evocations
of the other three elements that she does not represent. To this
effect, Doña Ana is compared to the sun (fire) in the first reference
made to her: "Gonzalo de Ulloa . . . / . . . / . . . tiene una hija
. . . / . . . / . . . que es maravilla / y el *sol* de las estrellas de Sevilla"
(vv. 1103–09: "Gonzalo de Ulloa . . . has a daughter . . . who is
both a marvel and the sun among the stars of Seville"). The allusions to this element in reference to Doña Ana continue: "donde
el puro *sol* se esconde" (v. 1139: "where the very sun conceals
itself"); "Veréis la mayor belleza / que los ojos del *sol* ven" (vv.
1265–66: "You will [be able to] see the greatest beauty that the
sun has ever set eyes upon"); and "y el mundo *se abrase* y *queme*"
(v. 1277: "and let the [whole] world burn up and perish in
flames"). At the conclusion of Doña Ana's primary episode, the
Marqués de la Mota expresses astonishment as he approaches
her house, in a scene in which the intertextuality with Tisbea's
previous episode cannot be ignored:

> Desde aquí parece todo
> una Troya que *se abrasa,*
> porque tantas *hachas* juntas
> paren gigantes de *llamas.*
> Mas, una escuadra de *luces*
> se acerca a mí. ¿Por qué anda
> el *fuego* emulando al *Sol,*
> dividiéndose en escuadras?
>
> (1624–31)

> [From here I perceive what appears to be
> another Troy set ablaze,
> for so many burning torches
> give birth to giants of flame.
> But, a squadron of lights
> moves this way. Why is [this] fire
> [trying to] emulate the sun [above],
> by dividing itself into squadrons?]

Earth and water also find a place in Doña Ana's realm: *"enterrado /
me tiene mayor cuidado"* (vv. 1251–52: "[to be] interred in [the]
earth worries me much more")—as Mota exclaims in reference
to her; and

Don Juan:	Pues, ¿dónde ha estado?
Mota:	En *Lisboa,*
	con su padre en la Embajada

                                                                (1258–59)

[*Don Juan:*	Then, where has she been?
Mota:	[She's been] in Lisbon,
	in the Embassy, with her father.]

(Lisbon, as Don Gonzalo has explained to the king previously,
"parece una gran ciudad / adonde *Neptuno* reina"—vv. 737–38:
"[Lisbon,] it seems, is a great city, where Neptune reigns
[supreme]").

Lastly, in the case of the *villana* Aminta, references to the other
three elements that she does not represent can be found:

Músicos:	Lindo sale el *Sol* de abril,
	por *trébol* y *toronjil;*
	y aunque le sirve de *estrella*
	Aminta sale más bella.
Batricio:	Sobre esta *alfombra florida,*
	adonde, en *campos* de *escarcha*
	el *sol* sin aliento marcha
	con su *luz* recién nacida,
	os sentad, pues nos convida . . .

                                                                (1684–92)

[*Musicians:*	April's sun rises ever so radiantly,
	as [do] clover and eglantine [in its wake];
	but although the sun serves as Aminta's rising star
	Aminta herself rises yet more splendidly.
Batricio:	Upon this blossoming carpet,
	on which through dewy fields
	the sun gently advances
	with its newborn light,
	please be seated, for it invites us . . .]

And, although this variety of references to the distinct elements
continues—"por eso *se baña* y pinta / de más colores el *prado*" (vv.

1700–1: "for that reason the meadows bathe and adorn themselves with a myriad of colors"); "*Montes* en casa hay de pan / *Guadalquivides* de vino / . . . / y entre ejércitos cobardes / de *aves*" (vv. 1752–56: "At home there are mountains of bread and rivers of wine, as flowing as the Guadalquivir . . . and amidst cowardly armies of birds")—it is once again the element of fire that dominates by means of its well-known evocations, since it is the game of love that the characters are dealing with at this point. Alternating with the refrain of the musicians—"Lindo sale el *Sol* de abril" ("April's sun rises ever so radiantly")—Batricio and Aminta converse as follows:

> *Batricio:*   No sale así el *Sol* de Oriente
>   como el *Sol* que al Alba sale,
>   que no hay *sol* que al *sol* se iguale
>   de sus *niñas* y su frente;
>   a este *sol* claro y *luciente*
>   que eclipsa al *sol* de su arrebol;
>   y así cantadle a mi *sol*
>   motetes de mil en mil.
>
> *Aminta:*   Batricio, aunque lo agradezco,
>
>   . . .
>
>   mas si tus *rayos* me das,
>
>   . . .
>
>   tú eres el *sol* por quien crezco.
>
>   (1708–22)

> [*Batricio:*   The sun does not rise in this way from the Orient
>   as the sun rises at dawn,
>   for there is no sun like the radiant sun
>   of her pupils and her forehead;
>   to this bright and luminous sun
>   which eclipses the brightness of the very sun;
>   and so, sing a thousand serenades
>   to her, my sun.
>
> *Aminta:*   Batricio, although I [must] thank you,
>
>   . . .
>
>   but since you shine your rays on me,
>
>   . . .
>
>   you are the sun for whom I wax.]

The correspondence of the elements with the female characters of *El burlador de Sevilla*, and the phenomenon of the "trans-elemental imagery," continue throughout the play. In the final act, three of the women, complaining of their misfortunate amorous adventures with Don Juan, prepare to appear before the king, in their intent to seek retribution for their social misfortunes (Doña Ana is not included, for reasons stated explicitly in the text: "que a Doña Ana no debía / honor, que lo oyeron antes / del engaño"— vv. 2953–55: "for he [Don Juan] did not owe Doña Ana any honor, since his trick had already been known beforehand"). For each one of them, as has been mentioned, fire ultimately reigns supreme for reasons which are intrinsic to the story itself—the story revolves around the central theme of Love and its effects. At the same time, however, each woman continues evoking the traces and associations of her respective element. Isabela, the principal possessor of fire, complains now of the "noche al fin tenebrosa" ("very dark night after all") in which she appeared at the beginning, recognizing that night is contrary and opposite to the essence of her element, "antípoda del *Sol*" (vv. 2146–47: "the sun's antipode"). For her, the world of the elements has now completely changed, and has adopted a negative character:

> El *mar* está alterado
> y en grave *temporal;* tiempo [se] corre;
> el abrigo han tomado
> las *galeras*, Duquesa, de la *torre*
> que esta *playa* corona.

(2154–58)

> [The sea is disturbed
> and tempestuous; the weather ready to unleash a storm;
> the galleys, Duchess, have headed
> for the shelter that the tower
> that crowns this shore offers.]

Tisbea, whose episode makes her representative of water (and fire), converges with Isabela in her misfortune, and also comes to view her characteristic element in a negative light:

> ¡Robusto *mar* de España,
> *ondas* de *fuego*, fugitivas *ondas*,
> Troya de mi *cabaña*
> que ya el *fuego* por *mares* y por *ondas*
> en sus abismos fragua
> y [en] el *mar* forma por las *llamas* [de] *agua!*
> ¡Maldito el *leño* sea
> que a tu amargo *cristal* halló camino . . .

(2184–91)

[Oh robust sea of Spain!
Oh waves of fire! Oh fugitive waves!
Oh you, my cabin, another Troy,
which fire has engulfed in seas and waves,
as it forges in its abismal womb
waves of flames!
Accursed be the ship
that found its way across your bitter crystal [surface]]

Aminta, for her part, remains the typical *villana*, "cristiana vieja . . . / hasta los huesos" (vv. 2686–87: "[she is] a staunch old Christian . . . to the [marrow of her] bones"), characteristically associated with earth, and proud of her *"hacienda"* (v. 2688). It is in the convergence between Isabela and Tisbea, then, given the preponderance of the elements that these two characters represent, where we observe most clearly the effect that the "exchange of elements," as Wilson has termed it (37), produces in this work. What begins as a chance meeting en route to the court between two women who complain of their amorous griefs, soon becomes a series of striking similarities—Isabela must *"llorar* mientras tuviera vida"* (v. 2177: "weep all the days of my life"), while at the same time "una pescadora . . . / . . . / . . . dulcemente *llora*" (vv. 2178–80: "a fisher woman . . . weeps tenderly")—and ends up in a situation in which they share the same words, complaints, emotions, and lover, thus fusing themselves, as projections that they are of their own respective elements, in one same lament:[8]

Isabela:	¿Por qué del *mar* te *quejas*
	tan tiernamente, hermosa pescadora?
Tisbea:	Al *mar* formo mil *quejas*,
	dichosa vos, que en su tormento agora
	de él os estáis riendo.
Isabela:	*También quejas* del *mar* estoy haciendo.

(2196–2201)

[*Isabela:*	Why do you so tenderly complain about the sea,
	lovely fisher woman?
Tisbea:	It is true that I have a thousand complaints about the sea,
	Lucky are you, who in the midst of such a storm
	can afford to laugh.
Isabela:	I too against the sea am complaining.]

A bit later, in the same conversation, what begins as a curse from the mouth of Tisbea—"¡Mal haya la mujer que en hombres fía!"

(v. 2235: "Miserable is the woman who puts her trust in men!")—
ends up being appropriated by Isabela, who exclaims exactly the
same imprecation, word for word and point for point in three
subsequent moments (vv. 2243, 2249, and 2261). These two
women, at the end "en . . . compañía" (vv. 2220 and 2260: "in
. . . [each other's] company"), have formed one voice, they have
become one person, with one same complaint. The perpetrator
of the misdeeds causing their affliction is also one and the same.
Fire and water have been fused together. In addition, earth—the
"playa" (v. 2158: "beach"), the *"cabañas"* (vv. 2186, 2203: "huts"),
"esta *tierra*" (v. 2227: "this land"), etc.—and air—"los *vientos*" (v.
2194: "the winds"), the *"viento"* (v. 2203: "wind"), "las *aves*" (v.
2207: "the birds"), etc.—have also experimented this process of
fusion. All the four elements now appear fused together.

If, as we have seen, the four female characters of *El burlador de
Sevilla* represent the four elements, this "mixture or confusion of
the elements," in Wilson's words (46), must clearly be seen to be
deliberate. It would be highly unlikely that a "dramatist-
theologian" (Lundelius 13) of the caliber of Tirso would be unfamiliar with the classical idea that "el número cuatro conforma al
universo" (Rico 47: "the number four conforms the universe").
Tirso was also undoubtedly aware of the case of his famous contemporary, Góngora—in whose writings "we [also] find many
cases of this confusion of the elements" (Wilson 46)—, and of this
writer's "constant preoccupation with the four elements in his
poetry" (Woods 154). Likewise, he would have been influenced
by an atmosphere in which, "under Góngora's lead as ever, poets
began to adopt imagery in which the expected divisions between
the four elements were rejected" (Woods 118). What Tirso attempts to attain by this is, as Wilson proposes in the case of
Calderón, to enhance the effect of violence and motion (46).
Woods confirms this idea:

> Trans-elemental images were also used by the baroque poets to add
> a sense of excitement to situations and phenomena which on the
> surface appear more ordinary. They draw attention to some of na-
> ture's subtle patterns which cut across the anticipated divisions and
> contrasts between the four elements. (124)

As Calderón would do later, the author of *El burlador de Sevilla*
lets "the confusion of the elements tell their own story, merely
letting the creature or attribute of one element be that of another,"
the conflict being "due to the intervention of the supernatural"

(Wilson 37). And it is here where the appearance of the figure of Don Juan gains significance. His figure, his image as *burlador*, is the direct result of this "mixture or confusion of the elements." *El burlador de Sevilla* can be viewed as a daring prefiguration of what years later would be seen in the Calderonean mythological drama *La estatua de Prometeo*. In Tirso's work, Don Juan Tenorio is found at the beginning in a dark interior space, parallel to the cave in which Pandora, Prometheus's statue, is also found. In Don Juan's case, this is a room in the royal palace. In this setting, our protagonist is presented as still without a definite identity: "¿Quién soy? Un hombre sin nombre" (v. 15: "Who am I? [Just] a man with no name"). As in Pandora's case, Don Juan, a prefigurement of the statue at whose hands he will later perish (the statue of the Comendador), becomes an image formed by the four elements, represented in this case by the four women whom he encounters during the course of the play, the play being, effectively, his life as *burlador*. The play's title aptly refers to the significance of this life as *burlador* in the play, for it serves as its definitive axis. By the time Don Juan meets the fourth woman, Aminta,— "con ésta cuatro serán" (v. 1815: "with this one, it makes four [women]")—he now has a name and identity of his own:

> Yo soy noble caballero,
> cabeza de la familia
> de los Tenorios antiguos,
> ganadores de Sevilla.
> Mi padre, después del Rey,
> se reverencia y se estima

(2066–71)

> [I am a noble gentleman,
> [the] head of the great Tenorio family,
> [the] conquerors of Seville.
> My father, second [only] to the King,
> is honored and esteemed
> [before all other men at court]]

Aminta gives herself to him—"Tuya es el alma y la vida" (v. 2125: "My soul and my life are [now] yours"); "Tuya soy" (v. 2140: "I am yours")—and it is at this point, following her romantic encounter with Don Juan, that the "statue," the figure of the *burlador*, is made complete. Don Juan is represented as a "figura diabólica" (Feal 9: "diabolic figure"), harking back to the previous reference to the role of the supernatural during this period. This portrayal can be seen in references to him as "enroscada culebra" (v. 140: "a writhing snake") at one point, and as a "víbora" (v. 2231: "[venomous] viper") at another. The likening of Don Juan to the serpent, which is a symbol of, among other things, androgyny[9] (Don Juan, as has been mentioned, does not have a defined identity when he first appears in Isabela's room), also makes this figure come to embody the characteristics of cunning, deceit, evil, false appearance, sensuality, temptation, treachery, and renewal/rebirth. The *burlador,* a therefore Promethean figure who obviously is not completed in his encounter with the first woman, will return to darkness again and again, to the atmosphere of germination and transformation. It is for this reason that his adventures alternate between day and night. One after the other, the four women, in whom the four elements are represented, invest in him through empathy the features of their defining element—in this vein, the parallel between the different elements, humors, and temperaments should not be overlooked. Just as in the case of Count Dracula, our *burlador* must have a woman, a new woman each time, who for him will mean his very life. With each one of the encounters with a new woman, Don Juan, the unfinished and incomplete *burlador,* acquires a new element, a new feature which will serve to complete his image. Don Juan continues in this way until he completes himself as a whole, until he becomes the *burlador* of *El burlador de Sevilla.* At the end of the play, Don Juan, who is now a complete image, figure, or statue, and who encounters his nemesis (the statue, the figure of the Comendador), *is* the *burlador.* If Pandora is sent by Zeus as revenge and punishment against Prometheus for his crime and daring act, Don Juan appears as an emissary of society, and as "símbolo de ella" ("its symbol"). In fact, "en cierto sentido, Don Juan es casi un instrumento para llamar la atención a la corrupción de su sociedad" (Silverman as quoted in *El mito* 215: "in a certain sense, Don Juan is almost like an instrument [designed] to draw attention to the corruption present in his society"). The *burlador* functions as a sort of system of checks and balances for his society, in which woman, being the primordial symbol of society as its receptacle of honor (the most criticized and artificial convention of this society), produces a figure such as Don Juan (it is to be remembered that without "burladas" ["tricked/seduced (women)"]—either willing participants or not—there would be no "burlador" ["trickster/seducer"]). As Ruiz Ramón has stated, the mythical figure of Don Juan is charged with "desmitificar, con sola su presencia y con su conducta, el sistema, el código, los paradigmas colectivos, al parecer, vigentes en esa sociedad . . . ; la falsedad, en cierto modo, del sistema" (quoted in *El mito* 330: "demythologizing, through his mere presence and behaviour, the system, the social codes and paradigms present, it seems, in that society . . . ; [demythologizing] the [whole] false apparatus of the system"). With Don Juan's death, the circle, or cycle, is completed, as one "statue"/*burlador* succumbs at the hands of another (Don Gonzalo becomes a *burlador* as well, when he gives Don Juan a taste of his own mendacious medicine—"Dame esa mano, / no temas, la mano dame"—vv. 2833–34: "Give me your hand, have no fear, give me your hand"). Fire has been extinguished with fire, and the two "statues," to pay for the crime of being *burlador*, sink into the tomb. This "descensus ad inferos," (descent into hell) on the other hand, is nothing else but a visit to the "reino de los muertos" ("kingdom of the dead"), to "la morada de los dioses subterráneos" (Miras 236: "the abode of the subterranean gods"), so that, when the precise moment is deemed at hand, the myth can be reborn, the cycle can be restarted once again. Don Juan, the myth of the *burlador*, is always back, literally and literarily, judging from the long list of his literary successors that surface throughout the centuries. Once again man, the central figure of creation, (according to the sociotheological conceptions of the times) in an act of regeneration and recreation (keeping in mind that man has been created in the image and likeness of God, and that he constitutes, as per the Melothesian theory, a true microcosm in himself, could Divine Providence be behind all this?), utilizes, literally, the elements as "his servants, the instruments of his salvation" (Wilson 34). We therefore come to see that, just as the play's title indicates, *El burlador de Sevilla* is not the story of Don Juan, but rather the story of a *burlador*. It is not that Don Juan happens to be a *burlador*, but rather it is a *burlador*, *the burlador*, that happens to be named Don Juan.

Notes

1. "The system of the four elements—earth, air, fire and water—is perhaps the most ancient of the cosmogonies which have persisted through western thought" (Barkan 14).

2. The following parenthetical observation by Francisco Rico seems appropriate for even the most discerning readers of this work: "el pobre lector del *Timeo* nunca está muy seguro de si le hablan de teología o de astronomía" (19: "the unguarded reader of the *Timaeus* is never quite sure whether the book is about theology or about astronomy"). *El burlador de Sevilla*, like the *Timaeus*,

conflates astrology and theology, Pythagorean numerology and elemental theories present in Plato's dialogues, that are also found in the *comedia*.

3. All quotes from *El burlador de Sevilla* are taken from the Alfredo Rodríguez López-Vázquez edition.

4. In this sense, perhaps we should see a veiled reference to this system in the mention that Don Juan and the Marqués de la Mota make, in their fortuitous meeting, to *four* prostitutes: Inés, Constanza, Teodora, and Julia; and to the *two* sisters: Blanca and "esotra" ("the other one"). See vv. 1204–40.

5. This phenomenon, as M. J. Woods recognizes, had already been advocated by E. M. Wilson in his important study "The Four Elements in the Imagery of Calderón" (37).

6. For a better idea of the different terms traditionally associated with each one of the four elements, see the "list . . . of the ingredients that Calderón used in . . . [his] metaphorical recipes" that Wilson provides in "The Four Elements in the Imagery of Calderón," page 43. Although this reference may seem anachronistic in character, in reality it works perfectly since, as Wilson himself recalls later in his article, "Calderón did not invent this metaphorical procedure . . . He probably derived it from a study of the works of Góngora" (43), who happened to be involved in the creation of his major, and most revolutionary works around the same time period in which *El burlador de Sevilla* appears.

7. See note 6 for explanation of the emphasized words.

8. Of the seven letters of the Duchess's name and the six of the fisherwoman's, five of them are shared by both, thus presenting all the trappings of a palindrome—speaking of fusions. However, since this is a theatrical text destined primarily for spectators and not for readers, the effect of this palindrome would not necessarily have been observed by Tirso's spectators.

9. It is curious to note how, in some editions of this work, as is illustrated in Rodríguez López-Vázquez p. 83, when the King arrives at the room from whence Isabela's screams emanate, he asks "¿Quién *eres?*" and Don Juan responds "¿Qué ha de ser? / *Un hombre y una mujer*" (vv. 21–22–23: "Who are you? / What do you think? ([Just]) a man and a woman"), a reply that illustrates the underlying androgyny of Don Juan.

The Devil, The Tower, and The Hanged Man: The Hermetic Tarot of the *Numancia*

Ronald J. Friis

The archetypal images of the tarot deck have long held the interest of writers and artists throughout the world. Aside from their common association with divination or fortune-telling, the cards are famous for their attractive and varied designs. They are spellbinding miniature works of art replete with a multilayered symbolism attributed to the occult sciences of astrology, alchemy, and numerology. The tarot has also been interpreted in the context of Christianity, the Kaballa, the Hebrew alphabet, and Egyptian as well as later mythologies. During the Renaissance, the tarot was used for gaming, divination, and as an aid in the *ars memoria*. In the twentieth century, the tarot, like alchemy, has attracted the attention of Carl Jung and his followers due to its rich archetypal images. In literature, these tarot symbols, like archetypes, often become manifest in characters and situations that have no relation to cartomancy; the messages of the tarot have universal associations that transcend the concrete illustration of any single card. In fact, upon beginning study of the tarot, one is surprised by the often conflicting interpretations assigned by experts to the cards and the variable depictions of different decks.

Of the tarot's relation to literature, Cynthia Giles writes: "The tarot provides a storehouse of images from which can be assembled a symbolic representation of almost any human drama, from *Hamlet* to one's own life" (xiii). Thus, in applying the symbols of the tarot to the *Numancia*, we need not assume previous knowledge of the cards by Cervantes, even though recent scholarship has unearthed convincing arguments regarding the Hermetic tradition in his work.[1]

The earliest reference to playing cards of any kind in Europe dates from 1332, when Alfonso XI, ironically enough, banned them from the kingdoms of Leon and Castile (Butler 3). The oldest surviving tarot decks, the Italian Visconti cards, date from around 1440 (Giles 12), and circa 1500 we have an ordered list of the Major Arcana, produced by a Franciscan friar in Italy (Giles 9). Art critics and mythographers such as Sylvie Simon and Joseph Campbell have noted the presence of tarot cards and themes in the *Inferno* of Dante and the *Gargantua* of Rabelais (Simon 107, Giles 12). Jean Pierre Étienvre, who has meticulously documented the history of playing cards in Spain, notes that Spanish playing cards differ greatly from the tarot and signals that the decks found in Spain as early as 1528 were Italian in origin (299). While Louis C. Pérez reminds us that: "con la invención de la imprenta a fines del siglo XV, se empiezan a manufacturar [naipes] de papel, y por consiguiente la baraja se pone al alcance de todos y no hay hogar ni pícaro sin ella" (140; with the invention of the printing press toward the end of the fifteenth century, paper cards began to be manufactured and, consequently, the decks became available to all and there wasn't a house or a rascal without one). In spite of the fact that "authorities agree that the major arcana were not known in Spain before the end of the eighteenth century"[2] there are many instances when Cervantes may have come in contact with the cards (Étienvre even dedicates a whole chapter in his *Márgenes literarios del juego* to cataloguing mentions of playing cards in Cervantes's work). The first instance is in 1569 during his visits to the Vatican as envoy to Cardinal Acquaviva; ironically, during this time, the Vatican's libraries, frescoes, and vaults represented the world's premiere forum for Hermetic texts. One account mentions a strong resemblance between tarot images and frescoes in palaces such as Schifanoia in Ferrara. Between battles, Cervantes was still living in Italy in 1575, precisely the time and place when the tarot flourished. All this occurred before he was captured and imprisoned in Algiers, another place out of the reach of the Inquisition where he may have seen the cards. The orientalism of Cervantes's work is testament to the fact that he spent all of his formative twenties and his early thirties outside of Spain. In fact, the ban on the tarot in the peninsula was so strenuous that there wasn't even a Spanish word for the cards: "¿Para qué una palabra, si no ha de usarse?" writes Étienvre (300; Why have a word [for the tarot] if it could not even be spoken?). Biographical polemics aside, Marquino's necromancy scene in the second act of the *Numancia* contains a series of archetypal tarot images that serves to create and later fulfill a prophesy of the city's destiny.[3]

The origins of the tarot are usually attributed to an initiation right of Thoth, the Egyptian god of writing, among other arts (Butler 7). Of Thoth, Barbara Watterson (1984, 181) writes:

> Thoth was not only the scribe of the gods; he was their messenger. Hence, the Greeks identified him with their own messenger of the gods, Hermes, and renamed his town of *Khemenu*, calling it Hermopolis (City of Hermes). During the Graeco-Roman period, Thoth was worshipped by both Greeks and Egyptians as Hermes Trismegistos (Thrice-great Hermes).

Mythographers such as Robert Graves and Thomas Bulfinch recognize Thoth/Hermes as one in the same and Bill Butler also sees a direct correlation between the many faces of Hermeticism and the cards of the Major Arcana (12–13). In "Plato's Pharmacy," Jacques Derrida stresses the association of Thoth ("an archetype of Hermes, god of cryptography no less than every other -graphy" [93]) not only with writing and memory but with death. The cloudy origins of Thoth, his reemergence as other gods, and the magical, occult elements he is known for, are exploited by Derrida in his deconstruction of *logos* and, as we shall see, parallel the Hermetic message of the *Numancia*.

As for the deck itself, the tarot is comprised of seventy-eight cards divided into the Major and Minor Arcana. The twenty-two cards of the Major Arcana, or Trumps Major, are the most commonly known due to their powerful and direct imagery. Here we find The Emperor and The Empress, The Lovers, The Fool, The Wheel of Fortune and Death—the Arcanum with no name. The Major Arcana have a more forceful message than the other cards in the deck and stand out in a reading much like capital letters in a written sentence, one could say they have more presence. Regrettably, the Major Arcana have disappeared from the playing cards of today, although they are still found in tarot decks. Many theories claim that our modern playing cards are descendants of the wands, cups, swords, and pentacles of the tarot's Minor Arcana, while Étienvre claims that the Spanish deck is, for the most part, unrelated to the tarot and other European cards (300). The cards of the Minor Arcana have lesser and somewhat more controversial divinatory meanings than the iconic Trumps Major. When seen together in a reading, the interpretation of either Arcana is dependent upon both the surrounding cards and the context of the divination. Although there are several traditional and countless personal methods of reading the tarot, the Ancient Celtic Method is the closest thing we have to a standard.

In his fundamental text, *The Pictorial Key to the Tarot,* A. E. Waite writes "this mode of divination is the most suitable for obtaining an answer to a definite question" (299). The Ancient Celtic Method involves ten cards dealt from a deck shuffled three times. Six cards are placed in the shape of a cross with four cards situated in a vertical row to the left or right. The cards are then read in the order of their placement, from one to ten, in accordance with the divinatory meanings assigned to both the card itself and its situation in the pattern. This specific method of reading provides us with a framework which we can apply loosely as we explore the archetypal tarot images in the *Numancia.* As it happens, the division of the cards into the cross and the vertical row corresponds to the textual cadence of Marquino's invocation of the dead and the subsequent prophecies spoken by the Corpse in the play.

In the second act of the *Numancia* we are presented with five different omens: the building of a fire and augury of its smoke, the sacrifice of a ram, the appearance of a comet, two eagles fighting in midflight, the materialization of a demon, and then Marquino's necromancy. Despite earlier prophetic speeches by the allegorical figures Spain and the river Duero, each of these omens points to the loss of the city and pushes the people of Numantia further into despair. At this point, Marquino enters the set with Milbio who leads him to the tomb of a recently buried boy and explains: "Murió de mal gobierno: / la flaca hambre le acabó la vida, / peste cruel, salida del infierno" (945–48; He died "Of almighty Famine- / That cruel snapping pest, born out of hell!").[4] In light of the earlier failed sacrifices and auguries, Marquino is the last chance to change the Numantines's fortune. After sixteen years of battle, the Romans have decided to encircle the walled city and starve its citizens into submission. This fallen youth represents the first victim of the latest Roman tactic and holds a symbolic value far greater than that of one man. By dying of hunger, his fate becomes the collective destiny of the entire city. When Marquino summons Pluto, god of the underworld, and attempts to resurrect the boy, he is simultaneously attempting to save all the Numantines.

Marquino begins his magic spell with the prelude:

> Está muy bien, y es buena coyuntura
> la que me ofrecen los propios signos
> para invocar de la región oscura
> los feroces espíritus malignos.

> Presta atentos oídos a mis versos,
> fiero Plutón, que en la región oscura,
> entre ministros de ánimos perversos,
> te cupo de reinar suerte y ventura;
>
> (957–64)

["That's to the good. Propitious signs favor me at this juncture / From their dark realm to call fierce evil spirits.

Now give attentive hearing to my verse, You ministers to souls that are perverse! May luck and fortune bless you and obey, Even if you be unwilling, what I say upon this dire occasion."]

In describing the Ancient Celtic Method of divination, some writers hold that before dealing the first card of a fortune, a card called the Significator should be chosen by the reader to represent the Querent, the person requesting the fortune.[5] Other authorities maintain that due to its Trump number (zero) The Fool should always be chosen as the Significator. The Fool is drawn as a carefree young man who is on the threshold of adulthood, as well as on the edge of a deep gorge.[6] He is a figure of transition, of passing on and through. In alchemical terminology, he is the *materia prima;* for Jung, the Trickster. Since the subject of this reading is a young man being summoned to a long journey back from Hades and a city at its most crucial moment of transition, The Fool is fitting.

The Significator is entirely covered by the first card of the tarot reading, in this case, The Devil (Pluto). This first card represents the principal influence upon the matter at hand. When Marquino summons Pluto, the Devil of the Greeks, he is knocking at the doors of hell and requesting the release of the soul of the corpse before him. Besides the natural association of the Devil with necromancy, Marquino has followed Milbio's idea that this plague of hunger had risen from hell. The Devil is the principal influence upon this divination. He has already claimed his first victim and he will possess all the Numantine's souls if they should succumb to the siege. In the play, the embodiment of The Devil is Scipio, leader of the Roman forces. In some decks, The Devil, with horned head, holds a sword by the blade in his left hand. Nichols comments: "It is obvious that his relationship to his weapon is so unconscious that he would be unable to use it in a purposeful manner, meaning symbolically that his relationship to the male Logos is similarly ineffectual" (262). The overly proud Scipio in a similar fashion has decided upon hunger, rather than further battle with weapons to defeat the Numantines.

Marquino continues his spell with: "te cupo de reinar suerte y ventura; / haz, aunque sean de tu gusto adversos, / cumplidos mis deseos . . ." (964–66; "May luck and fortune bless you! And obey, / Even if you be unwilling, what I say"). These verses are a plea to take the destiny of the corpse and the city into his own hands. Although Scipio, The Devil, is in control of fate, there is always the outside chance that the city's luck could change. When the element of skill has been eliminated, chance is all that remains. This situation evokes the ancient ideas embodied in The Wheel of Fortune. The second card of a reading is laid horizontally across the first and represents the nature of the obstacles in the matter. Since the Numantine soldiers are too weak from hunger to fight, they must rely upon outside sources to save themselves. The Wheel of Fortune, Trump Ten, depicts the battle of "fate versus freewill" (Nichols 179) on a wheel surrounded by esoteric figures. Luck is upon us and is suddenly gone, only to return later like the rotation of a huge wheel. Still, the positive side of this "eternal return," the message hidden in the orations of Spain and the Duero, cannot yet be revealed to the Numantines.

Further into his incantation, Marquino demands that Pluto release the soul of the corpse from the darkness of Hades and that it "salga, y torne a la luz del mundo nuestro" (975; return to the light of our world). This and the later "vuelve a ver el sol claro y sereno" (1026; "Return to see / the sun serene and clear") are clear references to Trump Nineteen, The Sun. This, as the third card of the fortune, lays at the head of the Celtic cross and represents the ideal outcome of the matter. It portrays a naked child riding on horseback under a brilliantly rayed sun in an attitude of victory and renewed innocence. In our reading, resurrection and the sight of sunbathed flowers of the card is obviously the best possible outcome for the Corpse's soul. The Sun is also a card of news, which Marquino requests as "Y ha de salir, salga informada / del fin que ha de tener guerra tan cruda" (977–78; "let him bring information / Of this harsh, bitter siege's termination").

The fourth card of a reading, found at the base of the cross, represents the foundation of the matter. The issue is resurrection, both of the boy and the collective whole and Marquino, master of this destiny, is clearly an embodiment of Trump Fourteen, Temperance. This card, in the Rider-Waite deck, is an androgynous angel figure standing with one foot in a river and the other on

Temperance from the Rider-Waite Tarot deck.

land. In its hands it holds two cups and is "pouring the essences of life from chalice to chalice" (Waite 124). In order to hasten the reluctant corpse's exit from Hades, Marquino performs a ritual with waters. He begins by bathing his lance in clear water and striking the dead boy's tombstone. This brings a rumble from the earth but not the body itself. Next, he proceeds to scatter about black waters, which raises the corpse from the ground and leaves it laying speechless at his feet. Finally, Marquino opens a flask of water made golden with saffron, sprinkles the corpse and whips it once, bringing it temporarily back among the living. Marquino, like Temperance, stands at the crossroads of two worlds. He has one foot in the water and the other on land. He is near a path that springs from the river and shoots straight up to the sun. Temperance's blonde hair shines amid a field of yellow flowers as he pours water from his golden chalices. It is no wonder that Nichols names him the "Heavenly Alchemist" (250). Indeed, Marquino too has performed an alchemical transmutation by raising the dead with his golden waters of life. He has brought the body out of the river of death and put it on a pathway to the Sun.[7]

At this point, the Corpse rises from the ground and begins to speak. His words prophesy the future of Numantia in symbols that once again recall those of the tarot. First he tells that although he now lives, shortly he must return to death: "antes me causas un dolor esquivo, / pues otra vez la muerte rigurosa / triunfará de mi vida y de mi alma" (1061–63; "For death a second time with bitter strife / Must triumph o'er my spirit and my life"). Here we find the fifth card of the fortune, the Ten of Swords, an influence that has just passed. According to Butler, the fifth and sixth cards of the Celtic Method refer to the Querent, while the remaining cards refer to the question (194). Despite its graphic design, Waite stresses that the Ten of Swords "is not especially a card of violent death" (234). Other authorities maintain that it is a card of transition. Both interpretations are appropriate here; the first reflects the twice repeated fact that the boy died of hunger and was not in any way bruised or mangled (946, 956). The second also holds true because even though the Corpse lives to speak his last words, his fate is identical to that of the figure pierced by all ten of the card's swords. Shortly, he too will lose the last rays of sunlight afforded him and will sink back into the night.

This night is, of course, death. Trump Thirteen, or Death, is often referred to as the Arcanum with no name due to its number and vivid imagery. Butler cites its origin in the Black Plague of the fourteenth century (159). It is a deceiving card in many respects, and the ideas it embodies are key to the Corpse's prophecies. Death is the sixth card of the fortune, it tells the future of the Querent and, in this case, of the city itself. For the Corpse, this card signifies the return to Pluto. In the broader sense though, it heralds the downfall of Numantia. It is here that death becomes certain for the Numantines, as the boy tells "del lamentable fin, del mal nefando / . . . de Numancia" (1069–70; "the lamentable end / On which the doomed Numantia can depend"). However, if Death is taken only at face value it represents a grave misreading of this complex card. The Death Card, like all of the prophecies of the necromancy augur the same fate. The Numantines must and will die, but it will not be in vain, for far in the future they will live on in the memory of later Spaniards. Still, Marquino cannot see that far at first and he misreads the future by falsely predicting the result of the spinning Wheel of Fortune.

The first six cards, placed in the form of the Celtic cross, have defined the question of Numantia's fate up to the time of the necromancy and have laid clues for the future. The final four cards, the vertical row to the right of the cross, are to be found in both the Corpse's predictions for the city and later in the text itself. These cards pertain neither to the present, nor the past, but to the future and will become manifest in the progression of the plot. When the Corpse speaks precisely of Numantia's destruction, it is the first time that an answer is provided to Marquino's original inquiry. According to Butler, this is the function of the seventh card of a reading, to answer the question. When the Corpse mentions the city by name, we are reminded of its structure. Numantia is an enclosed, walled city surrounded by the Roman siege. It stands alone on the Castilian plain to await a now-certain death. In tarot symbolism, the Corpse speaks of The Tower of Destruction, Trump Sixteen. This card depicts a burning tower being struck by a comet or lightning bolt. The parallels between The Tower and the fate of Numantia are uncanny. Firstly, Waite stresses that the destruction inherent in the card's design is only a superficial and temporary ruin. Once again, this is the essence of Cervantes' tragedy: that immediate destruction at the hand of the Romans is only a temporary state and that the bravery of Numantia will live again in the memory of a future and greater Spain. The flames that shoot from the top of The Tower coincide with this message through their purging and cleansing properties. For the Numantines, fire will prevent the Romans from looting the city's belongings:

The Tower from the Rider-Waite Tarot deck.

> En medio de la plaza se haga un fuego,
> en cuya ardiente llama licenciosa
> nuestras riquezas todas se echen luego,
> desde la pobre a la más rica cosa.
>
> (1426–29)

["Right in the central square, we'll make a fire / In which we'll burn all that those swine desire"]

One Numantine later describes how "sus llamas sube hasta la cuarta esfera" (1651; "Blazing and hungry conflagration, which, / Fed with our riches, soars to the fourth sphere") adding a transcendent quality to the fire. This *ekpyrosis* affirms both the blind destruction of The Tower and the Death card, as well as their inferred and important resurrectional qualities.

Amid the Tower's scene of ruin, Waite indicates the importance of the card's two falling bodies, "the living sufferers" (135), who are thrown from the city's walls. In the third act, the lovesick Leonicio and his friend Marandro vow to get food for the dying Lira by vaulting Numantia's walls and raiding the Roman camp. The fourth act opens with Quintus Fabius's report of this deed to Scipio. He tells of the bravery and ferocity of the two Numantines as they slew all the guards that stood between them and the food storehouse. Interestingly enough, he compares their speed to a "rayo ardiente" (1756; "red-hot lightning") and a "cometa reluciente"(1758; streaking meteor from heaven). This image forms an important part of The Tower of Death and is recurring throughout the *Numancia* as a bad omen (844, 1756, 1758).

Near the end of his prophecy, the Corpse speaks of "el amigo cuchillo, el homicida / de Numancia será, y será su vida"(1079–80; "The sword of friends will deal the fatal blows / And be the murderer of this great city"). At first, this riddle puzzles the listeners; it's not swords but starvation they fear. In the fourth act, Cervantes provides the answer to this puzzle as Lira comes upon a soldier chasing a woman with a naked blade. Before striking her a deathblow, he explains that the Numantine senate has passed a decree condemning all the city's women to death lest the Romans steal them. This provides the eighth and ninth cards of the Tarot fortune in a vivid manner. The eighth card, the Eight of Swords, portrays "a woman, bound and hoodwinked, with the swords of the card about her" (Waite 238) and tells of the "influence of immediate friends . . . one's house" (Waite 303). For others, it is the card of daggers, repression, and fire. The situation illustrated on the card is clearly being playing out in the *Numancia*. The blindfolded and bound woman refers to the inevitability of death and the finality of the Senate's decision, while the proximity of the swords about her tell of the immediacy of fate.

The ninth card of the fortune also involves "el amigo cuchillo" and exposes the final "hopes or fears in the matter" (Waite 303). Butler maintains that this card of the fortune defines the Querent on all levels. The Four of Swords embodies the Numantine decision to steal the Roman triumph without fighting to the death. For Waite, it is a card of "vigilance, retreat, solitude" (246). By turning their own swords against themselves, Numantia is forced to face fate alone. Waite continues that it is a card of "exile, tomb and coffin" (246). Truly, the walled city is soon to resemble the tomb of the card and become nothing more than a large sarcophagus for its citizens.

Thus far, the prophecies of the necromancy have stressed negative outcomes. Still, the reader must not forget the words of the Corpse: "No llevarán romanos la victoria / de la fuerte Numancia, ni ella menos / tendrá del enemigo triunfo o gloria (1073–75; "Neither the Roman / will win the victory, nor o'er her foeman / Will strong Numantia ever vaunt the glory"). After the mass suicide, Scipio enters the city lamenting the fact that "Con uno solo que quedase vivo, / no se me negaría el triunfo en Roma" (2235–36; "If only one of them / Is left alive, then they will not deny me / A triumph back in Rome"). If not a single soul remains alive, then the Numantines will have successfully undermined Scipio and robbed him of his triumph. The Romans find their last chance for true victory when Bariatus, the last Numantine survivor, is seen hiding in a tower. The entire tragedy hinges on this one boy. If he is taken prisoner by the Romans, then the bravery of the city will have been in vain. Scipio, like a tempting Satan, offers him freedom and riches if he will submit and sell the souls of the entire city. Bariatus replies that it is death and not the Romans, that has triumphed over his people. He then denies "el deseo de seguir tu suerte" (2371) and declares that he will follow his fellow Numantines and take his own life:

> Pero muéstrase ya el intento mío;
> y si ha sido el amor perfecto y puro
> que yo tuve a mi patria tan querida,
> Asegúrelo luego esta caída.

> (2388–91)

["Now let me show you my intention. That / I loved my dear–belovèd country purely / And perfectly, let this fall be proof"]

In his suicide, Bariatus represents The Hanged Man, Trump Twelve, the tenth and final card of the Tarot reading. Butler states that "This card totals all the other cards and is read as if all the cards progressed toward it in the manner of a story" (196). The majority of authorities identify The Hanged Man as he who "sacrifices himself for others in complete self-abnegation" (Simon 40). While Waite asserts that "It has been falsely called a card of martyrdom," he later states that whoever can understand the card "will know that after the sacred Mystery of Death there is a glorious Mystery of Resurrection" (119). Bariatus comes to embody all of the qualities of this figure by defying the luck ordered by The Wheel of Fortune and not succumbing to the Devil's seduction. In every sense, he is the culmination of the entire play, the climax of the plot, and the finest example of Numantine bravery and loyalty. Bariatus, like The Hanged Man, is smiling until the end, he has inherited all of the *brío* of his people and has put their wishes above his own. The cross from which the figure on the card is suspended is made of living wood, for it, like the city, will survive the death of the martyr and live to grow and prosper in the future.[8]

Throughout this reading, one cannot ignore the sometimes contradictory nature of the tarot's messages. Cards such as Death, The Tower, and The Hanged Man that appear on the surface to carry unfavorable meanings conspire in the end to provide an optimistic message. Still the same qualities we find in the communications of the tarot are equally present in the text in question. In the *Numancia*, a series of negative omens and a mass suicide give way to future greatness. What's more, the text that we now enjoy did itself disappear for nearly two hundred years and, like the Numantines, reappear to greater glories than it enjoyed in its own time.[9] Its message is one of life through death, one as the absolute prerequisite of the other. This duplicity of meaning evokes Derrida's reading of the myth of Thoth (Hermes) and his observations on the nature of writing, Thoth's gift. Of Thoth he writes:

> Sly, slippery, and masked, an intriguer and a card, like Hermes, he is neither a king nor a jack, but rather a sort of *joker*, a floating signifier, a wild card, one who puts play into play. This god of resurrection is less interested in life or death than in death as a repetition of life and life as a rehearsal of death. (93)

Just as the Hermetic, archetypal images of the tarot assume a new form and underscore the symbology of the *Numancia*, Thoth,

The Hanged Man **from the Rider-Waite Tarot deck.**

Derrida writes, "is never present. Nowhere does he appear in person" (93). In the text, we find traces of Thoth in the double meaning of the auguries and the confusion of their prophecies. We find embodiments of Thoth's invention, the tarot, as subtexts to the play's double message and we find Marquino, the necromancer and dealer of the cards, as a likeness of the Egyptian god.[10] Derrida describes Thoth as "the passage between life and death . . . The god of writing, who knows how to put an end to life, can also heal the sick. And even the dead" (94).

Whether or not Cervantes consciously or subconsciously applied tarot images the archetypes of the tarot that surface in the *Numancia* reveal more than just a curious overlap of imagery but rather they deepen and help illuminate the double meaning of the play's prophecies. The complexity of Cervantes's commentary on the subversion of the Roman victory by the Numantines is further illuminated by recognition of the presence of prophecy as *pharmakon* in the text. This knowledge is the motivation behind both Bariatus's suicide and the "feliz remate" spoken by Fame at the conclusion of the tragedy.

NOTES

1. See Frederick De Armas, *Cervantes, Raphael and the Classics*.
2. In his article "The Two of Coins: An Unheeded Omen in *El Buscón*," Heiple cites Alfred Douglas and Étienvre on this point.
3. I would like to take a moment to clarify my perhaps "unorthodox" use of the tarot. In this study I will be utilizing the "face value" of the cards, i.e., the pictures, symbols, and colors themselves in addition to the divinatory meanings assigned by Waite, Butler, and others. Often, these two views are conflicting. For example, a card with a seemingly negative message may be assigned a positive reading by experts. In the context of the *Numancia*, however, these sometimes contradictory meanings merge to foreshadow the conclusion of the tragedy; Numantia must be destroyed and all of its people killed in order to subvert the Roman triumph and insure the future fame of the episode in history.
4. All English translations in quotations are from Eric Bentley and Roy Campbell's *The Siege of Numantia*, those not in quotations are my own.
5. I will be basing my description of the Ancient Celtic Method of Divination mostly upon Waite's *The Pictorial Key to the Tarot*. Deviations from Waite's (at times minimal and ambiguous) explanations will be signaled in the text.
6. References to the cards themselves are taken from the "Rider Tarot Deck," which were conceived by A. E. Waite and correspond best to his interpretations in *The Pictorial Key*. There are a wide variety of intriguing tarot decks on the market and many authorities suggest the creation of a personalized deck with an assimilation of personal and traditional colors and symbols.
7. For an exploration of the tarot in relation to alchemy and rights of passage,

see Chester S. Halka *Melquíades, Alchemy and Narrative Theory: The Quest for Gold in Cien años de soledad.* Lathrup Village, Michigan: International Book Pub., 1981. Halka discusses the Fool as *materia prima* that is transmuted through the course of the deck and the novel.

8. Curiously, The Hanged Man has been identified with Jesus Christ, while the suicide of the pagan Bariatus would clearly not be sanctioned under Church law in the future Spain the play heralds.

9. Jean Canavaggio writes: "Pero sólo nos han llegado *El trato de Argel* y *El cerco de Numancia,* a través de copias manuscritas defectuosas, encontradas en el siglo XVIII en el polvo de las bibliotecas" (107).

10. According to Butler, the Magician is normally associated with Hermes and Marquino does (obviously) also share many of the qualities of that card.

Star-Crossed Love: Spheres of Reality in Ruiz de Alarcón's *La verdad sospechosa*

Carolyn Nadeau

In the *Star Trek* episode, "A Matter of Time," Captain Picard, Data, and a young ensign of the ship find themselves victims of a hologram created by Sherlock Holmes's nemesis, Professor Moriarty, who is himself the central figure of another, related hologram. Because he desires to escape permanently his "false" holographic world and become "real," he takes control of the *Enterprise* computer and jeopardizes the ship and its crew until his new reality is secured. Unbeknownst to Moriarty, Picard and the others create yet a third "reality" that simulates a universe in which Moriarty can travel. Believing it to be the real universe and not a holographic illusion, Moriarty leaves his first hologram behind, enters into the third hologram, and relinquishes control of the ship's computer. Captain Picard, Data, and the ensign are able to exit their series of holograms and return to their own world. The episode closes with Picard's philosophical question, "Are we real or an insignificant part of someone else's elaborate scheme?"

This theme of defining and controlling one's reality is central to Golden Age drama, most notably in Calderón's *tour de force*, *La vida es sueño* in which Segismundo struggles to understand the relationship between life and dreams. In *La verdad sospechosa*, the characters, particularly the central figure García, also exist between a series of realities and fictions. However, they are not defined by holograms or dreams, but rather by suspect truths that García and other characters in the text sustain. While the *Star Trek* episode allows for the possibility of a higher, unknown force that controls what we understand as reality, *La verdad sospechosa* inscribes that force in the text through the "writing" perceived in the stars. The focus of this paper is to uncover the higher, astrological allusions that influence characters and situations in the play, most notably the García-Lucrecia-Jacinta love triangle.[1]

Although critics have studied astrological imagery in the works of Alarcón, the emphasis has been primarily on other plays. In tracing the astrological influences in *El dueño de las estrellas*, Augusta Espantoso Foley notes that the opening scene takes place at the shrine of Apollo (93). Frederick de Armas demonstrates the astrological basis for *Las paredes oyen*, and reveals Apollo's significance for the love triangle between don Mendo, don Juan y doña Ana (1993). Apollo, then, is an established figure in several of Alarcón's plays. Indeed, Joseph Silverman has pointed out that Alarcón, like the servant Tristán in *La verdad sospechosa*, sought employment at the court and, in all probability, studied astrology and was friendly with those who became astrologers. Alan Paterson has discussed astrological implications in this play but only in terms of the women of the court that Tristán describes to his recently arrived master. Finally, with respect to the theatergoing public, de Armas states that: "el público del siglo diecisiete estaba muy al tanto de los elementos astrológicos y de su trasfondo mitológico" (1993, 121; The seventeenth century public was well aware of the astrological elements and their mythological background).[2]

In *La verdad sospechosa*, García, Jacinta, and Lucrecia's love triangle is complicated by a series of realities including greater astrological forces that influence human destiny, García's fantastic lies, and Jacinta's cautious lie about her identity. Some critics have argued that García's final marriage to Lucrecia is of little significance because the two women are so "undistinguished and indistinguishable" (Poesse 70). Others view it as an act of divine justice that punishes García for his compulsive lying (Pasto 233). My own reading of the play will show that their marriage is inevitable.[3] García is an Apollo figure, the sun god, whose search for love is unknowingly divided between two women, Lucrecia and Jacinta, who, in turn, represent the "Ptolemaic" planets, the moon and sun, respectively.

As the play opens García is described as a young man whose only vice is "no dezir siempre verdad" (156; not always telling the truth).[4] He has recently returned to Madrid from Salamanca where he had been a student of the humanities. García's capacity to devise elaborate, albeit false, descriptions of his life and experiences, along with his intellectual pursuits at university, align him with the sun god, Apollo, who embodies poetry, philosophy, and the pursuit of learning.[5] The connection between lying and poetry is best understood by recalling Plato's notion of imitation: that the poet, by imitating an imitation, is doubly displaced from the truth.[6] García's description of the summer heat: "El *calor*, / del *ardiente* y *seco* estío" (4–5; The heat of the burning and dry summer), brings to mind a fierce sun and again, Apollo, who rules this planet. Don Beltrán, García's father, also refers to his son in terms of the god Apollo when he remarks on his son's return from Salamanca: ". . . ayer a Madrid vino / de Salamanca el mancebo, / y de invidia el rubio Febo / le ha abrasado en el camino" (901–4; yesterday the youth came to Madrid from Salamanca and the blonde Phoebus, full of envy, has burnt him on the way). Beltrán is modestly excusing García's burnt skin, yet his comment also reveals that Phoebus's sun has been transferred to García; he is now an Apollo figure.

In the fourth century, Proclus classifies the macrocosm/microcosm relationship according to planetary spheres. He points to their physical and ethical influence on humans (Klibansky 158). Later, in A.D. 885, Abû Ma'sar attributes planets to corresponding temperaments of humans (Klibansky 131).[7] While the astrologer from Baghdad was still highly influential during the Spanish Golden Age, the conceptions of the Renaissance philosopher Marsilio Ficino proved to be even more important for the Spanish playwrights of the seventeenth century. Ficino explained that people could be influenced by a particular planet in two ways: either by being born under that planet's sign or by associating oneself with those planetary qualities and thus creating an affinity between oneself and the planet. By applying Ficino's second notion of influence to García, we can see how his imaginative fabrications can be linked to heavenly forces. His lying aligns him with Apollo and harnesses the power of the sun god.

García's newly created realities are constructed around the expectations society has for him. To Jacinta, he lies about his profession and falsely claims an exhalted economic position as an *indiano peruano*. To his friend, don Juan, he lies about women and elaborates an amazing tale of courtship and late-night feasting on the banks of the Manzanares. To his father, he invents his marriage to a fictitious doña Sancha and news of their soon-to-be son. Finally, to his servant, he exaggerates his valor describing the duel he fought against don Juan; he also lies to Tristán about his linguistic capacity, claiming that he speaks ten languages fluently. Both the sword and the word are instruments of defense for men whose identities are measured by the honor code. In short, García lies about every aspect of the traditional male role in society: economic status, marriage, family, and honor.

García is not the only one who lies in the play. After Beltrán learns that his recently arrived son is endowed with the capacity to weave together fiction and reality, he expresses his anger by accusing those at the court of being equally deceptive: "En la corte, aunque aya sido / un estremo don García, / ay quien le dé cada día / mil mentiras" (185–88; Even though at court don García may represent an extreme, there are others who will lie a thousand times a day). Furthermore, Jacinta, the woman with whom García thinks he is in love, also invents untruths. In act two at Lucrecia's balcony, she deceives García, pretending to be Lucrecia. Then, at the church in act three, she denies that she is playing such a role. Jacinta is coolly calculating; she always weighs the situation to her advantage, regardless of the truth.[8] Both Jacinta and García, like Captain Picard and Professor Moriarty, create new realities in an attempt to control their surroundings favorably. A closer look at the main characters in *La verdad sospechosa* reveals the ambiguous nature of reality. Although some of the characters believe they might be in control, the text of the play shows the greater influences of the heavenly bodies.

Characters' names reveal mythological and astrological signs in the text. In the Middle Ages, Isidore of Seville believed that the etymology of a name presented the essence of its meaning.[9] Catherine Larson reminds us that, "the institution of naming relates to language's ability to identify, describe, and make real" (96). Lucrecia's full name is Lucrecia de Luna, thereby directly associating her with the Ptolemaic planet, the moon and Apollo's twin sister, Diana, born of Zeus and Leto. According to Plato, in the *Symposium*, the basis of love is the search for one's half, that is, one's twin.[10] García, the symbolic sun god, searches for his complement and twin, Diana, the moon goddess, who appears, not as one might think as his beloved Jacinta, but rather as Lucrecia de Luna, whose surname reveals her astrological identity.[11]

Another example of the importance of Diana, the moon goddess, occurs when García explains to Tristán why he lies: "Nómbrenme a mí en todas partes, / y murmúrenme siquiera; / pues, uno, por ganar nombre, / abrasó el templo de Efesia" (863–66; Let them name me everywhere, and let them gossip about me; there was one who, in order to gain fame, burnt the temple at Ephesus). García is comparing himself to Erostratus, who burned Ephesus, which housed the temple of Diana, and thus earned him his fame. In this way, the myth suggests that García will earn his fame, as Erostratus did by consuming the moon goddess with flames, by consummating marriage to his moon goddess, Lucrecia.

On García's first day at the court, he spies two beautiful

women, Jacinta and Lucrecia, and falls desperately in love with
one of them, who the audience/readers know to be Jacinta. Tristán, García's servant, immediately warns him of the possibilities
of another woman and a greater love: "advierte, señor, si aquella /
que tras ella sale agora / puede ser sol de su aurora / ser aurora
de su estrella" (420–24; Notice, sir, if that one who emerges after
her may be the sun of her dawn, the dawn of her star). He defines
the women in planetary terms and warns that the other may be
even more luminous than the first. Tristán then is the first to
suggest that Lucrecia is the planetary figure who is better suited
to García. Immediately following this encounter, García describes
Jacinta—although he mistakenly calls her Lucrecia—in astrological terms:

> Si es Lucrecia la más bella,
> no ay más que saber, pues ella
> es la que habló, y la que quiero;
> que, como el autor del día
> las estrellas dexa atrás,
> de essa suerte a las demás,
> *la que me cegó*, vencía.

(558–64)

[If Lucrecia is the most beautiful one, there is nothing else I need to
know, since she is the one who spoke and the one I love. Like the
author of the day who leaves all other women behind. She who
blinded me has won.]

García errs in naming Lucrecia, "el autor del día" (the author of
the day), the sun, for it is Jacinta that he is describing. Her power
to blind, "la que me cegó" (she who blinded me), evokes darker,
saturnine images. In both astrology and alchemy, Saturn was considered a black star and a *sol niger* (Jung 75). In the García-
Lucrecia-Jacinta triangle, Jacinta is a black sun, hence, a Saturn
figure, who connotes frustration in love and suggests an unhappy
outcome for her and García. In a groundbreaking article on saturnine melancholy in *La estrella de Sevilla*, James Burke describes the
forlorn love associations with the mythic god: "a planet often
unfriendly and associated since pre-Ptolemaic times with the tradition of dubious love affairs. . . . Thus, astrologically speaking
the marriage . . . is fated never to be" (1974, 145–46). The relationship between García, who represents Apollo, the sun god,
and Jacinta, who represents Saturn, the *sol niger*, is also astrologically doomed from the start.

Jacinta and Lucrecia are best friends. This intimacy and the fact that Jacinta constantly disguises herself as Lucrecia, suggests that the two women are another twin pairing in the text. Indeed, Isabel, Jacinta's servant, reminds her of their close friendship. Jacinta herself refers to Lucrecia as a type of soul mate: "es amiga mía; / tanto, que me atrevería / a afirmar que en mí y en ella / vive sólo un coraçon" (2599–602; She is so much my friend that I would dare to affirm that in her and in me there lives only one heart). This shared "corazón" both portrays the women as twins and as two that share one love: García. Lucrecia defines Jacinta in terms of her solar beauty: "al mismo sol obscureces" (2363; you darken the sun itself). Again, images of darkness suggest that Jacinta is a black sun, a saturnine figure that frustrates love between two people. Although Jacinta is obviously not meant to be with García, she is, at the same time a sun figure and as such, a twin to Lucrecia, the moon figure. Together they form a solar-lunar complementary between which García is caught.

Spellbound upon meeting the two for the first time, García refers to himself as Atlas: "Esta mano / os servid de que os levante, / si merezco ser Atlante / de un cielo tan soberano" (437–40; Use this hand so that I can raise you up, if I deserve to be an Atlas to such a majestic heaven). Atlante, or Atlas, is best known for the punishment he endured of bearing the weight of the world and the vault of the sky on his shoulders. Elizabeth Hamilton explains: "Bearing this burden he stands forever before the place that is wrapped in clouds and darkness, where Night and Day draw near and greet one another" (66). This passage at once reveals Jacinta's celestial nature and her star-crossed conflict with García. Jacinta, the sun, and Lucrecia, the moon, are the figures that García can approach but never fully reach. Throughout the play his love is frustrated by this solar-lunar dynamic.

Jacinta's name further underlines her ill-fated relationship with García. Recalling the myth of Apollo and Jacinto (Hyacinth), Apollo and Zephyr, the god of the west wind, were in love with Hyacinth and, during a discus-throwing game, Zephyr, in a jealous rage, changed the winds and caused Apollo's discus to hit Hyacinth, instantly killing him. Thus, Apollo's love for Jacinto was cut short. From a mythological perspective, then, the love between García and Jacinta is ill-fated while the love between García and Lucrecia, echoing the reunion of the twins Apollo and Diana, is harmonious.

In *La verdad sospechosa* the varying levels of reality indicated by astrological subtexts in the play and the elaborate lies of the main characters convert truths into lies and lies into truths. García unknowingly lies as he repeatedly refers to Jacinta as Lucrecia. A typical scene of García's confusion between Jacinta and Lucrecia takes place at the end of act two, at Lucrecia's balcony. As Lucrecia is the moon, García appropriately arrives at her house at night. Previously, during the day, he and his father had ridden to Jacinta's house, again accentuating the sun-moon dichotomy in the text. On the balcony, Jacinta feigns her identity so she can talk to García without jeopardizing her honor or her marital prospective to don Juan. García petitions Lucrecia, who is really Jacinta in disguise. Fending off her accusations of his lying to her, García implores Jacinta (who feigns being Lucrecia) to believe in him. He rightly refers to Lucrecia (whose identity Jacinta has assumed) as a perfect moon.[12] The real Lucrecia, not Jacinta incognito, is lunar perfection. García is addressing Jacinta, and thus, unwillingly lies. Yet, if we take at face value his signified, he thinks and says he is talking to *Lucrecia*, then his lie is actually the truth. Lucrecia is a perfect moon who will not be eclipsed in her amorous efforts.

Through the use of astrology and linguistic games, Alarcón embroils his audience in a debate over the nature of truth and lies. Larson points out that, "Language . . . subverts García's controlling role in the same situations he has been trying to manipulate" (97). She and others suggest that García has selected the wrong signifier for the right signified.[13] Paterson writes, "Like a metal filing cast into a magnetic field, García's error is charged and orientated; it acquires a significance that grants to the outcome a sense of near-logical necessity. Pledged by his word, spoken and written, to the name Lucrecia de Luna, then Lucrecia de Luna he will and does marry" (362). However, from an astrological perspective, García does indeed have the right signifier; it is the signified that has been star-crossed. Lucrecia is the right name for García; Jacinta is the wrong figure.

Another intersection of astrology and García's lies occurs in his fabrication of his shotgun marriage to doña Sancha in Salamanca. Here, García's supposed lie ultimately foreshadows his own destiny. He explains to his father why he married doña Sancha to preserve her honor and his own life. Unknowingly, then, he is revealing the true outcome of his Madrid love affair. His lie becomes the truth. The difference between his false marriage and the real one are the underlying astrological elements. The Salamanca-marriage scene is encoded with traditional imagery associated with Saturn, that is, the watch and lead (of the pistol).

When doña Sancha's father unexpectedly visits the secret lovers, García's watch conspicuously sounds on the hour. García curses Father Time (1600–1601), who, as Klibansky points out, is Kronos, the Greek god that corresponds to Saturn (151–59). Sancha tries to retrieve the watch to show her father it is only a gift from her cousin, but García's pistol accidentally fires a lead bullet. Jung explains that Saturn's metal, lead, acted as a purifier that, "could aid the individual to attain virtue through repentance and expiation of sin" (cited in Burke 1974, 149). By exposing García's hiding place, which leads to his forced marriage to doña Sancha, Saturn has betrayed García two times; yet this planet also leads him to the more virtuous path of marriage. Moreover, Saturn, the black sun, is incompatible with García's own sun image. While both the false marriage of García's "lie" and the real marriage at the end of the play are forced on the protagonist, the Saturn-invested marriage is not harmonious with García's Apollo image and in this way differs from García's real marriage to Lucrecia.

There are other indications throughout the play that allow us to see the shift of importance from Jacinta, García's supposed love interest, to Lucrecia, the woman he will marry. First, John London notes that the setting, "underlines the increasing emphasis on Lucrecia which is necessary in order to portray her love for don García and so lead to her eventual marriage to him" (45). As the play advances, the setting revolves more and more around Lucrecia. The end of act one closes at Jacinta's house but the close of act two and again of act three take place at Lucrecia's house. Second, Lucrecia's house is appropriately situated on "la calle *victoria*" (Victory Street), suggesting a victorious outcome for her. In the final scene both Lucrecia's father, don Juan, and García's father, don Beltrán, offer García the alternative of death or marriage to Lucrecia. Death and victory are also pitted against one another in an earlier scene. When García is dueling with Juan, he foreshadows his final conflict by saying: "tengo de hazer / como quien soy, no bolver / sino muerto o vitorioso" (1813–15; I have to behave like who I am and not return unless I am dead or victorious). In effect, these are the choices don Juan and don Beltrán give him: die or marry Lucrecia whom we recognize as *la victoriosa* (the victorious).

Another indication of this shift in focus from Jacinta to Lucrecia is the rising tension the two friends experience as both women realize their strong feelings for García and see the other as a potential threat. At first, Jacinta asks Lucrecia permission to disguise herself as her friend and Lucrecia willingly consents, as she has not yet explored her feelings for García. Later, their love interest in García provokes feelings of competition, until finally one accuses the other of betraying their friendship and neither of them trusts the other. Their turbulent relationship draws attention to García's unknowing predicament of confusing their identities, a predicament of which the audience is fully aware, but that García himself will only understand at the drama's close.

Finally, García's special relationship with Lucrecia is underscored by the fact that she is the only person to whom he never lies. While the stories he tells Jacinta are either outright lies, (*el indiano*, for example), or unintentional lies due to her identity switch, the letters he writes to Lucrecia are true in spite of the fact that the receiver, the signified, is not who he thinks it to be. In the letter García writes to Lucrecia he states: "dime si serán creídas, / pues nunca mienten las obras" (2450–51; Let me know if my words will be believed, for actions never lie). This letter reveals two important developments of García's lying. First, in contrast to the Platonic dichotomy of holding speech to be innocent and writing to be deceptive, García's truth is clearer in his letters than when he speaks in person because he is removed from the confusing signifieds (the women Lucrecia and Jacinta).[14] Second, Larson has pointed out that this phrase represents a radical change for García who had previously "scorned the value of noble deeds" (105). The value placed on action over words is a sign of García's attempt to remain noble within the deceitful world of which he plays such a colorful part. It is not that the audience is offered hope that he will reform for he continues to lie to those around him till almost the close of the play, yet, he realizes that words, both truth and lies, are less effective than action for communicating the truth.

Notes

1. In Ruiz de Alarcón's play, *La verdad sospechosa*, we find many of the problematic elements that enrich Golden Age dramas. Harold Veeser and Catherine Larson have studied the conflict between the oral and the written text; James Burke, the importance of clothing (1975); and Robert Fiore and Alva Ebersole explore the father-son dynamics. Other intriguing articles include Mary Malcolm Gaylord's reading of the play as a journey of desire, its mimetic nature and the suspect nature of truth, and Geoffrey Ribbans's analysis of the nature of García's lies and its relation to theme, structure, humor, and social convention.

2. For more on characters from Alarcón's plays interested in astrology, see de Armas (1993, 120n. 8).

3. Many critics have debated the significance of the play's ending. Some

argue that García deserves punishment. DiLillo, for example, suggests that the play's theme is "rooted in moral consciousness and responsibility" (254), and that García's "lack of moral and social concern" (259) leads to his downfall. Ribbans believes he deserves his punishment because of his "arrogance and wilful pride" (215). However, others are less severe and sympathize with how García arrived at his fate. Fiore, for example, suggests that García's psychological motive for lying is based on his relationship with his father. For him, no one is punished harshly (20–21). Fothergill-Payne goes so far as to say that García does not deserve to be punished: "No merece castigo sino una admonestación que le despabile y le enseñe a tener más discreción y prudencia" (589). Many other critics address the play's *denouement* including Burke who, in discussing the interplay between medieval and modern stances on the faculties of reason and the imagination, questions any moral reform at the end of the play (1986).

4. All citations are from the Martel edition.

5. For more on the characterization of Apollo see, Morford (155–78, esp. 177).

6. In Book 3 of the *Republic,* imitation is described as impersonation and used to discredit Homer. Later, in Book 10, it is used in a broader, though still negative, sense of producing a copy of something else. While the theory of imitation is much more complex, this notion of imitation as a distortion of the truth is most commonly associated with Plato. For more on the theory of imitation in Antiquity, see Gerald Else. For imitation in the Renaissance, see G. W. Pigman III's classic study.

7. The relationship between the planets and humanity is also explored by Vettius Valens in the 2nd century and the Neoplatonists, particularly Macrobius and Proclus in the 4th century, among others. For more on the history of astrology in European thought, see Klibansky.

8. For interpretations of Jacinta's character, see Gaylord who highlights her prudence (234). Fothergill-Payne refers to Jacinta as a "cortesana por excelencia" (595). Pasto calls her, "rational and practical" (233) and suggests that she is the character with "the most control over her own destiny" (233). Madrigal does not have as optimistic an opinion. For him, Jacinta is as despicable as García: "don Juan y Lucrecia, dotados de cualidades positivas y merecedores de algo mejor, ambos contraen matrimonio con opuestos. . . . don Juan con una mujer calculadora y materialista" (131).

9. Isidore of Seville's work, *Etymologiarum libri,* discusses etymology as a part of grammar. See Curtius (495–500).

10. For more on the search for one's twin, see de Armas (1995).

11. Fothergill-Payne discusses the significance of Lucrecia's name but does not mention the astrological connections (592).

12. On the burning of Diana's temple at Ephesus, see de Armas (1996a).

13. Gaylord also stresses the wrong signifier. She explains that García is punished becasue of his error of "getting the girl's *name* wrong" (225).

14. Elias Rivers explains that, in general, the *comedia* treats writing as shameful while orality is respected as an honorable transaction.

Part 2
The Metamorphic Tradition

The Mythological and Astrological Subtexts of *La fundadora de la Santa Concepción*

Nancy Mayberry

La fundadora de la Santa Concepción, (*The Founder of the Holy Conception*), a two-part play by the Toledo playwright Blas Fernández de Mesa, is found in a partially holograph, autograph manuscript dated 1664.[1] It deals with the life of Beatriz de Silva, the Portuguese founder of a convent in Toledo which represented the first order dedicated to Mary's Conception. The historical facts concerning the life of Beatriz are well known today because the saint was formally canonized in 1976. At that time several manuscripts and published histories from the sixteenth and seventeenth centuries were brought to light (Gutiérrez, Omaechevarría).[2] One such biography by Sor Catalina de San Antonio (12), published in 1661, mentions Mesa's play proving that the 1664 copy is a late version.[3] That biography, called *La margarita escondida*, and the other chronicles of the age all relate her life story as follows:

Born in Portugal in 1424 to a noble family, Beatriz came to Spain as lady-in-waiting in the retinue of Isabel, the Portuguese princess who became the second wife of Juan II of Castile. Beatriz was extremely beautiful, and at court her beauty caused turmoil and jealousy. Some chronicles claim that even the king was enamored of her thus provoking the jealousy of the queen, Isabel. The latter, motivated by this jealousy, had Beatriz shut up in a trunk where she remained for three days and nights without food or water. When the queen finally revealed the answer to Beatriz's disappearance, and opened the trunk, all expected to find that Beatriz had died. Instead she emerged with the tale of a miracle. The Virgin Mary had come to her aid in gratitude for Beatriz's devotion to the Immaculate Conception. In some versions, Beatriz was ordered to found the convent in Toledo during this vision; in others, it occurred later on the road to Toledo. There, two monks mysteriously appeared to Beatriz and ordered her to found the new convent as the first order dedicated to Mary's Conception. Their symbols revealed them to be Saint Francis of Assisi and Saint Anthony of Padua. In Toledo, Beatriz, for over thirty years, tried in vain to get permission from Rome for this new order. But no new ones were being allowed, and the doctrine of the Immaculate Conception was still in dispute. However, a new pope, Sixtus IV, a Franciscan whose order supported the doctrine, and encouraged by letters from Queen Isabel's daughter, finally signed a papal bull granting the foundation. The documents were lost at sea during a shipwreck, but miraculously reappeared in Toledo. Other miracles occurred as Beatriz finally successfully founded her order, and died dressed in the new blue and white habit of the Orden de la Concepción in 1492.

All known dramatic versions of Beatriz's life also follow this basic outline.[4] It is difficult to imagine how a playwright could successfully forge a mythological subtext to such a plot. Blas de Mesa does, however, weave several myths into the play that parallel and inform the first literal level of meaning. It is well known that mythographers, Biblical commentators, and rhetoricians discerned multiple levels of meaning in the writings of their age. The traditional four-fold method advocated by St. Augustine, found a historical or literal meaning, an allegorical level, a prefigurative level, and a moral meaning (Augustine, 3). Thomas Aquinas also discussed a *sensus literalis, sensus allegoricus, sensus anagogicus,* and a *sensus moralis* in sacred writings.[5] While the historical and moral levels of this saint's play are easily discerned, the classical myths that illustrate the allegorical and prefigurative levels are less obvious.

On the allegorical level, a series of myths of metamorphosis parallel the change of Beatriz from lady-in-waiting to saintly founder of a new order. All these legends deal with love affairs in which an innocent love object is pursued by a powerful figure, usually a god, and wherein the unwilling objects are all ultimately transformed. The first myth deals with Apollo's pursuit of Daphne. She appealed to her father and escaped Apollo by being turned into a laurel tree. From that moment on Apollo used the laurel as his attribute and the triumphant crown of poets. A second myth tells of the west wind or Zephyr's capture of Chloris whom he abducted to an island where she was changed into the goddess of flowers, Flora. The Venus and Adonis legend tells of how Cupid accidentally wounded his mother Venus with one of his arrows, causing her to fall in love with the beautiful youth Adonis. Mars, in love with Venus, grew jealous, and disguising himself as a wild boar, killed Adonis whose spilled blood Venus changed into the red flower known as the anemone.[6] Intertwined with these myths is the story of the conflict between Venus and

Mars, representing the conflict between love and war, letters versus arms, the poet versus the soldier. The prefigurative level is found in two horoscopes, one dealing with Alvaro de Luna and the other with Isabel I.[7]

The first hint of these myths on the allegorical level occurs when the king, Juan II, first sees Beatriz. The king had never met his intended, the marriage having been arranged by Don Alvaro de Luna. On first seeing the retinue from Portugal, the king considers himself wounded by Cupid's arrows and falls in love with the wrong woman, Beatriz rather than Isabel. In the legend, Venus's love for Adonis was the result of an accidental wounding by one of her son Cupid's arrows. In the play the king questions the identity of the beautiful lady wearing a white plume in her headdress in the following terms:

> La que saber desea mi cuidado
> es la que trae con garbo más lucido
> la airosa pluma de cristal rizado
> que anima los arpones de Cupido
> de quien su frente corva es arco bella.
>
> (221–25)[8]

[My concern is to know the one who is wearing with magnificent elegance the proud feather of curling crystal which animates Cupid's harpoons and whose curved forehead is the beautiful bow.][9]

White and crystal are immediately associated with Beatriz, the colors of purity, the attribute of the Virgin Immaculate. Cupid's arrows, here called *arpones*, wound the king, and in effect transform him from a soldier into a poet. In a later conversation with Don Alvaro, the king admits himself disinterested in the wars in his kingdom, comparing himself to smitten heroes of mythology, noting the parallels not only with the Mars-Venus struggle, but comparing himself to Apollo and his love for Daphne.

> Si grandes héroes disculpan,
> a Marte mira depuesta
> la loriga, que con Venus
> celosamente pelea.
> Mira como sigue a Dafnes
> el Padre de los poetas.
> Oyele después cantar
> a un Laurel tristes endechas.
> Que un niño ciego y desnudo

> con solamente una flecha
> las armas postra a sus pies
> y sin letras a las letras.
>
> (617–28)

[If great heroes provide an excuse, see Mars with his shield abandoned as he jealously fights with Venus. See how the father of poets pursues Daphne, and listen to him afterwards sing sad laments to a laurel. For a blind and naked child with only one arrow prostrates arms at its feet, and without letters, conquers letters].

The arms-versus-letters motif is taken up in the allegory of Mars laying down his arms to struggle with Venus, while the king, conquered by Cupid's weapons, becomes Apollo, a love-stricken poet. In the allegory, Beatriz becomes the pursued Daphne who is transformed into the symbol of triumph, the laurel. Later, Don Alvaro tells Beatriz "Laurel es vuestra merced en quien my Rey idolatra" (1252–53). (Your grace is the laurel whom my king idolizes). Interestingly enough, a portrait of Beatriz attached to the manuscript, shows Beatriz with a leaf in her hand. Iconographers identify this leaf as the palm branch, the symbol of victory.[10] Thus, the laurel and the palm both represent symbols of triumph. The pagan myth pinpoints the symbol of the triumphant poet, while the Christian icon represents the triumph over death.

The king's remarks occur during a poetic contest called to celebrate Beatriz's supposedly miraculous cure of a child's nose bleed.[11] Each of the assembly narrates a poem or epigram on the event. Don Alvaro's poem refers to the myth of Chloris.

> Cloris por azules venas
> Beatriz con cinco azucenas
> los claveles recogía
> y a sus amantes promete
> la madre de los amores
> de blancas y rojas flores
> en su mano un ramillete.
>
> (1017–23)

[Chloris through blue veins, Beatriz with five lilies picked up the carnations, and the mother of love promises her lovers a bouquet of white and red flowers in her hand.]

This poem, and in fact the whole play, is filled with both flower and color symbolism. The Chloris referred to in Don Alvaro's poem is the name of the nymph who became the goddess of flowers. In the poem, the red blood is turned into a carnation, which Beatriz picks up, while the mother of love, Venus (the owner of the island of flowers) gives her a bouquet of white and red flowers. Beatriz's fingers are white lilies, one of the medieval icons of the Virgin Immaculate. During the vision, the Virgin orders Beatriz to clothe herself and her nuns in the colors white and blue, symbols of purity also found in the poem.

The color blue has an interesting double meaning. It is used most often to refer to the queen's jealousy, as in the line "que arroja puntas azules" (1071) (for she is throwing blue darts). In act 3 the servant sings a *letrilla* in which she refers to the blue flowers of the queen's jealousy:

> (*Canta*) Las flores del romero
> bella Isabel
> hoy son flores azules
> mañana serán miel.

(1873–76)

[The rosemary flowers, beautiful Isabel, today are blue flowers, tomorrow they will be honey.]

The song is an attempt to humor Isabel out of her depression caused by her jealousy of Beatriz and the king. While the color blue in this sense is jealousy, in reference to Beatriz, it refers to the color of the nun's cloak she will eventually wear.[12] The color red in Alvaro's epigram, the metaphor for blood, is obvious for Beatriz will shed her blood before being transformed. It may also recall the red anemone, the flower into which Adonis was transformed. Thus, the epigrams dealing with the nosebleed foreshadow Beatriz's shedding of blood before her transformation.

The myth of Zephyr's abduction of Chloris is referred to again in a later scene. The queen is in Beatriz's room and hearing the king enter, blows out the light. In the resulting darkness the king mistakes the queen for Beatriz and pledges his love, referring again to the Chloris-Flora myth. Mistakenly thinking he is addressing Beatriz, the king says:

> Si temes a la Reina
> contigo iré adonde Flora peina
> con oloroso peine de retama
> su pelo de junquillos que derrama
> en el jardín isleño.
> A Chipre dulce dueño

> es de Venus, patria de las flores
> donde todo es delicias, todo amores.
>
> (1658–65)

[If you fear the queen, I will go with you to where Flora combs with her comb of scented Spanish broom her hair of jonquils which she spreads upon the island garden. At Cyprus the sweet owner is Venus, the native land of flowers where everything is delights, everything is love.]

Again the king compares himself to Zephyr and his abduction of Chloris to Venus's island, the kingdom of flowers. Interestingly enough, Beatriz's biography also conferred upon her the name of a white flower, the margarita, or daisy.[13] A musician in act 3 likewise refers to Beatriz by that name:

> A la mejor Margarita
> que dio ijar a Valencia
> por celos del Rey su esposo,
> mató en palacio la Reina.
>
> (2084–87)

[In the palace the Queen out of jealousy of the king her husband, killed the best Margarita that appeared in Valencia.]

When first questioned concerning the identity of his mistress, the *gracioso* (clown figure) described Beatriz in these words:

> Sirvo a una señora
> tan bella que han presumido
> que es flor que se le ha caído
> de su tocado a la Aurora.
>
> (323–36)

[I serve a lady who is so beautiful that it is presumed that she is a flower that has fallen from the headdress of the Dawn.]

Thus, the flower symbolism links Beatriz again to the transformation legends of mythology. She is not captured or abducted by the king, but is transformed by the Virgin Mary into the founder of a new order dedicated to the Virgin's Immaculate Conception.

The final myth and the one that is the most prominent in the play is the Venus-Adonis story. Myth, allegory, and visual and oral representation commingle in a very powerful scene. The queen had ordered one of the courtiers to bring her his dagger,

and with it she forces Beatriz from her room and along a corridor.
The walls of the corridor are decorated with tapestries, and the
queen asks Beatriz:

> ¿Qué historia, Beatriz, contienen
> los lienzos de esa antesala?
> (*Ap.* Muy bien sé que es la de Adonis
> mas afecto la ignorancia.)
>
> (1348–51)

[What history, Beatriz, do the tapestries of this anteroom contain?
(*Aside* I know very well that it is the one about Adonis, but I'm
feigning ignorance.]

Beatriz replies:

> La tragedia es de Adonis
> y de Marte la venganza
> por celos que le dio Venus
> de uno y otro a un tiempo, Dama.
> En uno, montero el joven
> los llanos bate y montañas
> y en otro Marte celoso
> en jabalí se disfraza,
> y provocado de Adonis
> quitó a sus celos la causa
> con los agudos colmillos;
> y en la sangre que derrama
> tiñó sus cándidas flores
> Venus de color de nácar.
>
> (1352–65)

[The tragedy of Adonis, together with at the same time the vengeance
of Mars on account of the jealousy Venus gave him, milady. In one,
the young hunter beats the plains and mountains, and in the other,
jealous Mars disguised as a wild boar and provoked by Adonis, removed the cause of his jealousy with his sharp horns, and in the
blood that spills Venus tinted the pure white flowers the color of
mother of pearl.]

In this story with the same theme of a powerful figure pursuing
an unwilling victim, there is the added element of jealousy, and
wounding, as well as the conversion into a flower. When the
allegory is applied to Isabel, the king, and Beatriz, there is a
curious gender inversion in the Mars-Venus struggle. Obviously,

it is the queen who is the warlike figure Mars, whose jealousy persecutes Beatriz, the innocent recipient of Juan's love. In the play, the queen uses a dagger (the sharp horns of the *jabalí* (boar) in the legend) to force Beatriz into the closet where she will remain for three days and nights.[14] In the process she wounds Beatriz in the hand. The spilling of blood is an addition to the plot not found in the biographies, but the wounding makes the story more in keeping with the blood that turns into a flower. In the legend of Adonis, the flower is red, but there is a significant change of color in the version described by Beatriz. Here the flower is the color of nacre, white, or mother of pearl rather than red. Again the white symbolism is necessary both for the color of the nun's habit Beatriz will eventually wear, as well as for the white flower attributed to Beatriz in her biographies.[15]

Throughout the first part of the play the Mars-Venus conflict is represented in the fierce queen Isabel who represents the masculine Mars, while the king, Juan II, is linked to the feminine Venus, the goddess of love, as well as to Apollo, the god of poets. The queen is continually associated with the sword, the dagger, and the weapons of war, obvious phallic representations of the queen's masculine aggression.[16] Her jealousy is often represented in terms of weapons, as in the lines of the *gracioso* who reports that "la Reina arpones la tira / por debajo de las cejas." (954–55) (The queen is throwing harpoons at her from under her eyebrows.) The lines recall the harpoons that wounded the king earlier and that were Venus's son's arrows, rather than Mars's weapons of war. The king on the other hand, in both history and the play, is represented as somewhat effeminate, so disinterested in politics that he turns the government over to his favorite, Don Alvaro de Luna. He much prefers to write poetry and to pursue his love of Beatriz. His rejected queen bitterly realizes that he is like Paris who awarded the golden apple to Venus, not Juno goddess of war (1457). The queen, however, blames the king's weakness on Beatriz. In the scene where the queen imprisons Beatriz, she refers to yet another myth. She informs Beatriz that like queen Omphale who forced Hercules to spin thread like a woman for a year, so she has feminized the king:

> Y tú estorbas que el segundo
> Alcides luche en campaña
> que divertido le tienes
> hilando copas de lana.

(1498–1501)

[And you prevent the second Hercules from fighting in the field, for you have him diverted, spinning hanks of yarn.]

The king himself confesses to Alvaro his love of Beatriz in terms of a defeated soldier: "al templo de amor conduce / arrastradas mis banderas." (591–92) (leads to the temple of love, my flags dragged along) and again "porque amo la prisión y gusto de que me venza." (599–600) (because I love the prison and am pleased that she defeats me). In the scene of the poetic contest the king is portrayed as so anxious to participate that he even refuses to hear a war report from his *alférez mayor* (military captain). When Beatriz is reported missing, the monarch delivers a raving speech in which he is willing to see his whole kingdom conquered rather than lose Beatriz. It is Don Alvaro de Luna who must take over the reins of government and rule for the bewitched king, who like Hercules, has undertaken the feminine role represented by spinning.

The role of Don Alvaro is especially interesting in the play. Like Beatriz, he suffers from the queen's jealousy. From the moment he met Isabel, he sensed a hidden sword and metaphorical references to swords and daggers connect Don Alvaro and Beatriz (Mayberry, 1986). Beatriz survives the queen's jealous attack, but Alvaro dies beheaded, largely at the queen's behest.[17] A curious horoscope in the play tells of how Don Alvaro's ignominious end was determined by the stars.

> A un astrólogo pidió
> que observase en su horizonte
> su nacimiento y supiese
> por los astros brilladores
> en qué lugar moriría,
> y hechas las observaciones
> le respondió, que en cadalso,
> y en un lugar deste nombre
> jamás entró, y era suyo,
> que tarde se reconocen
> en la próspera fortuna
> equívocos deste porte.

(II, 293–304)

[He asked an astrologer to observe his birth on his horizon, to find out from the brilliant stars in what place he would die, and once made the observations he replied that in Cadalso (a pun for in Spanish this means also "on a scaffold"), and in a place by that name he never entered, and it was his (fate) for mistakes of this kind are recognized late in one's prosperous fortune.]

These lines occur in the second part where the *alférez mayor* narrates the death of Don Alvaro on a scaffold.[18] Alvaro is linked to Beatriz through the imagery of the blades, dagger, and weapons wielded by the jealous queen against both her husband's amorous object, Beatriz, as well as his favorite, Don Alvaro. Beatriz is able to escape the queen through her transformation into a nun. Alvaro trusts in earthly power and the king's friendship, neither of which save him from his fated end on a scaffold. The queen's jealousy is much stronger than the king's weak-willed defense of his friend, again representing the gender inversion in the Mars-Venus myth.

This Mars-Venus conflict is not resolved until the second part. There Isabel I, the daughter of Juan and Isabel of Portugal, fulfills both roles. She is represented as both a warrior, triumphant in the wars against the Moors, yet a model of feminine domesticity, wielding the spindle and the sword with equal skill.[19] Thus, the third level of meaning, the prefigurative, or prophetic, deals not with Juan II and his jealous queen, or even with Don Alvaro, but with their daughter Isabel. It is she who becomes Beatriz's mentor and champion, and through her intervention with the pope finally brings about the permission to found the order.

Throughout the two parts of the play, another horoscope, linking Isabel to Virgo and ultimately Astraea, represents the prefigurative level of meaning. We first learn of the horoscope shortly after the birth of Isabel in Part I. Beatriz directs her servant:

> Tráeme el curioso papel
> que pronostica a la infanta
> en la cuna gloria tanta,
> para alegrarme con él.

(1178–81)

[Bring me the curious paper that foretells for the princess in her cradle so much glory, so that I may entertain myself with it.]

The servant Leonor complies and describes the paper:

> Juicio, que han hecho
> astrólogos de importancia
> de doña Isabel, y dice
> será la señora infanta

> conforme a sus ascendentes,
> Reina, marcial, rica y sabia.
> Con su favor, y en sus días
> el signo Virgo señala,
> que una nueva religión
> tendrá principio en España
> a honra y gloria de la Virgen.
>
> (1222–32)[20]

[Judgment that astrologers of importance have made of Doña Isabel and it says that the lady princess, like her ancestors, will be a martial, rich and wise queen. With her favor, and in her time, the sign of Virgo indicates that a new religion will have its beginnings in Spain to the honor and glory of the Virgin.]

As Frederick de Armas has carefully documented, Virgo was the sign attached to Astraea. This was the goddess who returned to earth to restore justice and a golden age.[21] The prefigurative level uses the return of Astraea to refer not only to the founding of the order and its future success, but as an astral-imperial myth foretelling the triumph of the newly united kingdom of Spain under one religion and the Catholic kings. But as De Armas also points out, while normally an imperial myth foretelling the triumph of an empire as a golden age, in her Christian garb, Astraea/Virgo also became an allegory for the Virgin Mary (20). Thus, Beatriz interprets the horoscope as foretelling the queen's support in bringing a new religion into Spain. Religion here appears to have a double meaning, referring both to Spain's religious unity under the Catholic kings, as well as to the new order in defense of the Immaculate Conception.

For centuries a debate had raged all over Europe concerning the exact moment in time Mary had become immaculate; at her conception, in her mother's womb, at the moment of her birth, or the moment of the annunciation (O'Connor). While all agreed that Mary herself was sinless and Immaculate, the moment of this granting of sinlessness was in dispute. Blas de Mesa's play was rewritten in 1664 in honor of a papal bull by Alexander VII decreed in 1661.[22] The *Bula Solicituda* put a stop to the debate by declaring that the doctrine represented the feeling of the Catholic Church, and therefore all opposition to it was prohibited, even though the belief was never officially made dogma until 1854. Therefore the horoscope refers to a first step in the process of the dogma's promulgation. Beatriz's order, officially called in the papal bull the order of the Conception, was the first such order permitted and thus represented an important triumph for the immaculatists. The foundation represented, therefore, an important historical moment in the development of the doctrine. In his study of hagiographical drama, Josep Lluis Sirera claims that prophecies such as the one found in the horoscope are common in saint's plays providing a bridge between the time of the saint and the time the play was composed, read or performed. Mesa's audience would have viewed the founding of the first order to Mary's conception as a triumph for the doctrine, if not a new religion, and thus an appropriate vehicle for celebrating the pope's 1661 pronouncement. Thus, the horoscope prefigures not only the time of the Catholic kings, but the time of the play's rewriting in 1664.

The horoscope also neatly resolves the Mars-Venus struggle, and the gender confusion noted in the first part. There Isabel's mother was fierce and warlike and her consort an amorous poet. The queen had in fact likened the king to Hercules who spent a year spinning wool out of love for Queen Omphale. The gender confusion found Isabel identified with the vigorous and fierce, the king with the passive and amorous. This binary opposition is clearly evident and not resolved, for the queen's opposition to Beatriz persists at the end of the first part. The new queen, Isabel, in the second part is shown to have resolved the binary opposition, for she is both martial, as indicated in the prophecy, but also a loving consort proud of her spinning. The gender inversion of the first part is resolved in the resolution of both male and female in the person of Isabel I. A curious line leaves no doubt of this strangely hermaphroditic behavior as the queen describes herself as "tomando ora la espada, ora la rueca" (II, 989). (Now taking the sword, again the distaff.) Both the Spanish and the English contain a sexual play on words dealing with the phallic sword and the cleft instrument used to hold flax or wool while spinning. The latter is a symbol for the female sex in general. Isabel, the queen of the second part, instead of jealously persecuting Beatriz, supports her and is in fact instrumental in helping Beatriz found the first order dedicated to Mary's Conception.[23] Instead of writing poetry as her father did, she is depicted as taking an active role against the enemies of Spain, while retaining her feminine persona as faithful supportive wife to her husband, letter-writer to the pope, and therefore partner with Beatriz's enterprise.

Thus, Blas de Mesa manages to illustrate the literal and historical level of meaning with mythological and astrological subtexts. The myths of transformation parallel the change of Beatriz from innocence pursued to innocence triumphant. The Mars-Venus conflict is resolved in the figure of Isabel I, while the horoscope raises Beatriz's individual triumph to the level of an imperial and religious culmination. Thus, the subtexts bring us neatly full circle back to the literal level of history not only in reference to the time of the Catholic kings and the foundation of the first order to Mary's Conception, but to the historical climate of the date of the play's rewriting in 1664.

Notes

1. While relatively unknown today, Blas Fernández de Mesa was a well-known dramatist and poet in his own time. He was praised by Lope de Vega in the *Laurel de Apolo* (191) and by Agustín Moreto in the play *No puede ser* (187c–188a). Montalbán described him as follows: "Blas de Mesa, a pesar de ocupaciones mayores, las [comedias] hace con primor; tanto que no tiene que envidiar a cuantos hoy las escriben en España (Barrera, 154). (Blas de Mesa, in spite of greater occupations, writes them [plays] with elegance; so much so that he need not envy any who write them today in Spain). The "greater occupations" referred to by Montalbán were those of the political post held by Blas de Mesa in Toledo, that of city treasurer (Mayberry, 1982).

2. Gutiérrez's work lists a bibliography on Beatriz's life beginning in 1512. The list includes ten works from the sixteenth century, and eighteen from the seventeenth (383–86). Mesa could have had access to any number of these.

3. For a complete discussion of the various manuscripts, possible dates, and their authors, see my article "Blas Fernández de Mesa," 1982.

4. Mesa's play was not the only dramatic version of this saint's life. Tirso de Molina wrote a play entitled *Doña Beatriz de Silva* which was published in his *cuarta parte* (fourth-part) in 1635. Two early manuscript versions of the first part were erroneously attributed to Lope de Vega and Tirso de Molina. See Mayberry, 1982. The manuscript attributed to Lope de Vega is entitled *El milagro por los celos* (The Miracle on account of Jealousy) and was reprinted by Menéndez Pelayo in the *academia* edition of Lope's plays. Its similarities with Tirso's play are the result of their common historical sources. See Mayberry 1984.

5. For a full discussion of this method, see the work by Henri de Lubac.

6. A description of these myths may be read in *Bulfinch's Mythology.*

7. Another prefiguration occurs in the second part, where Beatriz plays the role of Esther in a play within a play that dramatizes Esther as a prefiguration of the Immaculate Conception. This prefigurative level is not related to mythology but to scripture, and represents a more anagogic level. See Weiner (36).

8. All quotes and line numbers are from my edition.

9. All translations from the Spanish are my own.

10. Cirlot identifies the palm branch with fecundity and victory (237). St. Anthony and St. Francis prophesied to Beatriz that she would be the mother of many children. She objected that this could not be so because she had dedicated her chastity to God. Her children were of course the nuns of her order.

11. Poetic academies and contests of this sort were very popular in the Golden Age. See Rodríguez Sánchez de León.

12. The nuns of this order still wear this habit as it is described in the vision in chronicles as well as in the various plays.

13. *Margarita* may also mean pearl, also usually white, and one of the attributes of the Virgin Mary. The biography that refers to Beatriz as *La margarita escondida* is referring to the hidden pearl, one of the iconographic symbols of the Virgin Immaculate. For a complete list of the Virgin's attributes, see Bourassé.

14. The change from a trunk to a closet was necessary for staging purposes. Some scenes take place inside Beatriz's prison.

15. Even modern biographies have continued this method of referring to Beatriz. The archbishop of Toledo, in a prologue to Gutiérrez's *Santa Beatriz de Silva*, (11), writes: "Beatriz de Silva es una flor de exquisita fragancia . . ." (Beatriz de Silva is a flower of exquisite fragrance).

16. There is a recurring motif throughout the first part dealing with the symbol of the sword, knife, or blade. In each case the mention of these objects foretells the beheading of Don Alvaro as well as the wounding of Beatriz. See Mayberry, 1986.

17. This is both dramatized in the play and based on the chronicles of the time.

18. Interestingly enough, this horoscope is supposedly historical, for it is documented in Mariana's *Historia* and was repeated in ballads and other plays on Don Alvaro. See Mayberry, 1993.

19. In a very interesting scene in the second part, Isabel's consort teases her about the Archbishop of Toledo who bragged to Alfonso of Portugal that he (the archbishop) would make Isabel return to her spinning. The incident is again found in Juan de Mariana's *Historia*, p. 191.

20. It is well known that Felipe II had his horoscope cast, but I have found no historical mention of this horoscope in connection with Isabel I.

21. The genesis of such a horoscope concerning Virgo may be traced back to Virgil's *Fourth Eclogue* often called the Messianic Eclogue. Christian exegetes believed that the prophecy in that eclogue was that of the birth of the Christ child. Lines 4–10 of the eclogue are translated into English as follows: "Now is come the last age of the song of Cumae; the great line of the centuries begins anew. Now the Virgin returns, the reign of Saturn returns, now a new generation descends from heaven on high. Only do thou, pure Lucina, smile on the birth of a child, under whom the iron brood shall first cease, a golden race spring up throughout the world! Thine own Apollo now is King!" Cited by de Armas, (1986, 6).

22. The *aprobaciones* (approvals) of both the first and second parts refer to the celebrations of the papal order.

23. The chronicles of the age as well as the modern biographies confirm Isabel's intervention. The papal bull granting the foundation is still extant and even mentions the role of the queen in helping the order's establishment. See Guitérrez's reproduction of the bull *inter universa* (367–71).

Myth and Metamorphosis in Tirso's
Privar contra su gusto
Christopher B. Weimer

Tirso de Molina's *Privar contra su gusto* (*The Reluctant Royal Favorite*) must certainly be numbered among his many unjustly neglected plays.[1] This thinly veiled portrait of Spanish *privanza* and politics during the early seventeenth century receives scant critical attention, while the meager scholarship actually devoted to the text focuses primarily on its value as a historical artifact or didactic tract. Pedro Muñoz Peña, for example, perceives a parallel between Tirso's fictionalized King Fadrique of Naples and Felipe III of Spain and contends that Tirso sought to eulogize the executed courtier Rodrigo Calderón with his laudatory depiction of the *comedia*'s protagonist, the reluctant *privado* Don Juan de Cardona (488–89).[2] William E. Wilson agrees that Fadrique represents Felipe III but regards Don Juan as a portrait of the Duke of Osuna, a Spanish viceroy of Naples recalled to Madrid in 1620 and placed on trial for charges fabricated by his political enemies; from this perspective, one supported by Battista J. Galassi in the preface to his critical edition (Tirso 1971, 3–48), *Privar* is Tirso's response to Osuna's opponents. Blanca de los Ríos (Tirso 1959, 1069–75), also perceives the unfortunate Duke's fate woven into the threads of this *comedia* but believes that Tirso's primary intent was to satirize the favor temporarily enjoyed by Quevedo at the court of Felipe IV. Finally, Gerald E. Wade and Ruth Lee Kennedy present the most persuasive arguments to declare the play a political prescription aimed at Felipe IV and his favorite, the Count-Duke of Olivares, the primary models for King Fadrique and Don Juan. With the exception of Galassi, the aforementioned critics address few literary or aesthetic concerns in their analyses. On the contrary, they appear primarily interested in questions of historical contextualization, regarding *Privar* mainly as an *espejo* valuable for its preserved images, for whatever information contemporary Hispanists can glean from it concerning Spanish politics of the early 1620s.

Despite the obvious value of such inquiries, my purpose here is not to address this critical dispute. *Privar* is indeed an important example of didactic commentary on *privanza* and might well constitute Tirso's portrait of court figures in his day, but it merits study from other perspectives as well. Although Galassi asserts that the author's prescriptive intent limited the psychological depth of the play, leading the Mercedarian to portray Juan de Cardona as "the perfect *privado*" and to sketch the other characters only to the extent necessary for them to serve as effective foils for the exemplary protagonist (Tirso 1971, 36–37), this study will argue that Tirso does more than merely populate the work with unidimensional characters to be guided like marionettes through his dramatized lessons for Felipe IV and the Count-Duke. Nor, for that matter, does *Privar* even limit itself to political questions. The play is also a romantic comedy depicting intricate mating dances between two aristocratic couples: King Fadrique's pursuit of Leonora de Cardona, sister of his reluctant *privado* Don Juan, and the confusion-plagued romance between Juan and Fadrique's sister, the *Infanta* Isabela. By interweaving the work's political dimensions with these romantic intrigues and by taking advantage of the additional opportunities for character development that the latter two plotlines present, Tirso demonstrates his frequently remarked talent for "psychological range and penetration" (McKendrick 116) and ensures that *Privar* will be far more than a formulaic, conventional *comedia de privanza*. Most significantly for the purposes of this study, the playwright finds inspiration in classical mythology for his two amatory plotlines. The primary models utilized by Tirso in this play are the accounts of Daphne's flight from Apollo and of Diana's revenge upon Acteon, both of which would have been available to the Mercedarian in the most fundamental and prominent mythological source of all: Ovid's *Metamorphoses* (I.452–567, 14–18, and III.138–252, 55–58, respectively).[3]

The enormous influence exerted by the Roman poet's output on Spanish literature, especially during the Golden Age, has already been well documented.[4] Thanks in part to the far-from-faithful but best-selling prose "translation" by Jorge de Bustamante, *The Metamorphoses* was Ovid's most popular work in Spain.[5] Among practitioners of the *comedia*, both Lope and Calderón knew Ovid's text well enough to draw repeatedly upon its many tales as a source of plots for their mythological dramas; still more significant is their use of Ovidian subtexts, metaphors, and similes in countless other plays (Schevill 211–25). The classical erudition which Tirso displays throughout his works leaves little doubt that he also knew *The Metamorphoses* well, and the text of *Privar* contains an explicit reference to the Roman author's *Remedia Amoris* (*Cure for Love*): when Don Juan de Cardona laments his silent passion for Fadrique's sister Isabela, he declares, "Remedios Ovidio escribe / contra amor; pero son largos" (1266–67: "Ovid offers remedies for love, but they are lengthy").[6] Clearly, it should not surprise us to discern an Ovidian palimpsest beneath *Privar contra su gusto*'s romantic intrigues.

Privar begins with the first of its many mythological allusions: the action opens in the forests surrounding Naples with the stage direction, "*El Rey, de caza, y Leonora, retirándose de él*" (preceding v. 1: "The King in hunting attire and Leonor retreating from him"). This initial scene, throughout which the young Neapolitan king Fadrique attempts to woo Leonora de Cardona in spite of her efforts to escape him with her honor intact, immediately recalls a host of literary precedents. The figure of a damsel, nymph, or huntress fleeing through a bucolic setting in defense of her chastity is a staple of the pastoral tradition; this figure's varied incarnations in Renaissance and Golden Age Spanish literature range from Camila in Garcilaso's *Égloga segunda* to Cervantes's Marcela in *Don Quijote*. As the encounter between Fadrique and Leonora develops, however, Tirso's source for the scene will become apparent: Daphne's famous flight from the god Apollo. According to Ovid, Cupid repaid Apollo's arrogance toward him by shooting the nymph Daphne, daughter of the river-god Peneus, with an arrow causing her to abhor love and by shooting Apollo himself with a contrary dart afflicting the sun-god with an irresistible passion for her. Dominated by that passion, his first experience of amorous emotion, Apollo pursued Daphne relentlessly. On the verge of being captured she cried out to her father for help, and Peneus complied by transforming her into a laurel tree. In a subsequent scene of the *comedia* Leonora's brother Juan will invoke the legend when he describes a beautiful woman bathing in a river; explicitly referring to the sun illuminating her body as *Apolo*, he declares:"y él todo ojos, / lo que en Dafne no pudo, aquí divisa" (172–73: "and he all eyes, that which Daphne denied him, here he espies"). This metaphor confirms the Mercedarian's knowledge of the tale, the primary source of which throughout Europe was *The Metamorphoses* (Barnard 1989, 5). Ovid's lighthearted treatment of this famous myth, described by Mary E. Barnard as "a serio-comic story of unrequited love with strong echoes of the trappings of Roman erotic elegy" (1987, 19), inspired

Spanish authors ranging from Garcilaso to Quevedo to pen their own versions of the story. Even before any words are spoken onstage in *Privar*'s opening scene, the unnamed pursuer's hunting garb and weapons link him with Apollo, the divine hunter whose prowess was the stuff of legend. Indeed, Ovid introduces the deity in *The Metamorphoses* as *deus arquitenens*, the "Archer god" (I.441, 14), and relates Apollo's ill-advised mockery of Cupid for presuming to wield the bow and arrow:

> Mischievous boy, what are a brave man's arms
> To you? That gear becomes my shoulders best.
> My aim is sure; I wound my enemies,
> I wound wild beasts; my countless arrows slew
> But now the bloated Python, whose vast coils
> Across so many acres spread their blight.
> You and your loves! You have your torch to light them!
> Let that content you; never claim my fame!
>
> (I.456–62, 14)

The ensuing dialogue between Fadrique and Leonora repeatedly parallels the royal hunter's feelings, actions, and circumstances to those of the Greek god in Ovid. First, both texts constitute the urgent passions felt by Fadrique and Apollo as forms of lovesickness. Leonora describes Fadrique's ardor in precisely such terms when she justifies her refusal to hear his pleas:

> Señales da vuestro amor
> de que la enfermedad crece,
> pues todo enfermo apatece
> lo que le ha de estar peor.
> El favor
> que os hago, cura os aplique;
> que el no verme os está bien.
>
> (81–87)

[Your love shows signs of its infection growing, since the sick hunger for what is worst for them. May the favor that I do you effect a cure, for not seeing me will help you most.]

Fadrique likewise speaks repeatedly of *enfermedades* and *curas*, and we cannot help but be reminded of Apollo's entreaty that Daphne take pity on him and relieve his passionate ailment:

> The art of medicine I gave the world
> And all men call me "healer"; I possess

The power of every herb. Alas! That love
No herb can cure, that skills which help afford
To all mankind fail now to help their lord!

(I.521–4, 16)

Indeed, Barnard asserts that Apollo's "subjection to Cupid renders him the helpless victim of *furor,* the erotic madness that afflicts all elegiac lovers, divesting them of self-mastery and reason" (1987, 24). There can be little doubt of the figurative metamorphosis involved in that subjection, for Ovid tellingly employs animal imagery when describing the god's pursuit of Daphne (I.533–39, 17). Barnard writes:

> It is true that Ovid identifies Apollo with a dog and Daphne with a hare by means of similes and does not actually "transform" them into these animals. But the way in which Ovid has fashioned his "cinematic," detailed description of the chase can only make the reader envision the god and the nymph bearing animal traits, especially Apollo who, as the target of the comedy, is dressed with "muzzle," "fangs," and "jaws," clawing at his sexual prey as he pursues her. (1987, 25)

These similes, then, associate the effects of lovesickness with the actual shapeshifting repeatedly depicted by Ovid throughout his poem. Moreover, Leonard Barkan has persuasively argued that the Roman author's text constitutes first encounters with amorous passion as partaking of the metamorphic principle (1986, 13–14). Fadrique's first sight of Leonora thus serves the same transformational function that Cupid's arrow did.[7]

Aware of the fear his uncontrollable ardor arouses in Leonora, Fadrique attempts to calm the noblewoman with assurances of the respect that he promises accompany his passion (5–10), just as Apollo likewise attempts to reassure Daphne that his pursuit is amorous rather than predatory (I.504–7, 16). When this tactic fails, both resort to disclosures of their true identities. Apollo, clearly hoping that knowledge of his divinity will render him more desirable in addition to alleviating Daphne's fears, cries out to her:

> Yet ask who loves you. No rough forester
> Am I, no unkempt shepherd guarding here
> His flocks and herds. You do not know—you fly,
> You madcap girl, because you do not know.
> I am the lord of Delphi; Tenedos

> And Patara and Claros are my realms.
> I am the son of Jupiter.
>
> (I.512–7, 16)

Fadrique likewise hopes to calm Leonora and win her heart with his self-disclosure, which would have come as a surprise both to the noblewoman and to the majority of Tirso's original spectators, who would most likely have been unfamiliar with the work: "Mirad que soy el rey. . . . Yo soy el rey don Fadrique" (90–91: "Look you, I am the king . . . I am King Fadrique"). Fadrique's royalty links him even more closely with Apollo than his announcement of it does. Not only was monarchy considered divine in origin, a ruler's duties corresponded to Apollo's traditional responsibility for human law and order (Smith 32). The connection between king and god is further developed by the two authors' subversively irreverent characterizations of them. Barnard has pointed out that Ovid's Apollo is a less-than-divine deity whose passion is exaggerated to the point where he becomes ridiculous: "The Latin poet degrades the arrogant Olympian converting him into a human, fatuous lover. The chase is the high point in his humorous treatment. We have a vision of a silly god wooing his elusive lady on the run, a picture of gallantry mixed with foolishness, pomposity with self-pity" (1984, 501).[8] Indeed, *The Metamorphoses* repeatedly and mercilessly humanizes the gods with its tales "of their loves and, more commonly, of their lusts, and the result necessarily had to be comic, even ludicrous at times, but not dignified and serious" (Welles 7–8). This comedy resulted naturally from the indignities inflicted by amorous abandon upon divine grandeur; Ovid himself, as Marcia L. Welles points out (8), declares explicitly in *The Metamorphoses*: "Ah, majesty and love go ill together, / Nor long share one abode!" (II.846–47, 50). Nor can human royal grandeur in *Privar* withstand passion's mockery. Even prior to the revelation of Fadrique's identity, this unknown *galán's* attempts to woo Leonora with a show of gallant ardor seem so overly impassioned that neither she nor the spectators can easily take him seriously; indeed, the noblewoman herself admonishes him with the words, "persuadís / exagerador, no amante" (45–46: "you plead excessively, not lovingly"). Even more comedy results from Fadrique's disclosure of his true identity, a tactic that succeeds no better than did Apollo's. When the boyish monarch reveals his identity to Leonora, the text specifies that he act "muy grave" as he does so (91: "very grave"). Such a stage direction is striking for its sheer rarity in the *comedia,* a genre in which playwrights rarely dictated specific emotional interpretations to their actors. This "muy grave" is in fact the single emotive line reading specified in the entire text of *Privar;* the remaining stage directions merely indicate when various *apartes* begin and end and to whom characters speak at certain moments in the play, along with the customary notation of entrances and exits. We can only conclude that Tirso considered the manner in which Fadrique reveals his identity absolutely essential to this opening scene's effect, and that effect is a masterfully humorous one: the extreme gravity with which Tirso demands that this boy-king unexpectedly announce his royalty to both Leonora and the spectators, after behaving from the moment of his precipitate entrance in such a comically overwrought manner, would certainly elicit far more mirth than awe from audiences. Just as Apollo's "desire to let Daphne know that he is no lowly peasant but a suitor of noble birth and high connections" results only in the god "revealing himself as an impotent, impatient fool" (Barnard 1987, 24), Tirso directs that Fadrique be portrayed in a similarly humorous fashion that renders him more risible than majestic.

Fadrique's resemblance to Apollo is implicitly strengthened by the use of the sun as a metaphor for the Neapolitan monarchy. When Leonora learns her suitor's identity, she tells him that she and her brother Juan live in seclusion outside Naples after the example of their deceased father, Don Pedro de Cardona, who acted as *privado* to Fadrique's own late father until palace slander and intrigue resulted in his exile from court. The metaphor she uses to relate his downfall is significant:

> Con vuestro padre privó
> el nuestro en tiempos pasados,
> y paró en lo que privados
> suelen: volaba, y cayó.

(112–15)

[Our father counselled yours in times past, and ended up as royal favorites are wont to do: he soared, and fell.]

Throughout the play both Leonora and Juan repeatedly describe Don Pedro's loss of his *privanza* with references to the myth of Icarus, who flew too close to the sun with his man-made wings and fell to earth when its heat melted the wax with which the feathers were fastened—and whose exploits are detailed in Book

VIII of *The Metamorphoses* (VIII.183–235, 176–78). A political Icarus, Don Pedro's ascent to power brought him too near to King Alfonso with similar results.[9] Fadrique, who now occupies his father's throne, is by extension the new "sun"; the text thus again equates him with Apollo the solar deity. Furthermore, even the obvious political parallel Tirso draws between his fictionalized monarch of Naples and Felipe IV of Spain further reinforces that parallel. Ruth Lee Kennedy makes the strongest case for this aspect of the text, describing Fadrique as "un joven rey, mucho más interesado en una mujer hermosa que en los asuntos de estado; un rey que prefiere traspasar el duro trabajo del gobierno a su privado, y está perfectamente dispuesto a pagarle en honores y mercedes con tal de quedar él mismo libre para sus amoríos" (1981, 234: "a young king, much more interested in a beautiful woman than the affairs of state, a king who prefers to delegate the hard work of government to his favorite, and is perfectly disposed to reward him with honors and favors in order that he himself might remain free to pursue his love affairs"). This description makes it clear that Fadrique at the play's outset, as Kennedy asserts, is in fact a sharply drawn portrait of Felipe himself in the first years of his reign. The fact that Felipe IV was styled the *Rey-Planeta*, a sobriquet linking him to the sun, fourth planet in the ptolemaic solar system, by extension makes Fadrique a sun-king analogous to Ovid's sun-god.

The parallel between Leonora de Cardona and Daphne is equally apparent. Leonora follows the nymph's example in refusing to surrender to Fadrique's passion. Daphne, of course, falls under the baleful influence of Cupid's arrow, which causes her to take refuge in the woodlands far from civilization:

> . . . . she flies the name of love,
> Delighting in the forest's secret depths
> And trophies of the chase, a nymph to vie
> With heaven's virgin huntress, fair Diana.
>
> (I.474–76, 15)

The misfortune suffered by Don Pedro de Cardona similarly affected his children, compelling them to shun the dangers of "civilization" and live in bucolic seclusion. When Leonora explains this to Fadrique, Tirso's text again echoes Ovid's:

> Mi ventura
> me destinó a habitadora
> destas selvas, donde gano

> cazadora,
> libertad con un hermano,

(106–10)

[My good fortune destined me to inhabit these forests, where as a huntress I enjoy freedom with my brother.]

Like the river-god's daughter, Leonora has sought refuge in a sylvan retreat; her self-characterization as a *cazadora* evokes Ovid's comparison of Daphne to Diana. The Cardona siblings' rejection of all that is associated with court life also leads inevitably to Leonora's fear of her obviously noble, though initially anonymous, suitor:

> Peligro el campo amenaza,
> todo es engaño en la caza,
> todo en la corte es fingido.
> Si venido
> habéis al campo a cazar
> de la corte, será en vano
> lisonjear,
> pues, cazador cortesano,
> no vendréis sino a engañar.

(12–20)

[The countryside threatens danger, for all is deceit in the hunt, all at court is false. If you have come from the court to hunt in the countryside, flattery will be in vain, courtly hunter, since you have come only to deceive.]

The lesson Leonora learned from her father's tragedy serves the same psychological function as Cupid's arrow, driving her into the forest and causing her to scorn Fadrique's attentions. Finally, just as Apollo's encounter with Daphne in the *Metamorphoses* ends with her frustration of his passionate intentions, *Privar*'s opening scene likewise concludes when Leonora succeeds in making her escape and thwarting Fadrique's designs.

However, Leonora's trials do not actually end here, as Daphne's do because of her transformation. Scarcely has she withdrawn from the young king's presence than he is attacked by several masked assailants. Two noblemen also exploring the sylvan countryside, Leonora's brother Juan and his friend Luis de Moncado, come to the king's aid and save his life. After Fadrique discovers that Juan is the unjustly disgraced Don Pedro's son, he insists on naming the unwilling nobleman his new *privado*; the king's abruptly conceived, intense desire for Don Juan's counsel, friendship, and presence at court is essentially a nonsexual infatuation corresponding to his passion for Leonora. Unfortunately for the latter, there is now no way she can avoid accompanying her brother to reside in the palace. Once the siblings have joined the Neapolitan court, the king's campaign for Leonora's favors is no less relentless than his campaign to conquer Juan's aversion to his *privanza* and to his new, unfamiliar life. Fadrique pursues his *privado*'s sister until she, like Daphne, cannot protect her virtue alone. Since Don Pedro is dead, her brother acts *in loco parentis* according to the custom of the day, and it is to Juan that Leonora turns early in Act II: "soy yo vuestra hermana, y temo / las violencias del poder" (1131–32: "I am your sister, and I fear power's violence"). Fearing Fadrique's apparently unquenchable attraction to her, Leonora begs Juan's assistance just as Daphne begged Peneus for his: "'Help, Father, help! If mystic power / Dwells in your waters, change me and destroy / My baleful beauty that has pleased too well'" (I.545–47, 17). The river-god, as we have noted, responded by transforming his daughter into a laurel tree. In Tirso's story, Juan likewise hopes that a transformation will serve the same purpose and to that end suggests the following strategy to his sister:

> Desdeñosa, manifiesta
> que enfado tu amor te da;
> menosprecia su cuidado;
> que un rey de todos querido
> tiene, como no ha probado
> lo que es ser aborrecido,
> el gusto tan delicado,
> que se muda fácilmente,
> Aborreceráte ansí.
>
> (1186–94)

[Show disdainfully that his love annoys you; scorn his attentions; a universally beloved king who has never known what it is to be hated has fickle interests that change easily. He will detest you thus.]

Yet this ploy does not present as simple a parallel to that of the river-god in Ovid as it might appear. Juan does hope that the scornful behavior he asks his sister to assume will protect her from Fadrique's unwelcome attentions and possibly terminate his own coerced service to the crown as well. From the young king's perspective, such a change of demeanor would indeed transform Leonora, whose deference to Fadrique's royalty since the first scene has apparently led her to adopt passive rather than assertive modes of self-defense. However, this—as Juan's use of the verb *manifestar* (to demonstrate) indicates—would in fact constitute no real transformation at all, merely the declaration of Leonora's true feelings which she has concealed beneath a cloak of courtly docility. The metamorphosis Juan actually hopes to effect—as signaled by the verb *mudarse* (to change)—is that of Fadrique, by transforming his dangerous fascination with both siblings into aversion. Juan here proves himself far more daring than Ovid's Peneus, who sought only to make his daughter invulnerable to Apollo's violent attentions rather than attempting to modify the god's perilous desire.

Juan's plan, despite its merits, is never put into action, for Leonora's attitude toward her royal suitor changes after she is (inaccurately) told by Don Luis de Moncado that Fadrique's intentions are in fact honorable and that he wants to marry her. Immediately tempted by the possibility of becoming Queen of Naples, Leonora becomes much more receptive to the monarch's interest. Tirso again rewrites his Ovidian model here: while Daphne never falters in her wish to be metamorphosed into an inviolable shape forever safe from Apollo's love, Leonora's Daphne-like terror of violation changes abruptly to interest in Fadrique. Such a transformation at this point in the action is scarcely a comic one, since it stretches Juan's resourcefulness to the limit. The king has locked him in a chamber with instructions to complete essential diplomatic documents, a transparent maneuver devised by Fadrique to prevent his favorite's interference with the nocturnal garden rendezvous to which he has invited the newly compliant Leonora. Escaping the locked chamber through a window, Juan dons a concealing hooded cloak, disguises his voice by holding a bullet in his mouth and goes to intercept Fadrique in the darkness: "Yo divertiré el amor / que su juventud provoca" (1885–86: "I will divert the passion provoked by his youth"). In the metatheatrical scenario which ensues, the *privado* proceeds to enmesh his opponents within a drama of his own devising in order to save himself and his sister, along with Fadrique and even Naples itself, from the dangers presented by the young king's irresponsibility.

When the men encounter one another, Juan amazes Fadrique with his intimate acquaintance of Neapolitan affairs and reveals to him a plot against the monarch's life, the facts of which the disguised *privado* was fortunate enough to overhear in the garden only moments before. Fadrique, believing his rescuer a guardian angel, benevolent spirit, or perhaps even a saint descended to earth, responds with even more gratitude and deference than he offered Juan after the nobleman aborted the assassination attempt in Act I. This sudden reverence toward his unknown mentor constitutes yet another infatuatory transformation on the young monarch's part, one that will finally yield positive results: he eagerly accedes to the counsel Juan offers, permitting the *privado* to secretly steer his young king toward responsibility and wisdom in both his personal and public lives. Indeed, Fadrique's newly instilled maturity soon leads him to judge his own dishonorable behavior, including his intentions toward Leonora, harshly; he describes his benefactor as "quien tanto / guarda mi vida y reino, y (en efeto) / quien juveniles vicios me reprime" (2731–33: "he who so guards my life and kingdom, and who in effect curbs my juvenile vices"). Nor is Fadrique the only one to verbalize this metamorphosis wrought by Juan: the *Infanta* Isabela, when she first speaks with her brother's anonymous adviser, asks him, "¿Sois vos / por quien el rey se gobierna?" (2921–22: "Is it you through whom the king now rules himself?"). In the drama's concluding moments Fadrique puts his new convictions into action by announcing his intention to wed Leonora. This establishes beyond all doubt that Juan's masquerade, along with his sovereign's susceptibility to the metamorphic power wielded by infatuation in in its various forms, has transformed Fadrique from an immature, self-indulgent youth into a monarch aware of his responsibilities to himself and to his subjects. Moreover, this final turn of events transforms Leonora de Cardona into a queen.

Even as Fadrique wooed Leonora de Cardona during *Privar*'s opening moments, her brother Juan was himself becoming entangled in an erotic web woven according to mythological patterns. Juan describes to his close friend Don Luis de Moncado in the second scene of the play (immediately prior to the assassination attempt against Fadrique) how he fell in love: when walking alone through the forest only shortly beforehand, he caught sight of an exquisite noblewoman undressing to bathe in the river.[10] Enraptured by her, Juan observed the unknown beauty's naked ablutions and dared, unseen, to steal one of her garters as a token of his good fortune. Such an encounter immediately brings to mind another Ovidian precedent: the hunter Acteon (grandson of Cadmus, founder of Thebes) unintentionally coming upon the goddess Diana while she bathed nude in a sacred spring.[11] In *The*

Metamorphoses, Diana acts swiftly to redress this breach of the barrier between the human and the divine. She transforms Acteon into a stag and sets his own dogs upon him; his hunting companions and hounds unknowingly tear him to pieces, much to Diana's sadistic gratification. The parallel between the two initial situations is obvious, and further examination of Juan de Cardona's voyeuristic encounter emphasizes Tirso's debt to Ovid. As Galassi notes (24), Juan describes the unknown beauty in exalted terms, referring to her both as "la blanca Aurora" (161: "the white Aurora") and "un ángel" (164: "an angel"). Not only do these metaphors assign her to the divine realm occupied by Diana, the reference to Aurora, goddess of the dawn, specifically recalls the Roman poet's description of naked Diana blushing "like the crimson dawn" (III.184, 56). The unidentified noblewoman, though she bathes alone, is later joined by what Juan describes as "un escuadrón de damas (digo estrellas)" (235: "a squadron of ladies, or better said, stars"), a group of metaphorically celestial ladies-in-waiting who correspond to Diana's own chaste attendants ennumerated by Ovid (III.165–72, 56). Moreover, the bathing beauty's reaction when she discovers the disappearance of her garter is significant:

> busca la liga, de mi amor reparo,
> y no hallándola, cóleras resiste,
> y registrando flores que despoja,
> hurtos de amor acusa en cada hoja.

(230–33)

[she searches for the garter, a tonic for my love, and not finding it, she struggles to control her ire, and shredding flowers as she searches through them, she declares each leaf guilty of love's theft.]

Throughout classical mythology, the huntress Diana/Artemis distinguishes herself for the ferocity with which she defends her own inviolability along with that of her followers and of her sacred preserves (Barnard 1987, 34). The nameless aristocrat's fury at the theft of her garter, fueled by the knowledge that the thief must have seen her naked, recalls Diana's reaction when Acteon views her unclothed body. Not only does Ovid assert that the deity instinctively looked for her bow and quiver upon perceiving the hunter (III.188, 56), he concludes his description of Acteon's gruesome death thus:

> And not until so many countless wounds
> Had drained away his lifeblood, was the wrath,
> It's said, of chaste Diana satisfied.
>
> (III.251–52, 58)

The bathing beauty's anger is no less intense, as Juan reports to Luis, and hardly less implacable, as Juan will discover shortly—at the same time he discovers that she is none other than King Fadrique's sister, the *Infanta* Isabela. This familial relationship offers still more evidence in favor of an Ovidian design on Tirso's part, since Diana was the sister of Fadrique's mythological counterpart Apollo.

Only moments after Juan completes his narration to Don Luis, the *gracioso* Calvo alerts them to the attack on Fadrique nearby. In the course of the struggle, Juan suffers an injured arm when he blocks with his own body a sword-thrust aimed at the king. Juan uses the garter he filched as a sling and accompanies Fadrique to the nearby royal *quinta*. When the grateful king insists upon naming him *privado*, against his vigorous protests, Juan's connection to Acteon becomes still more pronounced: Ovid's hunter often served as a Renaissance "emblem of the fate of those who peer into the secret cabinet of princes" (Bate 39). Ovid himself, whose tragic expulsion from Rome at Augustus's command very likely resulted from his too-intimate knowledge of court secrets, compares his own exile in his *Tristia* (*Sorrows*) to Acteon's fate: "Why did I see anything? Why did I make my eyes guilty? Why was I so thoughtless as to harbour knowledge of a fault? Unwitting was Actaeon when he beheld Diana unclothed; none the less he became the prey of his own hounds" (vv. 103–6). Clearly, a *privado*'s intimacy with his monarch always presented the same danger of seeing or learning too much, and thus Cadmus's grandson could constitute yet another mythological analogue for royal favorites. The dazed nobleman has not even recovered from the shock of his unwanted ascension in the court hierarchy when Isabela bursts onto the scene, agitated by the news of her brother's brush with death. She immediately notices her garter in Juan's possession and realizes the circumstances under which he must have obtained it. Their words once alone together leave no doubt concerning Ovid's influence. Juan declares her to have been "una imagen celestial" in his eyes at the river (530: "a heavenly image"), while Isabela's offended wrath is unmistakeably that of Diana: "profanado has el secreto, / que injurió tu desacato" (540–1: "you have profaned the secret that your disrespect violated"). The new *privado*'s reference to the divinity he perceived in Isabela and her description of his intrusion upon her privacy as a form of profanation prepare us for the intertextuality soon to be made explicit:

> *Infanta:* ¿Qué desacato o locura
> a tal parte te llevó?
>
> *Don Juan:* La de Acteón cuando vio
> de Diana la hermosura.
>
> (558–61)

> [*Infanta:* What disrespect or madness brought you to such a place?
>
> *Don Juan:* That of Acteon when he beheld Diana's beauty.]

Isabela does not immediately seek Juan's death but does repeatedly threaten him with the possibility during their dialogue, declaring that she shrinks from that penalty only because his rescue of her brother imposes an obligation which she cannot lightly disregard: "matarte será crueldad, / cuando tiene vida y ser / el rey mi señor por ti" (552–54: "to kill you would be heartless when my lord the king lives and breathes because of you"). Her violent impulses in that direction stem from the same source as the Ovidian goddess's: the desire to ensure that the inadvertent voyeur will not relate what he saw to others. Just as Diana mocks Acteon at the onset of his transformation into a mute stag with the words, "'Now tell / You saw me here naked without my clothes, / If you can tell at all!'" (III.192–93, 56), Isabela promises to have Juan killed should he not guard his tongue: "Por vida del rey mi hermano, / que os mande matar si habláis" (620–21: "I swear by the life of my brother the king that I will order your death if you speak [of what you saw]"). Tirso further foregrounds the question of verbal indiscretion when Juan rhetorically suggests that Isabela strike him blind for his offense:

> Sacarme los ojos,
> pues a divinos despojos,
> siendo humano, me atreví.
>
> (555–57)

> [Pluck out my eyes, since I dared, though merely human, to profane the divine.]

Acteon does not lose his vision in *The Metamorphoses*, but another mythological figure does: Tiresias (III.316–38, 60–61). The blind

Greek seer's fame as counselor to generations of Theban kings immediately constitutes him as a plausible analogue for Juan de Cardona, King Fadrique's new *privado*. The origins of Tiresias's blindness and gift of prophecy make his history even more relevant to Juan's current predicament. Some myths equate his transgression to that of Acteon: the goddess Athena deprived him of sight for having seen her bathing naked with his mother Chariclo in the fountain at Hippocrene.[12] Other tales—those from which Ovid derived his account—claim that Juno angrily blinded Tiresias after he sided with Jupiter in a wager concerning which gender finds more pleasure in love. The gods consulted him because he had lived both as a man and as a woman: born male, when Tiresias one day attacked two mating serpents with his staff he miraculously became female; when he encountered the same serpents again mating seven years later, he deliberately repeated his assault in the hope of returning to his original gender, a plan which proved successful. In all the myths he receives the gift of prophecy in compensation for his lost vision (Deveraux 44). This dual tradition makes Juan's allusion to the Greek seer's fate quite appropriate, since the nobleman has already beheld a puissant woman naked and is thus now capable of offensive verbal indiscretions concerning that experience. Moreover, knowledge of Tiresias's gender transformations as detailed by Ovid will later figure into the examination of Juan's masquerade as Fadrique's guardian angel.

Unfortunately for the *privado*, a misunderstanding soon persuades Isabela that he has betrayed her by divulging the anonymous bather's identity to his friend Don Luis; in reality, of course, the honorable aristocrat has done no such thing. Furious that Juan would dare to "imprudente profanar / sagrados de tal secreto" (1456–57: "imprudently profane such secret divine preserves"), she directs toward him a truly Olympian wrath and desire for vengeance. Toward this end she deceives Don Luis into believing that Juan in fact spied upon Clavela, the young lady-in-waiting whom Luis himself loves, naked at the river. Luis, furious at his friend's alleged betrayal, then imputes to Juan selfish motives for shielding his sister from Fadrique and tells the naive young noblewoman that her brother has rejected the king's legitimate request for her hand. To make matters even worse, the *Infanta* also informs Clavela that Juan is falsely boasting of having seen his friend's fiancee in such a compromising situation, deliberately exposing her honor to public mockery. Luis, Leonora, and Clavela unite against Juan due to Isabela's machinations, which thereby perform a function corresponding to Diana's metamorphosis of Acteon. That divine retribution transforms the once-beloved hunter into the object of his friends' and hounds' deadly hunt; blind to the prize stag's true identity, they pursue and destroy it. The *Infanta's* slander likewise transforms Juan de Cardona in his former allies' eyes so that they turn on him and seek his downfall, unaware that the object of their ire is nothing more than an illusion created by Isabela's lies and that the integrity, loyalty, and honor which constitute Juan's true essence still exist unaltered beneath his tarnished reputation.

The relationship between this plotline and Ovid's account in *The Metamorphoses*, however, is no simpler than the relationship between Fadrique and Leonora's interaction and that of Apollo and Daphne. Juan's negative transformation at the vengeful Isabela's hands—or at least that of his public image—is not the first change triggered by their bucolic encounter. On the contrary, Tirso makes it very clear that both nobleman and *Infanta* experience immediate amatory metamorphoses as a result of that incident. When Juan first narrates what occurred in his scene with Luis, he begins the account thus:

> Oíd milagros de amor,
> don Luis, porque admiréis
> mi dicha, y no os espantéis
> de que andando a caza amor,
> las libertades persiga;
>
> . . . .
>
> Ya no tengo libertad;
> perdíla; ya vivo preso.

(142–51)

[Attend the miracles of love, Don Luis, so that you may marvel at my good fortune, and be not frightened that when love goes hunting, it pursues one's liberty. . . . I have no freedom; I lost it; I now live a prisoner.]

Raymond R. MacCurdy points out that such scenes in the *comedia* contain more than an echo of the dynamics of courtly love (1959, 38). Here Juan invokes the time-honored "prisoner of love" motif and leaves neither Luis nor the spectators with any doubt concerning the exhilarating effects wrought on him by his first sight of the half-clothed Isabela—effects that led him to continue watching her as she finished undressing and bathed, then to steal her garter. Unlike Acteon, whose involuntary glimpse of Diana makes him the terrified, doomed prey in an all-too-real hunt, Juan de Cardona's initial sight of the *Infanta* converts him into the willing object of love's metaphorical pursuit. Furthermore, while Diana's reaction to the violation of her privacy is entirely angry, Isabela clearly has contradictory feelings toward Juan. Her sense of offense and her fear of his potential indiscretion conflict with the attraction she feels toward him, as her aside at the conclusion of their first conversation indicates:

> Quien me vio
> desnuda, siendo atrevido,
> ¿qué pena merece? Honor,
> no consultéis al amor;
> que dirá: Ser mi marido.
>
> (681–85)

[What does he who presumptuously saw me naked deserve? Honor, do not consult love, who would say: to be my husband.]

Isabela goes so far early in the second act as to send Juan a message encouraging him to declare his feelings toward her, though both the *privado*'s uncertainty and his concern for Leonora's endangered honor lead him to neglect the opportunity. Finally, the *Infanta*'s act III monologue, in which she resolves to ask Fadrique's supernatural adviser to avenge her dishonor makes her feelings and their origins manifest:

> Pudiera don Juan tener
> ventura, a saber callar;
> mas ya perdió por hablar
> lo que mereció por ver.
> Bien le empezaba a querer:
> hame ofendido hablador;
> no culpe, pues, mi rigor
> si solicito su muerte;
> que no hay desdén, si lo advierte,
> como el que nace de amor.
>
> (2863–72)

[Don Juan could have been fortunate had he known how to keep silent; but he already lost by speaking what he earned by seeing. I truly began to love him, but he has offended me with his indiscretion; thus let no one blame me for severity if I seek his death, for there is no scorn, if attention is paid to the matter, like that which is born from love.]

There can be no doubt that Juan's initial encounter with Isabela, along with her discovery of the garter-thief's identity, served as the catalyst for amatory transformations of them both. These transformations precede Juan's Acteon-like metamorphosis at Isabela's hands into the court pariah.

Acteon, unfortunately, has no power to remedy his condition. Juan de Cardona, on the other hand, does precisely that when he assumes the identity of Fadrique's alleged guardian angel. This figure, by virtue of the reverence and trust he inspires at the Neapolitan court, is able to disprove the misunderstandings and slanders that have disgraced Juan de Cardona; it is as if Acteon were somehow to communicate to his hunting companions the reality concealed beneath his cervine form and were thereby to reclaim his original human shape. We cannot help but think of Tiresias and his gender transformations here as well. As Leonard Barkan points out, the future seer stands out among the many involuntarily transformed characters of the *Metamorphoses* by himself effecting the return to his original masculine form with his deliberate second attack on the copulating serpents: "It is the special talent of Tiresias to have rather full insight into what has happened to him. Unlike some of the other figures who follow this paradigm, Tiresias comes to control the metamorphic power that had overtaken him" (1986, 42). Juan likewise takes action to reverse Isabela's slander, which concealed his exemplary nobility and distorted the other characters' perception of him just as Diana's transformation of Acteon blinded the hunter's companions and dogs to the true nature of the stag they pursued. Once having absolved himself of the charges against him, Juan concludes his metadrama by abandoning his disguise. He is rewarded with the *Infanta*'s hand, finally requiting their long-frustrated attraction. This marriage, along with that of Fadrique and Leonora, assures the *privado*'s future at court as well as his personal happiness: "El privado fui por fuerza; / mas ya lo seré con gusto" (3198–99: "I was royal favorite under duress, but now I so serve with pleasure"). Juan de Cardona's masquerade thus serves as *Privar*'s linchpin. This imposture connects the Ovidian source myths, for the *privado*'s disguise recalls both Daphne's shedding of her physical body in order to defend her essential identity and Tiresias's successful effort to reverse his gender switch; the analogy between Tiresias and Acteon furnishes the final link. The masquerade connects the two amatory plotlines as well, for Juan adopts his new persona as much to save Leonora from Fadrique as to save himself from the *Infanta*'s machinations; in addition, he has still a third motivation: to guide Fadrique toward a wiser, more responsible exercise of his authority. Juan's disguise therefore links *Privar*'s political and romantic plotlines by serving as a common factor in their resolutions.

Though *The Metamorphoses* clearly provided Tirso with models for *Privar*'s two romantic plotlines, it soon becomes equally obvious as we follow their development that the Mercedarian has no intention of slavishly following either of his Ovidian models through to their unfortunate conclusions. Instead, we can perceive the radical direction in which Tirso takes his revision of Ovid's text. The primary Greco-Roman myths underlying *Privar*, when stripped to their barest essentials, relate the deadly transformations suffered by those who come into unwanted contact with the gods. Daphne's metamorphosis into a vegetative state, after all, is hardly a desirable turn of events—although it saves her from Apollo's ardor, it does so in a disturbing, problematic fashion. Barnard writes that Daphne's "transformation becomes ambiguous, offering only a half-solution (and even this half-solution is extreme); according to the ruthless formula, her humanity must be destroyed so that her virginity may be preserved" (1987, 39). Acteon's death lacks even that ambiguity: for seeing Diana naked through no fault of his own, she deliberately metamorphoses him into a mute animal doomed to brutal slaughter. Tirso emulates Ovid by depicting the transformations experienced by two reclusive Neapolitan subjects as a result of unwanted interactions with their rulers, but makes those transformations notably positive, upward ones. Leonora does not enter a convent, which would seem the most apt Golden Age analogue to Daphne's metamorphosis. Instead, she ultimately becomes Queen of Naples. Nor does Juan suffer destruction at his friends' hands, despite Isabela's temporary determination that he share Acteon's fate. His elevation to the rank of *privado*, on the contrary, is made permanent at the *comedia*'s conclusion. Rather than destroying his Daphne and Acteon, then, Tirso bestows upon them entrance into the "divine sphere" with which they come into contact.

Moreover, Juan and Leonora experience changes beyond those of political power and social status alone, metamorphoses which make those changes possible but which are at the same time far more fundamental. Ever-mindful of their father's misfortunes during King Alfonso's reign, the siblings begin *Privar* leading sterile lives characterized by celibacy, bucolic seclusion, and extreme distrust of palace life. In the course of the drama, they fall in love and renounce their previous fearful isolationism in favor of love, marriage, and a glittering shared future at Fadrique's court. Nor does Tirso provide his Daphne and Acteon alone with such psychological transformations. Fadrique and Isabela, the royal siblings who parallel Ovid's Apollo and Diana, experience inward metamorphoses of their own in *Privar*. By the end of the play, Fadrique has been transformed from a comically over-wrought Ovidian deity into a desirable future husband for Leonora and a worthy counterpart to the traditional Apollo of myth "who stood for order, dignity, and moderation" (Barnard 1987, 27). And while Diana's wrath at Acteon's involuntary transgression is appeased only by his painfully protracted death, the love Isabela initially feels for Juan de Cardona, along with the evidence of his virtue provided by the supposedly divine emissary, brings about her final transformation from vengeful fury into the nobleman's betrothed. The presence of such psychological metamorphoses further emphasizes Ovid's impact on this *comedia*. According to Barkan, many characters in the Roman poet's mock epic undergo bodily transformations which serve as catalysts for internal revelation and change (1986, 14–15). There are no literal shapeshiftings in *Privar*'s nonmagical Neapolitan setting, but Barkan's study of Ovid, as previously noted, also discerns the metamorphic principle at work in many characters' first encounters with passion (1986, 13–14). Barkan calls such encounters "threshold experiences," a label he also applies to exogamic journeys like those of Europa and Io, and declares: "stories of metamorphosis are stories of pursuit, of travel, of unfamiliar and alien loves" (1986, 14). The central role played by the Ovidian dynamics of transformation in *Privar* now seems inescapable, for Barkan's statement encompasses virtually all the romantic and political turns of events resulting directly and indirectly from Juan and Leonora's fateful sylvan encounters with the willful royal siblings. The internal metamorphoses of selfhood and self-awareness ultimately experienced by all four primary characters confirm Melveena McKendrick's perception that "Tirso often strikes one as a dramatist interested above all in characterization but trapped by historical accident within what was primarily a theatre of action" (118).

In conclusion, a close reading of *Privar* reveals metamorphosis's central function in this text. Its most obvious manifestation, Juan's self-transformation into the guardian angel in response to the *Infanta*'s metamorphic slander and to his sister's dangerous change of heart toward Fadrique, serves as the device which resolves both the political and emotional questions onstage, thereby causing the genres of *privanza* drama and romantic comedy to coalesce within the action of the play and to fuse into two sides of one theatrical coin. Still more fundamentally, attention to the theme of transformation illuminates the relationship between *Privar* and Ovid's comic epic. Beginning by overtly imitating the myths of Daphne and Apollo and of Diana and Acteon, even while Tirso boldly rewrites those accounts—thereby, we might say, metamorphosing *The Metamorphoses*—he also draws upon the very nature of metamorphosis itself in those tales for his own dramatic ends. *Privar contra su gusto* is far more than an inconsequential love comedy or even yet another prescriptive *comedia de privanza* destined to fall upon inattentive royal ears. It constitutes nothing less than Tirso's intertextual engagement with Ovid's most famous work and his use of the Roman poet's mythological metamorphoses as the inspiration for his own characters' psychological and emotional evolution.

Notes

1. William E. Wilson and Ruth Lee Kennedy both believe this play to have been written in 1621. Blanca de los Ríos attributes it to at least a decade later due to her belief that the work mocks Quevedo, who was named royal secretary in 1632 (Tirso 1959, 1070).

2. Although *Privar* can be considered nominally historical given that a King Fadrique did rule Naples from 1496 to 1501, Galassi demonstrates that the play's events and characterizations have no further factual basis (Tirso 1971, 10–12).

3. References to *The Metamorphoses* will specify the cited book, verse numbers from the Miller edition, and pagination from Melville's translation.

4. See Rudolph Schevill, José María de Cossío, Marcia L. Welles, and Mary E. Barnard for the most useful explorations of Ovid's impact.

5. Bustamante's version, despite its flaws, was for many years the only widely available Spanish rendering of *The Metamorphoses*. Following the first edition, which carries no year of publication but appears to have been printed sometime before 1546, Bustamante's adaptation was reissued several times. Schevill declares, "No translator of a noted classic ever proceeded in a freer manner, no translation has ever been a greater fraud than this, if judged only from the standpoint of Ovid's text; no version, however, could better reflect the spirit of the age in which it was written" (152). Pedro Sánchez de Viana's 1589 verse rendering, though Schevill considers it worthy of attention, was considerably less accessible and popular. Consult Schevill 143–73 and 245–49 for details of these and other Spanish translations.

6. References to the text of *Privar contra su gusto* cite Galassi's critical edition by verse. All translations are mine.

7. The role played by vision in Golden Age Spanish theories of amorous attraction is well known. Halstead offers an in-depth study of this question with regard to Tirso's theater.

8. See Barnard 1987 for a fuller exploration of the tradition behind this comic mockery and the carnivalesque context in which it functioned (22–34).

9. Tirso is not the only Golden Age writer to utilize this myth when addressing court politics; another well-known example can be found in Góngora's 1613 "Soledad primera" (lines 125–34). Curiously in light of Tirso's anti-Gongorism (see Kennedy 1974, 99; 156–57; 168; 192; 262; 270), Galassi finds elsewhere in *Privar* strong evidence of Góngora's influence on this play, maintaining that Juan de Cardona's narration of his first encounter with the *Infanta* Isabela owes much to the poet's 1612 "Fábula de Polifemo y Galatea" (Tirso 1971, 24–28).

10. Though such an erotically charged encounter could not be enacted onstage for obvious reasons, poetic narrations by *galánes* of their fateful bucolic meetings with nude female bathers were a recurrent feature of Golden Age drama; according to Raymond R. MacCurdy, these scenes permitted playwrights to demonstrate their talents for painting Baroque word-pictures in verse and also compensated for the lack of pictorial nudes in the visual arts of the time (1959, 38–39).

11. MacCurdy contends that the Golden Age fascination with the bathing nude derived from three sources: the Biblical tale of David and Bathsheba, the Spanish quasi-historical legend of King Rodrigo's infatuation with la Cava, and—most popular of all—Ovid's account of the myth of Diana and Acteon (1982, 159–61). For a detailed exploration of this myth's evolution and variations, consult Barkan 1980.

12. Barkan traces this analogy between Tiresias and Acteon to Callimachus's *Hymns and Epigrams* (1980, 324).

Achilles: Gender Ambiguity and Destiny in Golden Age Drama

Anita K. Stoll

The history and myths of ancient Greek and Roman civilization are significant in the theater of the Golden Age, serving different purposes for the writers who turn to them for inspiration. These antique tales are used in the *comedia* as shorthand to evoke a particular feature of a character, as foreshadowing of the future, or to point to the classical models of the play and its characters. They also often served writers in expressing, through a subtle pattern of allusion which is not always readily obvious, their perceptions of underlying truths about human beings and about cultural attitudes. Plays reflecting these mythical perceptions may have had their origin in the purely unconscious process of the writer; they may reflect a cultural concern, or they may just be conscious repetitions of winning plot patterns.

The presence of the figure of Achilles from the story of the siege of Troy is an excellent example of this creative use of classic models by Golden Age writers. The fact that Achilles appears as the protagonist in name or by proxy in several *comedias* is therefore worthy of note and of inquiry into their contents. We find Achilles or his prototype used to dramatize the universal human concerns involving both physical, that is, gender-related, and metaphysical destiny in five plays: Tirso's *El Aquiles* (*Achilles*)(1611–12), Cristóbal y Monroy's *El caballero dama* (*The Gentleman as Lady*) and *Héctor y Aquiles* (*Hector and Achilles*)(1640), and Calderón's *El monstruo de los jardines* (*The Monster of the Gardens*) (1650–53) and his little-studied *Las manos blancas no ofenden* (*White hands do not Offend*)(1640).[1] Tirso's early play *El Aquiles* initiates this tradition, focusing first on the story of the early years of Achilles, particularly with reference to the physical aspect of Achilles's destiny, and points to Tirso's major influence on the drama written in subsequent decades. *El caballero dama* follows this lead in subject and tone. Monroy's second play deals with Achilles's later life and death. Calderón's plays suggest the influence of Tirso's earlier work, while the later play gives more attention to the hero's metaphysical destiny. This study will focus on the issue of the gender confusion associated with the early life of Achilles, and the classical tradition that inspired Spanish Golden Age dramatists to employ this archetypal figure as representative of the Renaissance preoccupation with gender definition.

Let us first consider the basic story of Achilles and its textual transformation through the centuries. The basic story of Achilles is as follows: He was the son of Peleus, the king of Thessaly, and Thetis, a sea nymph. Soon after his birth, his mother dipped him into the river Styx to protect his body from harm. However, the water did not touch the heel by which Thetis held him. He ultimately died from an arrow shot into this heel. Because of the prophecy that he would lead the Greeks to victory in the Trojan War but would not survive it, Thetis wished to hide him from the recruiting Greeks. She dressed Achilles as a woman and left him with Licomedes on the island of Skiros. As a lady-in-waiting to the king's daughter, Deidamia, Achilles wooed and won the princess. The clever Ulysses then discovered him and carried him off to war.

In order to illustrate the perennial and evolving interest in the Achilles legend, Catherine Callen King traces the addition and deletion of elements of his story and the evolution of attitudes developed toward the hero's persona as they change to reflect current concerns. Homer's version emphasized heroic values and an understanding of human mortality. Horace and Virgil portrayed him as "synonymous with war, the great destroyer of human achievement and happiness" (xvii). One of the *topoi* arising from this view is Achilles as "the be(a)st of the Achaians: the superlative warrior embodying total savagery" (28). It is only with the first century A.D. that the amatory motif begins to gain additional importance until, in some medieval versions, love comes to dominate Achilles' penchant for violence. In general, the important influences for Spanish literature are Benoît de Sainte-Maure's twelfth-century reworking of the sixth-century Dares's plot and the *Libro de Alexandre* (Book of Alexander), a version of Homer's *Iliad* that painted an Achilles consumed by pride. The presence or absence of such characteristics as pride, fierceness, or an inclination to the romantic, indicate the contemporary models influencing Golden Age reworkings of this major symbol in world culture.

The Achilles story has thus been a very productive one, and in the area of Spanish Golden Age drama, its considerable attention begins with its use by Tirso. An incident of the story of Achilles which attracted his theatrical bent was Thetis's dressing him as a woman. Since gender questions and confusions result from this practice of cross-dressing, it is logical to begin with some comments on this topic with reference to seventeenth-century Europe.

Gender membership and roles in the seventeenth century were in a state of confusion. An example of this is the belief that wearing the clothing of the other sex could alter the sex of the wearer. It was also believed that women were men who had lacked the necessary heat in the fetal stage to cause the appropriate genitalia to appear.[2] A volume appropriately named *Playing with Gender: A Renaissance Pursuit* provides an illuminating study of these attitudes and beliefs.[3] This mixing of the genders is observed especially in the theater, as evidenced in the Elizabethan and Jacobean periods in England, in which women's roles were played by boys, and the Golden Age theater in Spain with its extensive history of the *mujer vestida de hombre* (woman dressed as a man). Recent records of this theatrical presence have been studied in a comprehensive anthropological work titled *Crossdressing, Sex and Gender.*

While there are several possible models for Tirso's focus on the gender issue arising in the story of the youthful Achilles (Kromayor 168), Everett Hesse and William McCrary point out that Tirso's play follows closely the account of Achilles's early life as written by Statius, a poet of the second century, a period in which the amatory Achilles comes to the fore.[4] His version recounts the story, leaving off at the point of Achilles' departure with Ulysses for Troy. I quote from J. H. Mozley's prose translation, as Deidamia laments his departure:

> go and good luck be with thee, and come back mine! Yet too bold is my request: soon the fair Trojan dames will sigh for thee with tears and beat their brests and pray that they may offer their necks to thy fetters, . . . But I shall be a story to thy henchmen, the tale of a lad's first fault, or I shall be disowned and forgotten. Nay, come, take me as thy comrade; why should I not carry the standards of Mars with thee? (I. 579)

Their hypothesis is logical since this version is followed closely at the end of Tirso's play as Deidamia disguises herself as a man and follows Achilles to the battleground where she observes his infatuation there with the Trojan woman Policena.

Tirso appears to have been inspired by this version of the legend, likely driven by the *comedia* public's interest in the *mujer vestida de hombre,* present in up to a third of all plays of the period, according to Bravo Villasante. And since he was given to social satire, according to Halkhoree, Tirso makes of this story a farce, thus overlaying a major classical theme with contemporary concerns and interests.[5] The following discussion of scenes from the play illustrates the category of farce and provides material for comparison with later versions of the Achilles story.

The first appearance on stage of Aquiles is described in the following stage direction: "Salen Aquiles, que *ha de hacer la mujer vestida de pieles* con un birtón, y Quirón, . . ." (1946, I. 1912: Quirón and Aquiles, who should be played by a woman dressed in skins, appear on stage). Not only do we have a male protagonist played by a female actress who in the course of the play will dress as a woman in the attempt to hide, but Tirso adds yet another twist to the gender confusion. When in act 2 he (she) appears dressed as a woman, there are several scenes that emphasize the issue. In preparing her son for the role of a woman, Thetis has him practice walking on high heels. He replies

> Sólo dificulto andar
> sobre estos corchos, no quepo
> en ellos ni sé regillos;
>
> [I'm having trouble walking
> on these high heeled shoes, I don't fit
> in them nor know how to control them;]

Thetis answers:

> Todo es fácil a quien ama.
> Cuando estés en la presencia
> del Rey, haz la reverencia
> que te he enseñado de dama;
> vuélvela a ensayar aquí.
> (Aquiles hace una reverencia de soldado.)
>
> (I. 1921)
>
> [All is easy for the one who loves.
> When you're in the presence
> of the King, make a ladylike curtsey
> that I have taught you;
> try it again here.
> (Aquiles makes a soldier's bow.)]

The audience, knowing that this is a woman playing a man's role in which she pretends to be her own sex and has great difficulties with the "role," must have found this scene hilarious. Another example of the farcical gender confusion occurs in the playacting of the children's game of "señores y señoras" (ladies and gentlemen) suggested to Deidamia by the disguised Aquiles. "Finge que mi dama eres / y yo tu galán," (Pretend that you're my lady / and I your gallant) Aquiles-Nereida says, and the direction reads "(Hace que sale del vestuario)" (I. 1929: He pretends to come out of the discovery space). And then he (she) appears dressed as a man. The language of the play is suggestive of confusion and fluidity of both identity and gender. There is a high incidence in these speeches of "transformación" (transformation), "engaños" (deceptions), and "disfraces" (disguises) throughout the play.

Deidamia's decision to disguise herself as a man and follow Achilles to the battleground, suggested by Statius's version, and Achilles's infatuation with the Trojan woman, Policena, are the focus of the last scene. Here Deidamia witnesses the encounter in which Aquiles again falls in love at first sight. When Policena throws a glove from the Trojan wall to Aquiles, it is picked up by Deidamia, disguised as a man. The following exchange takes place after Aquiles asks for the glove.

Deidamia:	Yo he de matarme contigo antes que el guante te dé.
Aquiles:	¿Quién eres, hombre atrevido?
Deidamia:	Sabráslo si me buscares.
Aquiles:	¿Adónde?
Deidamia:	¡Traidor, en ti mismo!

(I. 1947)

[*Deidamia:*	I will die with you before I give you the glove.
Aquiles:	Who are you, daring man?
Deidamia:	You will know if you look for me.
Aquiles:	Where?
Deidamia:	Traitor, in yourself!]

Deidamia's replies make clear that the intention here is to provide a mirror image: the woman dressed as a man (Deidamia) mirroring the man (Aquiles) who is really a woman in male dress. These scenes illustrate how Tirso closely adheres to Statius's model and as well focuses on the Renaissance interest in gender mixing.[6]

Cristóbal Monroy y Silva's *El caballero dama*, is clearly a reworking of Tirso's play. It includes the same material, continues the gender confusion, and pronounces in its title its farcical intent.[7] While the many plot elements of the work make clear its obvious debt to Tirso's play, Monroy adds material that make the comedy of the play and the gender confusion even broader. The cast of characters includes "Aquiles, que lo ha de hazer una muger con nombre fingido de Aurora" (1: Aquiles, who should be played by a woman with the pretend name of Aurora). The stage direction for the first appearance of this character reads "Descubrese Aquiles en trage de Cavallero de caza muy galan, la espada desnuda y sangrienta, y viene baxando por el monte hasta llegar al tablado" (1: Aquiles is found in a very elegant hunting dress, with naked and bloody sword, and he comes descending from the mount to get to the stage). He describes his successful hunt, having killed a porcupine, and describes having left off the pursuit of a lion on being called by his tutor, Policarpio. Thus, with the first appearance of the protagonist the gender mixing is established, since the public knows this is a woman, while the boastful and bloody hunting demeanor is clearly male behavior. "He" appears again a short while later, as the stage direction indicates, "Sale Aquiles en trage de dama, suelto el cabello, sin chapines, arrastrando la ropa, en la mano siniestra un lenzuelo con sangre, en la derecha una daga, y el rostro salpicado de sangre . . ." (4: Aquiles appears dresed as a lady, with hair loose, without clogs, clothing dragging, in the left hand a bloody cloth, in the right a dagger, and with face spattered with blood). Even the stage props here bespeak of the confusion, the (male) dagger and the (female) bloody handkerchief.

There are many other signs of the obvious play with gender in Monroy's version. Both Deidamia and her brother, the king, fall in love with Aquiles. When the king pursues "her" too closely, "she" grabs his sword and defends "herself." When "she" refers to "herself" as "valeroso" (a valient man), the king is confused, replying "¿Qué dices?" (What are you saying?). Aquiles answers, "Tan valerosa, / no te espantes porque como están aora / turbados, señor, los sentidos todos, / no es mucho que yerra la lengua / . . ." (9: Such a valient woman, don't be alarmed because as things are so upset, sir, all the senses, it is not surprising that the tongue should err). This play with gender is also found in the subplot, which focuses on the confusion of the two comics Pulgón and Pistolete. One of the jokes Pulgón plays on Pistolete is tricking him into visiting the room of Pulgón's girlfriend, Laura.

Laura, of course, is Pulgón, who gets Pistolete to remove his clothes and wash his face in ink. At this point the king enters with light and discovers the disrobed and comically painted *gracioso*.

During Monroy's version of the playacting "señores y señoras," Aquiles, in male dress, is kidnapped and tied up by the king's aides. Needless to say, the king is very disturbed to find the object of his attentions dressed as a man, and more so when, after pleading to be a helpless lady in order to get untied, Aquiles draws his sword and they have an extended battle, in which Aquiles exhibits his valor and dexterity.

Cross-dressing and the play of gender recurs in two other plays dealing with Achilles: Calderón's *Las manos blancas no ofenden* and *El monstruo de los jardines*. These *comedias* also manifest the influence of Tirso's play with its focus on gender mixing and Achilles' youth. They were written well after Tirso's play, the earlier one the same year as those of Monroy y Silva. The earlier Calderonian play, *Las manos*, has as cross-dressed hero César, Príncipe de Bisiniano. His long narrative near the play's beginning is introduced by a song sung to please him. The two *damas* speak of their choice of theme to please César: "El de Aquiles, cuando está / sirviendo a Deidamia, pues / su letra otras veces es / la que más gusto le da" (1087: That one about Aquiles, when he serves Deidamia, since its words have previously given him such pleasure). Their song is intertwined with his commentary on the words. When they sing "para que sirva a Deidamia, / traje de mujer le viste" (in order to serve Deidamia, he wears woman's dress) he tells them to stop because:

> no por Aquiles, por mí
> se hizo . . .
> que presumo que soy yo
> quien en mujer transformó
> su madre, pues que desea
> que entre mujeres criado
> de Marte el furor ignore.
>
> (1087)

> [not for Aquiles, for me
> it was written . . .
> since I presume that I am the one
> whose mother changed him
> into a woman, because she wanted

> me raised among women
> so that I know nothing
> of Martial fury.]

He proceeds to describe why he sees himself as Aquiles: to spare him from combat, his mother brought him up in the company of women, has not allowed him to fish or hunt, nor carry a sword. His only pleasure is playing the harp. But he has seen his lovely cousin Serafina, and, in order to court her, he must escape from his mother. Since he must cross her bedroom to leave, he dresses as a woman, pretending to be a lady-in-waiting. He arrives at a place near Serafina's palace at the same time as Lisarda who, in order to follow her lover, Federico (who also wants to court Serafina), has dressed as a man. There is an accident after which Lisarda identifies herself as César, Prince of Bisiniana. The real César, still dressed as a woman, remains so since his identity has been co-opted. As such he is able to serve as lady-in-waiting to Serafina. With this courtly, aristocratic plot, Calderón is able to avail himself elegantly of the apparent societal interest in gender mixing without resorting to the broad farce initiated by Tirso's *El Aquiles* and expanded by Monroy y Silva.

The play opens with a scene reminiscent of Monroy y Silva's aggressive protagonist: Lisarda converses with Patacón, the servant of her lover, in an effort to discover his travel plans. Patacón would tell her if he knew:

> que estoy temiendo, y no en vano,
> cuando aquesa blanca mano,
> por blanca que es, me derriba
> dos o tres muelas siquiera
> como si tuviera yo
> culpa en que se vaya o no.

> (1080)

> [since I fear, and not without reason,
> that this white hand,
> for all its whiteness,
> may still knock out
> several teeth as if
> I were to blame
> for his leaving or not.]

Calderón introduces some order into the gender confusion through use of the "blanca mano," which serves as a marker in gender categories. This is the first mention of the *blanca mano* of the title;[8] the second is also one of violence uncharacteristic of a woman. When Federico goes to pick up a glove dropped by Serafina (perhaps an echo of Tirso's *Aquiles,* where, as we recall, Aquiles and Deidamia vie for the glove dropped by Polyxena), Lisarda, still dressed as a man, stops him, and strikes him. Federico takes out his dagger and starts to return the blow when he realizes who she is. In order not to challenge her to a duel and at the same time protect his honor for not doing so, he shows her hand to all:

> [Toma la mano a Lisarda, y la enseña a todos.]
> Sabed que . . . tiene esta mano,
> y siendo, como es, tan blanca,
> agravio no ha sido, pues
> las manos blancas no agravian.
> [Vase, llevándose a Lisarda.]

(1116)

> [(He takes Lisarda's hand, and shows it to all.)
> May you know . . . he has this hand,
> and being, as it is, so white,
> it was no affront, since
> white hands don't offend.
> (He leaves, taking Lisarda with him.)]

The third and final evocation of the "blanca mano" again relates to gender categories and even voices the idea of costume as a determining factor. When Serafina discovers at the end who César really is, she resolves the contest for her hand in his favor, addressing César:

> Príncipe, esta blanca mano
> tocaste tal vez: aleve
> ofensa fue que me hizo
> un disfraz, y es conveniente
> que sepan que aun de su dueño
> las blancas manos ofenden;
> y así, pues vos la agraviasteis,
> el irse con vos lo enmiende.

(1125)

> [Prince, perhaps you touched
> this white hand: I was betrayed

> by a disguise, and you should all know
> that white hands can even offend their owner;
> and since you have injured that hand,
> making it your own repairs the injury.]

The *blanca mano* motif at once presents a breadth of permissible female behavior and at the same time underscores in chivalresque fashion a clear gender distinction. Calderón has it both ways: he capitalizes on the popular theme of cross-dressing while remaining firmly grounded in an ultimately unbreachable gender distinction.

The play contains many more scenes that are amusing because of the ostensible confusion arising from the dual cross-dressing, another feature that Calderón may have adopted from Tirso, but that he employs in a much more refined fashion.[9] The story also relies on the technique of metatheater, a hallmark of all of these plays, since cross-dressing in itself is metatheatrical, that is, the representation of a role within the role on stage.[10]

In Monroy y Silva's second play involving the Achilles story, *Hector y Aquiles*, the playwright obviously concentrates on Achilles' metaphysical destiny, a point in the hero's life after the time of the masquerade, a period mentioned in the play only in passing. Here the focus is on Achilles' preordained fate of killing Hector and then succumbing himself. However, in this story, his love for Polyxena is his fatal flaw. He is lured to the Temple of Apollo by a letter written by Polyxena at the behest of Paris, who kills him there with arrows. He no longer has a god as parent and there is no mention of his being vulnerable only in the heel, a turn in the story stemming from Benoît de Sainte Maure's version (King 228).

Calderón's second use of Achilles' early history, apparently a decade later, has a much different tone. It does not create the sense of a courtly amusement that we find in *Blancas manos*. While necessarily presenting Achilles dressed as a woman in some scenes, as we know from his story and especially from the focus on his early years inserted by Tirso into the theatrical reality of seventeenth-century Spain, there is no supporting material for an element of gender confusion. With this play Calderón employed the story of Achilles' early history to presage his inevitable destiny, according to Alexander Parker (92–101) and Angel Valbuena Briones (1776). The use of the term "monstruo" to describe a character also praised for his beauty recalls the early *topos* from the *Iliad* in which he is the "be(a)st of the Achaians," and presumably echoed in its Spanish version, *El libro de Alexandre*. Frederick de Armas has shown how the play fits with the astrological knowledge of the seventeenth century and, with the presence of Astrea, the name given the cross-dressed Achilles, finds it an allegory, bringing the promise of harmony to the world beyond Achilles' destined end (1986, 197–211). This serious play belongs to the cycle of mythological plays and not with the farces of Tirso and Monroy y Silva and the light *comedia de capa y espada, Las blancas manos no ofenden*. Unlike the plays of Tirso and Monroy, it joins the two destinies, carrying the story far beyond the limitation to the early years through the miraculous appearance of Achilles' mother, Thetis, at the end of the play, who evokes his ultimate destiny.

The interest in this period in gender differences is evident in the writings of Fray Luis de León's *La perfecta casada* (The Perfect Wife) and in the writings of Juan Huarte de San Juan (Hicks 135–56, Heiple 121–34). The rapt attention of the playgoing public is manifest in the hundreds of plays featuring *la mujer vestida de hombre* and in the many futile attempts by authorities to prohibit the practice of the cross-dressed woman. Given this penchant, we may hypothesize that Tirso came across the account by Statius of Achilles' youthful masquerade and wrote the play we know as *El Aquiles*. We may also suppose that its success prompted Monroy y Silva to copy it, expanding on its sensational elements in order to please his audience. There is also evidence that Calderón may have been inspired by one or both of these works to use the plot in his plays, while in the mythologized version taking into consideration also extant versions to add the warrior aspect of the persona. Whatever the truth of these suggestions, the fact is that the classical story of the young Achilles struck a chord in the concerns and attention of the public of the day, and the image drawn by these dramatists is one that evokes the societal interest in the matter of gender.

The two plays that do not concentrate on gender matters (Monroy y Silva's *Hector y Aquiles* and Calderón's *El monstruo de los jardines*) focus on the other significant meaning of the Achilles myth for seventeenth-century Spain. The ultimate destiny of Achilles is the guiding idea in the other two plays, in one of which Calderón also injects a note of hope. This violent destiny is surely the reason for the evocation of the cause of the Trojan War, Helen, in act 1 of *El castigo sin venganza* (Punishment without Vengeance), as Batín, speaking to the Duke's son, Federico, criticizes the marriage of the Duke and Casandra: "No era mejor para ti / esta Venus, esta Elena?" (I. 639, 644: Was not this Venus, this

Helen, better for you?), and the reference to her errant husband in act 3. As the Duke of Ferrara returns from military success to face the unhappy consequences of his former life of dissolution and abandonment of his new wife, he is hailed as "el ferrarés Aquiles" (III. 96: the Achilles of Ferrara). This epithet encodes for the knowledgeable reader or viewer the foreshadowing of a violent and tragic conclusion.[11]

The true significance of classical models (and their reworkings) for the *comedia* is only beginning to be uncovered. Perhaps this is such a late discovery because Lope, in his *Arte nuevo de hacer comedias* (New Art for Writing Plays), disclaimed a debt to them. Although the poets of the Golden Age do not slavishly imitate the classical stories, they did not in fact forget them. They reshaped the essential material in such a way that they mirrored their own society. The employment of the young Achilles to express the interest in gender differentiation, and the image of the Achilles of the well-known preordained destiny, to work out the mysteries of human physical and metaphysical destinies are valuable examples of this creative imitation. Tirso de Molina's role in this development suggests a need to reassess the extent of his influence on theatrical development later in the century, as well as the need for continued study of classical influences in Golden Age drama.

NOTES

1. Doña Blanca gives this date for *El Aquiles* in *Obras completas* I, 1887. For the rationale of dates for Monroy's work see Astrid Kromayor's essay, 167. Monroy Y Silva also has two additional plays dealing with the Trojan story: *El robo de Elena* (The Kidnapping of Helen) and *La destrucción de Troya* (The Destruction of Troy). The dates for Calderón's plays are found in *Obras completas: Comedias*, 1079.

2. See Stephen Orgel's essay "Nobody's Perfect." This title is the final sentence spoken by Joe E. Brown to Jack Lemmon's cross-dressed character to whom he has just proposed marriage in the movie *Some Like it Hot*.

3. The purpose of the book is described in the "Introduction" as follows:

This book is a collection of original essays invited to elucidate a major *topos* of Renaissance culture—playing with gender. The volume as a whole provides literary and artistic evidence that the much-acclaimed Renaissance self-fashioning goes hand in hand with playful and creative experimentation with gender distinctions. (ix)

4. Everett Hesse and William McCrary jointly published an article in 1956 characterizing the action as the transformation of a child into a man symbolized by a Mars-Venus struggle. The protagonist was torn between his warlike nature and his inclination to submit this to the demands of love. Hesse later examined "Sexual Problems in the Achilles Plays of Tirso and Calderón." Most recently

José A. Madrigal described the play as "La transmutación de Aquiles: De salvaje a héroe (Tirso de Molina, *El Aquiles*)" (The Metamorphosis of Aquiles: From Savage to Hero).

5. All discussions listed previously in note 4 disagreed with Da. Blanca de los Ríos's assessment of the play as a farce, insisting instead that it was written as a serious drama. In the Twayne series *Tirso de Molina*, Margaret Wilson qualified it as "one of the oddest of Tirso's plays," highlighting the confusion and disagreement in the responses to this play (69). Jane Albrecht also characterizes the work as a farce in *Irony and Theatricality in Tirso de Molina*, 51–58. We must note that when Hesse and McCrary studied the play, there was much less available information regarding the prevalence of the interest in gender in the sixteenth and seventeenth centuries. Much of these attitudes have been brought to light relatively recently through studies of Renaissance English theater and life. One such valuable study is Jean E. Howard's "Cross-dressing, The Theater, and Gender Struggle in Early Modern England."

6. The effect achieved by this farce is very similar to that which Halkhoree detailed in his examination of *Don Gil de las calzas verdes* and other plays in *Social and Literary Satire in the Comedies of Tirso de Molina*. He illustrates how Tirso satirized many conventions by carrying them to a new extreme, including the theatrical one of the *mujer vestida de hombre*. For a more extended study of this play, see my "Cross-dressing in the Theater of Tirso de Molina."

7. In his study of the play "Sexual Aberration and Comedy in Monroy Y Silva's *El caballero dama*, Thomas O'Connor stops short of identifying the play as a burlesque farce, a category into which I believe it fits very well. See his study for an interesting discussion of inverted cosmic imagery.

8. This may also be an echo of Tirso's *La celosa de sí misma* (Jealous of Herself). Since it is said that Calderón's *tapadas* (veiled ladies) are the inspiration of Tirso's *La celosa de sí misma*, it is also possible that this *blanca mano* comes from the same play, where Melchor apostrophizes on Magdalena's beauty on his first encounter with her:

> Ventura, palabras deja
> aplicadas a tu humor,
> y en esa mano te queda,
> que es la que he visto no más.
> ¡Ay, qué mano! ¡Qué belleza!
> ¡Qué blancura! ¡Qué donaire!

(II. 1445)

> [Ventura, leave words
> applied to your humor,
> and keep it in that hand,
> which is all I have seen.
> Oh, what a hand! What beauty!
> What whiteness! What flair!]

His fixation with her beautiful hand is the base upon which the entire play rests, and stage action relating to a beautiful woman's hands is a central focus.

9. Valbuena Briones comments in the introduction to the play the extensive parallel structures of the work of which this is representative.

10. Roger Hornby describes this as the play within the play, whose effect is to create two sharply distinguishable layers of fiction so that the audience has

the experience of "seeing double," clearly noting multiple levels of action. This is the metatheatrical technique that is particularly relevant in this play and frequent in Golden Age drama.

11. See Debra Ames's article on Lope's *La villana de Getafe* for further discussion of uses of classical references.

The Harmony/Dissonance of Calderón's
El monstruo de los jardines

Thomas Austin O'Connor

The plot of *El monstruo de los jardines* dramatizes Aquiles'[1] dalliance with the *infanta* of Gnido, Deidamia, as the youth attempts to elude those who would compel him to depart in the Greek armada for the Trojan War. Calderón employs at the end of the play a basic convention of *comedia* writing, marriage as the symbolic representation of harmony restored to chaotic human and social relations, and through it creates a dramatic dissonance whose elucidation reveals a discordant and even contradictory view of Aquiles' rite of passage from boyhood to manhood. In addition, Calderón lays bare the underlying values of the heroic career to which Greek youth aspires and many mature Greek males have dedicated their lives, their fortunes, and their honor. In consequence, the price to be paid by all of them for entry into the pantheon of elite warriors and the value attributed by masculine society to their metamorphoses into the most noble manifestations of what men are capable of achieving on earth are problematized by a close scrutiny of the actual motives that drive the Greek nation to all-out war. Such a scenario contributes to making this work one of the most enigmatic plays ever written by the clearly disillusioned and deeply suspicious dramatist.

Aquiles is a youth who seeks to avoid the responsibilities of adult life by disguising himself as Astrea and hiding in Gnido amongst Deidamia's ladies-in-waiting.[2] Since some critics have viewed Aquiles' eventual acceptance of his socially defined duty as leader of the Greek expedition against Troy as the proper assumption of his authentically masculine nature and necessary integration into adult life (Hesse 1981; de Armas 1986), it is imperative to add at the outset this caveat: such a course of action also spells his death before the gates of Troy for a cause based on dubious moral motivation and questionable legality.[3] Aquiles is destined to lead a successful campaign against the enemies of the

Greek nation; however, looming behind this prophesied success, death stalks many warriors on both sides, including the youthful and rash Greek champion. The teasing out of the dramatic tension created by an assurance of success as a man of arms, but only at the price of forfeiting his very life, opens our eyes to the nature and character of this warrior society for which Aquiles eventually accedes to the dictates of destiny. Once the youth accepts his socially defined duty as a Greek male, he also internalizes a code of conduct, the Greek honor code, that proves itself to be destructive of life and love and everything good and sacred it once set out to uphold and preserve.

A significant dimension of the background action addresses Aquiles' origin and fate. The marriage of Peleo and Tetis was, in the first place, ordered by Júpiter to forestall his siring of a son who would become greater than the ruler of Olympus himself. In spite of being strongly attracted to the marine goddess Tetis, Júpiter felt obliged to marry her off as quickly as possible to a mortal. Pérez de Moya expressed the goddess's reaction to this enforced marriage thus: "Hacíasele de mal a Tetis, siendo deesa marina, haber de ser mujer de hombre mortal" (1928 II, 202; Tetis was not pleased being a marine goddess and having to become the wife of a mortal man). Tetis, recognizing the futility of resisting Júpiter's will, begrudgingly accepted her marriage to Peleo: "hubo de consentir en el casamiento" (II, 203; she had to consent to marriage).

Calderón configures this at-best ambivalent situation according to a well-known and, in the present circumstances, very significant pattern in his dramaturgy: Peleo rapes Tetis.[4] The deeply offended goddess then murders her attacker, a novel situation in Calderonian dramaturgy, and one not sanctioned by any known version of the myth. The rape of Tetis and murder of Peleo, in Calderón's dramatic rendition of the story, thus condition our responses to the play's eventual resolution. In the original version of the myth, the alienation of the couple occurred when Peleo cursed Tetis on discovering her roasting their infant son.[5] Calderón depicts the dramatic action in dark and lugubrious hues filled with ominous forebodings, for Aquiles was an "embrión de una violencia" (1998b; an offspring of violence).[6] Other myth plays in which rapes occur sensitize us to what is at stake.[7] Due to the providential guidance of Mercurio and Palas in *Fortunas de Andrómeda y Perseo* (*Fortunes of Perseus and Andromeda*), the latter was able to avoid a premature and tragic death, the inheritance of Júpiter's rape of his mother Dánae. Due to Liríope's ineffectual, imprudent, and cruel intervention to avert Narciso's fate in *Eco y Narciso*, the young man pays with his own death the price of Céfiro's rape of his mother. Death always stalks the offspring of rape, and the allusion to the rape of Aquiles' mother, Tetis, immediately alerts us to a potentially tragic issue, for her intervention in her son's life will more closely resemble Liríope's inadequacy and ultimate failure than Mercurio and Palas's prudence and remarkable success.

Once a child was born to Tetis, she attempted to read his fate in the stars:

> y hallé que al tercero lustro
> te amenaza la más fiera
> lid, la más dura batalla,
> la campaña más sangrienta
> de cuantas en tus teatros
> la fortuna representa.

> (1998b)

[I found that by your fifteenth year a most fierce battle will threaten you, the hardest battle, the bloodiest campaign of all that will be fought in the theaters of your fortune.]

Tetis interprets this revelation of Aquiles' fate only within the narrow context of imminent war with Troy. While this interpretation appears logical, even compelling, Tetis will soon learn that it also alludes to her son's passage from boyhood to manhood in the palace of King Polemio, where she herself placed him. Tetis originally wished to break fate's eyes (1999a) by raising her child of violence in complete seclusion and in the exclusive company of women. While her purpose, to avoid her child's prophesied fate, was, at face value, a good one, as was Liríope's, the nature of his upbringing contributes, ironically, to the creation of the very situation this fearful mother hoped to avoid. The interpretation of fate, whether one's own or that of others, and subsequent action that appears logical and necessary at the time, inevitably form the active and collaborative counterpart of an announced fate, the personal involvement required for its fulfillment, that oftentimes remains hidden from one's view. All Greek males are to be implicated in the upcoming war, and Aquiles, too, will enter it, but ill-prepared for what faces him. For he assumes the obligations of the Greek code of honor and its values without understanding that the price of vengeance demands the death of the avenger. With success on the fields of Ilium there will also come the destruction of Greek manhood, including that of the warrior chief, Aquiles.

Marte's oracle predicted that Aquiles' participation in the expeditionary force was essential for eventual victory:

> Troya será destruida
> y abrasada por los griegos,
> si va a su conquista Aquiles,
> a ser homicida de Héctor.
> Aquiles, humano monstruo
> de aquestos montes . . .

(1989b)

[Troy will be destroyed and burned by the Greeks, only if Aquiles takes part in the conquest and slays Hector. Aquiles, monstrous human of these mountainous lands . . .]

The oracle, however, conveniently omitted that Aquiles's own death was directly implicated in the endeavor. As Tetis was not capable of comprehending, goddess though she be, that her interpretation, intervention, decisions, and actions would contribute to the realization of Aquiles' fate, so too Marte's pronouncement conveniently brackets the young man's death at Troy, a victim of the cowardly Paris, thus underscoring the extent to which deceit, conscious and unconscious, will characterize all the actions of this play. The Greek warrior would not even be afforded a heroic death at the hands of an equal, such as Héctor. Toward the end of act 1, Aquiles deliberately tumbles down a mountainside in the attempt to elude his pursuers, and this fall proves to be both predictive of his acceptance of Marte's oracle and significative of his own participation in the fulfillment of his fate. Aquiles willingly assumes his *predicted* role in the Trojan War, thus transforming an announced fate into a personally directed course of action, in other words, his consciously chosen destiny.

The symbolic dimension of the action, never far from the rapid unfolding of events, is accentuated toward the end of the play. Once Aquiles accepts his role as chief warrior of the Greek forces, the essential participant in this punitive expedition against Troy, he sheds his heretofore protective, albeit shameful, feminine garb, declaring:

> Así yo, habiendo dejado
> la nupcial ropa de Venus,
> solo túnicas de Marte
> vestiré.

(2020a)

[Therefore, I, having shed the nuptual gowns of Venus, will dress only in Martial tunics in the future.]

In a dramatic world so starkly conceived, the gods of love and war represent distinct and conflictive values; and their respective axiological systems, the one here being necessarily exclusive and dismissive of the other, become part of the play's dynamics. At one point Aquiles forsakes Deidamia because she is scheduled to marry Lidoro, and his renunciation of her becomes ironically predictive:

> y pues me guardan los cielos
> para tragedias de Marte,
> no empiece por las de Venus.
>
> (2020b)

[And since the heavens are keeping me for the tragedies of Mars, I should not meddle in the affairs of Venus.]

In spite of this bravado, the dangers he confronts on the isle of Gnido are truly life-threatening. Yet, this young man willingly accepts equal, if not greater, dangers in his espousal of Marte's cause, for his rejection of Venus itself entails subtle dangers that the "manly" decision to abandon Deidamia brushes aside. When the *infanta* offers herself, body and soul, to the warrior, he responds:

> Pues cómo he de ir con esto?
> Piérdese vida y honor,
> fama y gloria. Mas qué es esto? *Clarín*
> La voz de Marte me llama.
>
> (2020b)

[Well, how should I proceed with this matter? Life and honor, fame and glory but . . . What is this? (A trumpet sounds) The voice of Mars calls.]

The representation of the youth's psychological struggle, clearly communicated in these scenes, requires little additional comment. Though attracted by Deidamia, Aquiles feels the greater claim on him now made by the "masculine" pursuits codified in Greek honor, war with Troy and total annihilation of their enemies. At this point he makes the personal decision to forsake love for honor, accepting thereby death's laurels on the fields of Ilium.

The traditional Mars-Venus struggle ostensibly represents two distinct modes of "being-in-the-world" at loggerheads, and this tension is evident in the character of Aquiles as well as in the masculine-dominated society he now wishes to join. Although he may experience a momentary reconciliation of these disparate claims on him, when acceptance of his martial duty translates into a socially approved marriage to Deidamia, *Monstruo*, nonetheless, underscores their fundamental incompatibility in the Greek world now dominated by the specters of death and destruction. Aquiles' marriage to Deidamia will be but a brief respite en route to complying with honor's uncompromising claim, his very life.

At first glance Venus represents the values of human and sexual love. However, on closer inspection, the goddess appears to uphold an exclusively sensual human existence and total dedication to life's pleasures. Can Aquiles continue to disregard the obligations of manhood to embrace such a life? Obviously he cannot. Correspondingly, must he accept the codes and values of Greek manhood as they are presented to him by Ulises? The play intimates, though not so obviously as in the first instance, that he does not have to; but apparently he will embrace them in their entirety as presented, thus making them his own. This starkly defined dichotomization of human life reduces human freedom to either sensual indulgence or martial madness. For the young man, exclusive dedication to Venus's values would epitomize an effeminate existence not worthy of him; but Marte's values, as constituted, stand for an equally warped, revenge-driven existence also not worthy of any reasonable man. However, he never gives due consideration to the implications of accepting the patriarchal option. While the acceptance of the Venus option represents distortion and incompleteness, the unconditional surrender to the feminine side of his character, the nonreflective espousal of the Marte option represents a similar outcome, death and destruction. In the first place, Aquiles assents to the destruction of the feminine side of his character and, in the second, he joins with others in proclaiming death as the ultimate value upheld in the Greek code of honor.

This traditional struggle between Venus and Mars raises the issue of the education of children and the extent of their human freedom in a society controlled by exclusively masculine values and dedicated to upholding at all costs a code of honor that undervalues life and exalts warfare and heroic death. At the conclusion to the play Aquiles marries Deidamia, and the happiness they experience appears to carry the day. However, Aquiles's happiness was made possible only by accepting his socially defined duty as leader of the Grecian expedition. Deidamia is permitted to marry him only because he will shortly depart for Troy. The exchange value of their marriage underscores its dehumanization of them both. For both these young people, service to the state and to patriarchal paradigms claims priority over personal happiness and critical thinking; and only in serving the state, one imbued with the values of Greek honor, can personal, albeit temporary, happiness be achieved. Society's definition of who they are, of what they are worth, and of what they will become is determinative for them as persons and citizens. Deidamia, as *infanta* of Gnido, may marry only when that marriage contributes to and fosters Gnido's state interests. Aquiles, as a young Greek male, is able to marry her only because this marriage will advance the Greek nation's political and moral objective, vengeance on their Trojan enemies.

The tragic irony of *Monstruo* is that neither the option symbolized by Venus nor that symbolized by Marte recognizes Aquiles', or Deidamia's, human freedom.[8] The former sidesteps the youth's need to assume his rightful place in adult society, while the latter slavishly chains him to a warped code of honor and to a deadly execution of the vengeance it proclaims as a sacred and national duty binding all Greek males. Aquiles' eventual tragedy proceeds from these limitations placed on his options for living and his potential for growth. His cry for freedom, heard earlier in the play, will go unanswered.

El monstruo de los jardines juxtaposes two distinct, disharmonious, and, in this plot configuration, mutually exclusive sets of values: those associated with honor, vengeance, and war, and those linked to life, love, and peace. While the action of the play attempts vainly to reconcile them, the Trojan War and its inevitable progression of events problematize what is conventional, and ultimately contradictory and unreconcilable, in the plot. This lack of synthesis reveals a fracture in the Baroque mindset, a disjunction of the Renaissance ideal of the harmony of opposites. Aquiles' engagement to Deidamia comes, ironically, only after his espousal of honor, war, and death. As a rite of passage for this offspring of violence, the events that comprise it reveal a truly monstrous reality at the core of society's values. For Aquiles participates simultaneously in two rites of passage, but, unfortunately, the one will, in the future, cancel the other. In the first and more conventional one, the young man espouses Deidamia, committing himself to her. At the surface level his marriage to the *infanta* represents his espousal of love, an encounter with "Woman As Death," the symbolic death of an immature and now inadequate masculine nature, as his manly and mature personality emerges from puerile egotism and adolescent self-centeredness. But a more fundamental rite of passage occurs at the same time, one temporarily hidden from our view and inspection. Aquiles's acceptance of the obligations of Greek honor brings him to an encounter with "Destiny As Death," the Trojan War, a predictive event that reminds us of what awaits him on Ilium's fields. In spite of the "optimistic" *desenlace* (denouement), for Aquiles' last words in the play are "Feliz soy" (2022b; I am happy), *Monstruo* is ultimately unable to reconcile the claims of honor and love, war and Deidamia, death and life.

In his introduction to the play, Valbuena Briones cites Antonio Minturno's comment on the concept of *admiratio:*

Debe admirarse aquellas cosas que conducen a la piedad o que producen el terror, y todavía mayormente aquellas cosas que siguiendo como consecuencia, suceden contrariamente a lo que se esperaba o deseaba. (1984b)

[One should admire those things that incite pity or produce terror, and even more the consequences that are to the contrary of what was hoped for or wanted.]

This is precisely what occurs in Aquiles' life after momentary happiness in the court of Gnido. Although he marries the *infanta* Deidamia, he will shortly be forced to depart for Troy to meet Héctor and his own death. The play subtly presents the following issue for our deliberation: Will the price the Greeks seem so willing to pay for their revenge of Paris's abduction of Helen be worth all the death and destruction it leaves in its wake? Tetis, blind as ever, predicts "trofeos, / victorias, triunfos y aplausos" (2022a; trophies, victories, triumphs, and applause.) for her son and the Greek armada; however, in the midst of this hymeneal celebration, death raises its gloomy specter. In the first scene of the play Lidoro had remarked, after having been cast shipwrecked upon the shores of Gnido: "pues desdicha no hay, no hay desconsuelo / que no enmiende el vivir" (1985b; there is no bad fortune or sorrow that can not be cured simply by living). Aquiles' predicted death reminds us that his initiation into sexuality and manhood is, at the same time, an initiation into the code of Greek honor with its demand, in this instance, for vengeance. Two of Deidamia's ladies had earlier sung: "¡Desdichado / del que no vive engañado!" (1991a; Unfortunate is he who does not live deceived), suggesting that, to be happy in this world, one must either be deceived by others or consciously embrace a life of illusion. Aquiles can be momentarily happy only when this curious admixture of deceit by others and self-delusion takes full effect. We are not, however, afforded this self-congratulatory luxury, and this is the source of our pity for Aquiles and for Deidamia. What begins for him on a happy note will inevitably end in self-annihilation and disaster. This knowledge produces our *admiratio*.

Notes

This study originally appeared in *Texto y espectáculo:* Selected Proceedings of the Symposium on Spanish Golden Age Theater (March 11, 12, 13, 1987) ed. Barbara Mujica (Lanham: University Press of America, 1989), 149–56. I gratefully acknowledge permission granted by University Press of America to publish a revised version of the study in this volume.

1. I have chosen to employ the Spanish names for the characters, as given in Calderón's play, rather than Anglicize them.
2. For a positive appreciation of the figure of Astraea in Calderón's dramaturgy, see de Armas (1986).
3. The question of what constitutes the necessary conditions for a just war is never seriously addressed. However, the issue that plagued the conde-duque de Olivares for over twenty years, and Spain throughout the second half of the seventeenth century, "the *falta de cabezas*—the lack of leaders" (Elliott 342), receives in this play a broad, dramatic treatment that includes the political and moral assumptions underlying imperial aspirations and the conquest mentality emanating from the top echelons of society.
4. It will be recalled that, in her resistance to Peleo's use of force, the goddess progressively transformed herself into water, wind, lion, and fire. These metamorphoses, nonetheless, proved to be futile. From this violent union Aquiles was born.
5. See Hathorn (1977, 353). Consultation of popular mythological references works, such as the *Espasa diccionario de la mitología griega y romana* (1996) and *The Penguin Dictionary of Classical Mythology* (1990), provides a sense of the narrative variety found in many myths, as well as myth's essential malleability, an attribute making these ancient stories very attractive to creative artists.
6. All references will come from the Valbuena Briones edition of the play (1969), and will be cited by page and column, indicated by "a" or "b."
7. For a study of the significance of the rape theme in Calderonian dramaturgy, see O'Connor 1991 and 1988.
8. See A. A. Parker's perceptive study of the play (1979).

Part 3
Representations of the Goddess

Three Faces of Diana, Two Facets of Honor: Myth and the Honor Code in Lope de Vega's *El perro del hortelano*

Hayden Duncan-Irvin

As Norman Austin states, "Myth purports to offer an adequate explanation for everything—for the elements and laws of nature, for social structures, ethics, and the dynamics of the individual psyche" (*Meaning*, 2). *Webster's New Universal Unabridged Dictionary* defines myth as "a traditional story of unknown authorship, ostensibly with a historical basis, but serving usually to explain some phenomenon of nature, the origin of man, or the customs, institutions, religious rites, etc. of a people: myths usually involve the exploits of gods and heroes." From time immemorial, humans have constructed myths in order to deal with phenomena that transcend the limits of understanding, and as a means of communicating ideas and concepts that might otherwise prove too difficult for articulation. The writers of the Spanish Golden Age were largely inspired by the myths of Classical Antiquity and while such influence is obvious in the title of some Golden Age works, others manifest their debt to the ancient myths more implicitly. This is certainly the case of Lope de Vega's *El perro del hortelano* (*The Dog in the Manger*), in which three types of myth are either implicitly or explicitly embedded in the action: classical myth, myth as a social structure, and deception as a form of myth.

The first type is instituted by direct references to the classical myth of Ícaro (Icarus) and Faetón (Phaeton), along with more oblique references to the goddess Diana, whose presence is evoked by certain characteristics and actions of the protagonist of the drama. The second type is the "myth" of seventeenth-century Spanish honor, which is the main motive of the action of *Perro*. And the third involves the "myth"[1] or tale fabricated by the servant Tristán. Tristán's *invención* intentionally provides a much-needed solution to Diana and Teodoro's problematic situation, and inadvertently exposes honor as a form of myth. These three types of myth will be examined in the present study (although not necessarily in the order in which they have been presented above) and certain aspects of our explication will be informed by Lacan's thoughts on law, desire, and his Imaginary and Symbolic Orders. While any definition of these terms is inevitably reductive in a study of this length, the following succinct explication is offered as a general context.

Lacan posits that all humans are born prematurely and that the consequent lack of motor control and coordination produces a sense of turbulence in the newly born infant. The sense of an integrated self is first achieved when the infant experiences some kind of reflection of itself (in a mirror or through the experience of a human form) and, subsequently, identifies with the reflected image. While the child enjoys a narcissistic relationship with the reflected image that gives it the illusion of a unified self, it hates the image that it cannot physically appropriate; that is to say, the ideal of a totally integrated self is an unattainable one. Since the reflected image is at once "self" and "other," the child "misrecognizes" itself because it discovers the "I" in an image that is "other" than or "alien" to itself. Thus, "misrecognition" has an alienating effect on the child. This period of images or the Imaginary determines the perception of reality that the child becomes aware of in an inverted way, and lays the foundation for all future human relationships that might be affected by jealousies, rivalries, aggression, etcetera, because of the narcissistic and alienating structuring of the "I."

During this period, the child enjoys an Imaginary dyadic relationship with objects, and with the body of the other (usually the mother or another nurturing individual). Desire—a psychic force that motivates the individual—now begins to mediate the child's awareness of self since the "I" identifies with the other and hence desires what the other desires.

At about eighteen months the child enters the Symbolic Order (the realm of signifiers, speech, etcetera), that is, it gains access to signification through the use of language. This period coincides with that of the Oedipus complex when the dyadic Imaginary relationship of mother and child is disrupted by the presence of the father. The child's position in the family, together with its entry into the world of language, determines its subjectivity and defines its sexuality. The law of the Name-of-the Father (which Lacan describes as being both *le Nom-du-père* and the *le Non-du-père*, that is, the Name-of-the Father which is also the **No**-of-the-Father) with its interdictory function "castrates" the subject by imposing the laws of culture and society. By the same token, the interdictory function of the law of the Name-of-the-Father also forces desire to be repressed and become unconscious desire, creating a lack-in-being—a consciousness of the limits of self, as it were—in the subject which is now "split" into the subject of being (*moi*) and the subject of conscious discourse (*je*). As a result of this lack-in-being, desire now structures the subject who searches for meaning through the use of language. In other words, desire is articulated through language whose Symbolic function provides endless substitutes for the true object of desire.[2]

As Henry Sullivan has noted in his discussion of what he terms a psychoanalytic poetics of the Spanish *comedia*, "the constraints of law push to inhibit and tame desire socially, while law must always contend with the pressure of desire to subvert its own claims" (Sullivan 1994, 223).[3] Sullivan draws attention to the fact that "the main actions of Golden Age Spanish drama concern law, expressed as issues of *power* politics, and the secondary actions concern *desire*, expressed as issues of love and passion" (224). In the case of *Perro* the dialectic of law and desire constitutes the main action, for it is precisely the honor code that restrains Diana, and delays her marriage to her secretary, Teodoro, until the end of the play. The "myth" of honor is the Symbolic element, the law of the Name-of-the-Father, which threatens to thwart desire (the natural process of love) when the Countess Diana and her secretary Teodoro fall in love with each other.

Marcelin Defourneaux correctly observes that

> for the Spanish dramatists, honor plays the same part as the Fates in Greek tragedy. They represent it as a mysterious power, looking down on everyone's life, forcing people to abandon their feelings and natural inclinations, sometimes forcing them to acts of sublime sacrifice, at others to the commission of crimes or terrible atrocities. But these must be regarded in the light of the provocation which caused them and the dire necessity of which they were the consequence
>
> (Defourneaux, 34).

Considered from this perspective, the honor code, as both a social and aesthetic convention, imposes a figurative "Thou shalt not . . ." on the free play of erotic/amorous relations, as well as on the crossing of social barriers. Nevertheless, this man-made construct is neither invulnerable nor absolute—at least within the fictitious world of the *comedia*—since it can be undermined by other "myths" such as Tristán's *invención* in the closing scenes of *Perro*.

We have already noted *Perro*'s references to three figures from classical mythology namely, the goddess Diana, Ícaro, and Faetón. At this point, we should like to focus on the individual figures and then illustrate how they function in interrelated fashion within the plot. Let us first consider the goddess Diana. She is most commonly known as the huntress, the goddess of chastity, the goddess of the moon. The Romans often identified her with the Greek goddess Artemis who, like Apollo is armed with a bow and quiver; in her aspect of light-goddess she had the same functions as Apollo and bore the epithet *Apollousa*, which means "destructress" (*The Larousse Encyclopedia of Mythology*, 121). She was sometimes merged with Hecate, a divinity of the Underworld who was originally a moon-goddess. Indeed the name "Hecate" seems to be the feminine form of a title of Apollo's—the far-darter (Larousse 165). One of the possible reasons for the merging of Hecate and Artemis might be attributed to their association with Apollo through name and function. With this fusion of Artemis and Hecate, it is not difficult, therefore, to understand why Diana is sometimes referred to as the goddess with three faces. Calderón de la Barca, for example, makes use of this triple-faceted image of Diana in *Celos aun del aire matan* (1660) (*Jealousy, Even When It Comes from the Air Can Kill*) when he has the goddess identify herself thusly:

> ¿No soy la *que* con tres rostros,
> siendo mis imperios tres,
> Diana en la verde selba,
> Luna en el azul dosel,
> y Proserpina en el negro
> centro, los mortales ven
> tal vez presidir opuesta,
> y favorable tal vez?
>
> (1039–46)[4]

> [Am I not the one whom, with three faces,
> since I have three kingdoms,
> Diana in the green forest,
> Luna in the blue canopy,
> and Proserpina in the black
> underworld, the mortals see
> rule sometimes adversely
> and sometimes favorably?]
>
> (117)[5]

The multiple aspects of the goddess Diana, which are derived from the fusion of Artemis and Hecate, also seem to have provided Lope de Vega with a model for the heroine of *Perro*, whose changing moods elicit such epithets as *tornasol mudable* (twisting sunflower), *veleta* (weather vane), *luna* (moon), *monstruo de mudanza* (monster of mutability) from Teodoro. A close reading reveals comparable traits between the mythological deity and her namesake of *Perro*. Lope's Diana has never married and her indifference to suitors permits one to posture her chastity, thus evoking a reference to the moon goddess's famed virtue. As goddess of the forests and woods, that is, goddess of the hunt, Diana is also known for the strict laws of chastity that she imposed on her companions who were duly punished when they disobeyed her. Although the Diana of *Perro* has no reason to chastise Teodoro and Marcela for breaking laws of chastity, she nonetheless puts an interdiction on their love for each other to suit her own purpose, and cruelly torments Teodoro by alternately luring and rebuffing him as she becomes the proverbial dog in the manger. Finally, the less desirable qualities of the goddess manifest themselves in the relationships that Diana has with those close to her. In the first instance, once she realizes that she herself is in love with Teodoro, she eliminates Marcela from the scene by locking her in her (Diana's) chamber. On another occasion, she sadistically demonstrates her love to/for Teodoro by hitting him so hard that he bleeds. And even after she has achieved her wishes (to make Teodoro her husband), she considers having Tristán killed in order to keep secret the fact that Teodoro's newly discovered "noble" bloodline is the result of a ruse designed by Tristán.

Like the goddess Diana who, in her aspect as light-goddess, had the same function as Apollo, Lope's Diana is cast in the role of the moon by Marcela who tells Teodoro, "todo lo sabe en efeto; / que si es Diana la luna, / siempre a quien ama importuna, / salió y vio nuestro secreto" (910–14): "In short, she knows; of course, since she's Diana / the moon is always meddling with us lovers. / She peeped, and saw our secret" [58]). Teodoro also draws on the moon reference as he complains to Tristán about Diana's inconstancy:

> Pues, Tristán, agora vino
> ese tornasol mudable,
>
> .   .   .   .
>
> esa Diana, esa luna,
> esa mujer, ese hechizo,

ese monstro de mudanzas.

. . . .

(1749–56)

[Tristán, a moment since, that twisting sunflower,

. . . .

that inconstant moon
well-named Diana, that bewitching siren,
that monster of mutability

. . . .

(75)

More important, however, are the references that are made to
Diana as the sun, particularly through the metaphors of the
myths of Ícaro and Faetón. For instance, Fabio presents Diana
with the hat that he has found on the staircase of her home. The
feathers of the hat are all burned because the hat had been used
to snuff out the light of a lamp as Tristán and Teodoro were
fleeing from Diana's house. In reply to Diana's comments on the
state of the feathers, Fabio exclaims:

> Ícaro ¿al sol no subía,
> que abrasándose las plumas,
> cayó en las blancas espumas
> del mar? Pues esto sería.
> El sol la lámpara fue,
> Ícaro el sombrero, y luego
> las plumas deshizo el fuego.

(125–31)

[Remember Icarus flew near the sun,
his wings were burnt, and he fell in the sea.
This hat was Icarus, the lamp the sun,
its feathers flamed, and it fell on the stair.]

(43)

Although Fabio is literally referring to the feathers of the hat
and to the lamp, the Ícaro metaphor is obviously a latent textual
reference that foreshadows for the viewer/reader the Teodoro-
Diana affair, since both the hat and the lamp are metonmynically
linked to Teodoro and Diana, respectively. The abundant feathers
that Diana had perceived in the darkness apparently belong to
Teodoro's hat, while the lamp is an item in Diana's house. Thus,
Teodoro is Ícaro and Diana, the sun. The reference to the Ícaro

myth is later echoed by Teodoro, who tells Diana, "Tristán, a quien hoy pudiera / hacer el engaño estatuas, / la industria versos, y Creta / rendir laberintos . . ." (3279–82: "Tristán, to whom Deceit should set up statues, / whom Mischief might immortalise in verse, / whom Daedalus, who made the Cretan maze / might well acknowledge as the greater master . . ." [111]) . He is alluding, of course, to the Cretan labyrinth out of which Daedalus led his son, Ícaro, just as Tristán has freed Teodoro (Ícaro) from what would otherwise have been a *huis clos* situation. This comparison invites speculation with regard to the future happiness of Diana and Teodoro. Has Tristán's plan to give him his passage to freedom from the social status that had previously debarred him from marrying Diana positioned him too closely to the sun? After all, Diana has been apprised of the truth and still is the sun, that is, a social superior to Teodoro.

The myth of Faetón also reinforces the sun metaphor for Diana, and is mentioned in the same context with the myth of Ícaro. Teodoro refers to both myths in a conversation with Diana, as he hints at the potential danger that can ensue when one's aspirations are placed too high:[6]

Diana:	que no ofende un desigual amando, pues sólo entiendo que se ofende aborreciendo.
Teodoro:	Ésa es razón natural, mas pintaron a Faetonte y Ícaro despeñados, uno en caballos dorados, precipitado en un monte, y otro, con alas de cera, derritido en el crisol del sol.

(815–24)

[*Diana:*	You say here that you fear, as an inferior, to offend one far superior; yet in love that cannot be, and you must be mistaken. It seems to me inferiors can't offend by loving; only hating gives offence.
Teodoro:	That's nature's logic; but the painters show Phaeton and Icarus hurtling from the heavens, one drawn by golden horses, then struck down, the other borne aloft on wings of wax, soon melted by the fierceness of the sun.]

(56)

Once again, Diana is in the place of the sun because like Apolo (Apollo), who grants Faetón the privilege of driving the chariot of the sun, in essence, she is attempting to grant privileges to Teodoro. However, unlike Faetón, Teodoro intuits the possible harm that can result when one undertakes an enterprise beyond the limits of one's ability.

One final reference to Diana as the sun strengthens the metaphor that is borne out in the myths of Ícaro and Faetón. As the marquis Ricardo approaches Diana's home, he espies the count Federico who is waiting to be received by Diana. Celio, Ricardo's servant, comments on Diana's beauty which he likens to that of the sun. Ricardo elaborates on the reference by drawing a parallel between Diana's review of her suitors and the sun's passage through the signs of the zodiac. Once again, the reference to *rayos de sol* (sun rays) evokes the image of Apollo and sheds light on the comparison between the protagonist of *Perro* and the light-goddess who shares the name and function of Apollo.

According to what has just been outlined above, the three mythological characters that figure in the action also have an important function in the myth of the honor code. The foregoing explication of the classical myths has shown that, metaphorically, they are linked by the representation of Diana as the sun. As the central figure both of the myths as well as of the action of *Perro*, Diana is placed in a position of authority. In other words, she is in the place of the father figure; the one who bears the Name-of-the-Father.[7] A full recounting of the tales of Ícaro and Faetón would reveal the names of the respective fathers, Dédalo and Apollo, who play an important role in their sons' respective destinies. Each father facilitates his son's ascent to higher realms and each son fails to heed the advice of the father: Dédalo cautions Ícaro not to venture too closely to the sun, and Apollo advises Faetón to steer a medium course when he drives the chariot of the sun. Each son's disastrous end is well known. However, the fact that these two fathers are not explicitly mentioned in the play suggests that they are eclipsed by Diana, who has appropriated the place of Apollo, that is, the position of the father figure. The validity of this suggestion is further strengthened by the fact that Count Ludovico, the only father to appear in the play, is not the father of a living son, because Tristán has fabricated the evidence that dupes Ludovico into believing that he has found his long-lost son. In essence, Tristán's manipulation of Ludovico renders the latter powerless. The only authority that he has left is the ability to bestow his inheritance on a fictitious son. Diana, therefore, is the only figure that bears the Name-of-the-Father. She is also the figure in whom the dialect of law and desire is foregrounded, since her sense of honor (derived from the Symbolic Order) is in conflict with her desire (in the Imaginary).

Diana and her household live in a fictitious Naples, a place that with its social conventions and laws seeks to represent the seventeenth-century Spanish code of honor. Like her fellow citizens, Diana is subject to the dictates of the honor code that forbid her to marry someone of inferior social standing. With the realization of her love for her servant Teodoro she is confronted with the dilemma that arises from the disparity between her social status and Teodoro's, and her rebellious, "¡Maldígate Dios, honor! / Temeraria invención fuiste, / tan opuesta al propio gusto" (2623–25: "Oh, Honour, / God curse you, foolish fiction[8] that you are, / so alien to our innermost desires" [95]) is an indication of the frustration that she feels. From a Lacanian perspective, this clearly demonstrates how law constrains desire socially, while desire constantly seeks to subvert law.

Within the Symbolic Order, Diana's interests lie in the strict observance of the honor code. Hence, she is disturbed to find that two men have intruded into the privacy of her home at night, thus putting her honor (her good name) at risk. Since she bears the Name-of-the-Father, she must fulfill her role in the Symbolic Order and thus act as a "Father" to Marcela, while at the same time denying her own debt to Teodoro:

> tú podrás con más secreto
> proseguir ese tu amor;
> que en la ocasión yo me ofrezco
> a ayudaros a los dos;
> que Teodoro es hombre cuerdo,
> y a ti, Marcela, te tengo
> la obligación que tú sabes,
> y no poco parentesco.
>
> (310–18)

[and you pursue your love with more discretion. When opportunity affords, I'll help you; Teodoro's sensible, and has been raised here in my house, and you, Marcela, kinship apart, have merited my favour.]
(47)

In addition to the above reassurance, Diana, as a figure of authority, promises to marry the two. Nonetheless, this interest and sense of honor that reside in the Symbolic are threatened by

Imaginary feelings of jealousy. When left alone, Diana muses on Teodoro's attributes and wavers between respect for the honor code and resentment of the restraints that it places on her freedom to love Teodoro:

> Mil veces he advertido en la belleza,
> gracia y entendimiento de Teodoro;
> que a no ser desigual a mi decoro,
> estimara su ingenio y gentileza.
>   Es el amor común naturaleza,
> mas yo tengo mi honor por más tesoro;
> que los respetos de quien soy adoro
> y aun el pensarlo tengo por bajeza.
>   La envidia bien sé yo que ha de quedarme,
> que si la suelen dar bienes ajenos,
> bien tengo de que pueda lamentarme,
> porque quisiera yo que por lo menos
> Teodoro fuera más, para igualarme,
> *o yo, para igualarle, fuera menos.

(325–38)

[I've often seen Teodoro's handsome face, often remarked his wit and manly beauty, and might admire his mind, his charm, his grace, were that consistent with my sense of duty.

Love is the common lot of all on earth; but I more highly prize my honoured name, I worship my nobility of birth, and must regard the very thought with shame.

Envy, I know too well, must be my fate, engendered by a joy I cannot share; with reason I resent my rank and state, and can but vainly wish in fond dispair, that he were more, and I not far above him, or I were less, and so could freely love him.]

(47)

Law and desire are clearly in conflict with each other. This conflict seems to reach a climax, at a later point in the play, when she violently slaps Teodoro. This action is a displacement manifested Symbolically (in the form of a physical upbraiding of her inferior) for what she is experiencing in the Imaginary (the frustration that arises from the mixture of love for Teodoro and jealousy of Marcela, hence Diana's aggressive action).

Teodoro is one of the first to recognize and identify her dilemma: "si Diana algún camino hallara / de disculpa, conmigo se casara. / Teme su honor, y cuando más se abrasa, / se hiela y me desprecia" (2539–42: "if Diana were to find some pretext, / any excuse at all, she'd marry me. / She's fearful for her honour; when her passion / is most inflamed, she cools and turns against me" [93]). These are the words that prompt Tristán to devise the plan that eventually remedies the situation—at least on the surface. The dialectical conflict between law and desire continues as Diana prevents Teodoro and Marcela from pursuing their love for each other, while she resists risking the ruin of her reputation (her *honra*).

The motive of preserving Diana's honor also occasions undesireable reactions on the part of two of her suitors, Federico and Ricardo. A negative aspect of the honor code (killing someone to preserve one's good name), is foregrounded when the two suitors decide to hire Tristán to murder Teodoro because the latter's relationship with Diana is an affront to Ricardo, who is supposedly Diana's chosen suitor. Federico tells Ricardo, "antes que desto se hable / en Nápoles y el decoro / de vuestra sangre se ofenda, / sea o no sea verdad, / ha de morir" (2398–402: "before there's talk of this all over Naples, / before your family reputation suffers, / whether it's true or not, he'll have to die" [90]). This contract to kill Teodoro is made in the Symbolic, but in the Imaginary, the motives of Federico and Ricardo stem from their jealousy of one who is a formidable rival. As in the case of Diana's slapping Teodoro, the aggression displayed by Federico and Ricardo is a manifestation of the workings of the Imaginary Order.

The negative aspect of honor manifests itself once more when Diana considers killing Tristán in order that the truth about Teodoro's "nobility" be buried forever. Nonetheless, it can be said that Diana upholds the positive aspect of honor, since she has already acknowledged that honor of the Symbolic Order (*honra*) is, after all, not superior to nobility of spirit (*honor*). After Teodoro confesses, "mi nobleza natural / que te engañe no me deja, / porque soy naturalmente / hombre que verdad profesa" (3294–97: "'my natural nobility / will not allow me to abuse your trust. / I am by nature one who tells the truth" [111]), Diana replies, "discreto en que tu nobleza / me has mostrado en declararte (3303–4: "You've been . . . shrewd to have made so candid a confession / and shown me your nobility of mind" [111]). This is her way of justifying her acceptance of Tristán's ruse as a solution to her dilemma.

Viewed from a Lacanian perspective, law still holds desire in place, because although Diana can now marry the man she wants, she can only do so through a solution that has been found in the Symbolic: Tristán's creation of a noble father for Teodoro, which makes Teodoro an acceptable husband for Diana according to the constraints of the honor code.

Viewed from the perspective of the honor code, the players of *Perro* have little control over their actions since they are bound by the Law of the Name-of-the Father—the honor code, which places an interdiction on marriage across social boundaries in order to keep the family name intact. It is only through the success of Tristán's strategem—the invention of the myth of Teodoro's bloodline—that Diana can marry her social inferior without tarnishing family honor. Ironically, it is Tristán's "myth" that informs Diana of Teodoro's noble spirit (*honor*) and highlights the myth of honor (*honra* as a social convention). In this light, it can be concluded that *Perro* constitutes a mythological sublimation and justification of the theme of honor (*honor*), i.e., nobility of spirit because, as Bruce Wardropper notes, "in this world . . . only moral values ("nobleza natural" as opposed to social appearances) are valid" (Wardropper 1967, 111). Thus, Diana's forgiveness of Teodoro for his share in the *engaño* is a celebration of spiritual nobility since, as Pedro Crespo (*El alcalde de Zalamea*, 1.874–76) reminds us, "el honor / es patrimonio del alma, / y el alma sólo es de Dios (honor is inherited property of the soul / and the soul belongs to God only" [my translation]).

El perro del hortelano can, therefore, be read as a work in which Lope employs myth in three different ways as a vehicle for presenting two facets of the honor code. The goddess Diana, with her three faces, provides the *materia prima* with which Lope de Vega constructs a play that exposes the convention of *honra* as a form of myth.

Notes

I would like to acknowledge Charles Oriel's influence on some of the ideas developed in this essay. Conversations with him concerning the depiction of the goddess Diana in Calderón's *Celos aun del aire matan* as representative of the honor code in all its negative aspects provided me with food for thought. Charles has also been very helpful in critiquing parts of the present work.

1. Toward the end of act 3, when Diana is told of how Tristán has beguiled the Count Ludovico into believing that Teodoro is his long-lost son, she refers to Tristán's story as an *invención*, which has synonyms *ficción, fábula, mito*.

2. The ideas summarized above are taken from Jacques Lacan (1977 and 1981).

3. Also see his 1990 article, in which he addresses the structure of Spanish classical drama from a Lacanian perspective, focusing in some detail on the relationship between Law and Desire in *La vida es sueño*.

4. All references to *Celos aun del aire matan* (*Jealousy, Even When It comes from the Air Can Kill*) are from the Matthew Stroud bilingual edition (1981).

5. All English translations of *Celos* (*Jealousy*) are from the Matthew Stroud bilingual edition (1981).

6. Louis C. Pérez has already noted that Lope links the Faetón and Icaro myths in order to highlight the hero's adventure and possible failure. He also mentions Diana's role as moon-sun: "Al terminar el primer acto, Lope vuelve otra vez a referirse al fracaso y 'a la empresa dudosa' de conquistar el cielo— Diana (Luna) que por medio de una metamorfosis metafórica Lope ha convertido en sol" (291).

7. As head of her household, Diana controls the lives of those who reside and work in her home. In the absence of a father or older brother, she decides her own destiny.

8. By having Diana address the honor code as "foolish fiction," Lope strengthens the plausibility of Diana's ultimate acceptance of Teodoro's newly discovered "noble" bloodline. Since Tristán's *invención* can expose the honor code as a form of myth, Diana realizes that *honra* is necessarily inferior to *honor*.

Astraea, the *Pax Christiana*, and Lope de Vega's *Santa Casilda*

Gordon Sumner

Like the majority of the *comedias de santos* (saints plays), Lope de Vega's *Santa Casilda* (*Saint Casilda*) is generally unknown, although it is a play of considerable dramatic craftsmanship. One of the more interesting aspects of this play is the mixture of hagiography and myth. Indeed, one particular deity is particularly prominent in this *comedia*. In *The Return of Astrea*, Frederick de Armas states: "Astraea, having survived medieval and Renaissance transformations, has become a multifaceted figure utilized by numerous writers during the Spanish Golden Age" (1986, 58). The literary debt that *Santa Casilda* owes to the myth of the goddess Astraea is enormous, and the purpose of this essay is to illuminate the relationships between Casilda in Lope's drama and the legendary Astraea. Moreover, this study aims at promoting further critical attention to a large subgenre of the *comedia:* the *comedias de santos.*[1]

During the Spanish Golden Age the goddess adopts many guises. De Armas explains:

> In her imperial and religious garb, Astraea is utilized during this period as a laudatory vehicle by authors who wish to portray the Catholic kings, Charles V, Philip II, and even Philip IV as a *dominus mundi* who will bring about world order and peace. Others such as Fray Luis de León and Miguel de Cervantes move away from the imperial goddess and prefer to view the golden age over which she presides as being actualized (1986, 58)

As this critic demonstrates, the treatment of the mythic goddess in the works of these authors is varied, and there are reoccurring ideas which can be succinctly summarized. Among the multiple roles and guises Astraea assumes are those as a maiden who is the embodiment of justice and truth and as the spiritual agent who symbolizes inner peace and harmony. Furthermore, Astraea is thematically associated with the *pax Christiana*, and in this function, she represents the return of a new golden age. Each trait of Astraea corresponds to a fundamental characteristic that underlines the actions and personality of Casilda. An examination of these correspondences will serve to illustrate the influences of the legendary Astraea upon the Spanish saint in Lope's *comedia*.

The myth of Astraea is very old and has its roots in classical culture. Ovid, Virgil, and Aratus, among others, allude to her in their works. In the *Phaenomena*, a book on the constellations, Aratus writes:

> After Helice, Arctophylax, very like a waggoner is borne along, commonly known by the name of Bootes, because he appears to drive the Wain of the Bear, and appears conspicuously bright. Beneath his girdle rolls Arcturus, the most brilliant of stars. Below both feet of the waggoner the Virgin appears, who holds in her hand the splendid star Spica. Whether she be the offspring of Astraeus, the reputed father of primeval stars, or of some other, matters not. There is another story current among men that she was at one time well acquainted with earth; nor did she shun the society of old men, or women, but mingled freely with them, although she herself was immortal; moreover, they call her Justice. Associating with old men at one time, in the market place, and at another in the open air, she by her wisdom, demonstrated the laws of State.
>
> (Singleton, 1958, 192–93)

Thus, Astraea is the virgin goddess who left earth to become the constellation Virgo. Virgil also refers to Astraea his Fourth Ecologue: "The great order of ages, begins anew; now the Virgin, now the rule of Saturn, now a progeny descends from heaven on high" (Singleton, 1958, 195). Astraea is this same virgin, and as the embodiment of justice, she will reign in the return of a new golden age. In *Journey to Beatrice*, Charles Singleton describes the development of the myth of Astraea, and makes clear the association between the goddess and justice:

> It seems quite probable that Ovid was familiar with Aratus' version of the myth of Virgo. Cicero translated a portion of the Greek poem, as did the poet Germanicus Caesar. The latter made almost a literal translation of the *Phaenomena*, and therein gave full attention to Astraea's role. Through him and Ovid, and yet others, the figure of Astraea or Virgo becomes firmly established in the meaning "Justice," a meaning which was known to men in the first age of mankind.
> (Singleton, 193–94)

In the first act of *Santa Casilda*, the fragile Moorish princess describes herself as a maid of fifteen years who suffers an unknown malady. She yearns for something which she cannot precisely identify. She has vehemently refused marriage with all the eligible Moorish princes because she intuits that they cannot assuage her malaise, and she declares:

> Un año me sirvieron
> dos reyes sarracinos,
> y con desprecio a entrambos
> pagué tantos servicios.
> Vino a verme Abenámar,
> Hijo del rey Marsichio,
> sobrino de mi padre,
> que me pide por primo.
> Y con tantos rigores
> y desdén tan altivo
> desprecio sus finezas
> que no sé como es vivo.
>
> (Lope de Vega, *Santa Casilda*, 562a)

> [For a year, two Saracen kings
> courted me,
> and for so much attentiveness
> I repaid them with scorn.
> Abenámar, son of the king Marsichio,
> and nephew of my father,
> came to see me,
> and as my cousin,
> to ask for my hand.
> I rebuked his suit
> with such coldness and
> haughty disdain that I
> do not know how he is alive.]

After a dream points the way to Christianity, Casilda's existential crisis is resolved, and she announces to her servants that she must visit the imprisoned Christians. Casilda takes food to them and asks them to provide her with instruction about themselves and their beliefs. Through an "imperial" gesture in which she vows to free the Christian slaves, Casilda commences her role as an agent of justice. At the end of the second act, the freedom of the Christians is a *fait accompli*. Gonzalo, a leader of these captives, recounts how more than three thousand slaves have gained liberty:

> Soltaron a los cristianos
> de la prisión que tenían
> que apenas crédito daban
> con el placer de la dicha.
> A todos hizo vestir
> de la manera que miras,
> y el Rey lo permite y quiere
> sin que a su gusto resista

(580b)

> [They let go the Christians
> from the prison which they had,
> and such was the pleasure of
> their good luck that they
> scarcely believed it. The king
> had everyone dressed in the
> manner in which you see, and
> he wishes and permits this
> without his desire being resisted.]

Casilda's identity as an agent of justice is emphasized dramatically in the third act when it appears that the devil has fatally trapped her in his web of treachery and deception. Abenámar, cousin and noble suitor of Casilda, has accompanied the princess on her journey to Castile where she hopes to find the miraculous lakes of San Vicente. Because the devil has metamorphosed himself and has fabricated fake letters, Abenámar erroneously believes that Casilda loves him and will openly reveal her love at an appropriate moment. Tarfe, another Moorish noble, similarly thinks Casilda loves him since the devil has likewise deceived him with another specious letter. In the letter, Tarfe learns that he must kill Abenámar in order to win the princess. Like Abenámar, Tarfe is a part of Casilda's retinue that makes the journey to Castile; both men anxiously await the occasion in which Casilda will announce her love. However, Abenámar mistakes a discussion of salvation for one of amorous declaration:

Abenámar: ¿Posible es que no eres mía?

Casilda: Tengo Esposo que me espera.

Tarfe: (Esto es por mi claro está.
¿Quién tuvo dicha come ésta)

Abenámar: Mataréle.

Casilda: No podrás.
             y guardate de sus fuerzas.

Abenámar: Gozaréte.

Casilda: Es imposible. (583b)

[Abenámar: Is it possible that you are not mine?

Casilda: I have a husband and Lord who awaits me.

Tarfe: (This is clearly a reference to me; who
              ever had such fortune as this?)

Abenámar: I will kill him.

Casilda: You cannot.

Abenámar: I shall have and enjoy you now.

Cailda: It is impossible.]

As Abenámar is about to rape Casilda, Tarfe considers this scene
as his cue to kill his rival and draws his dagger to strike. In spite
of this attempt to defame her honor, Casilda mercifully alerts
Abenámar to Tarfe's approaching blow and thereby saves her attacker. Although both men furiously accuse her of having lied,
the princess summons divine intervention against this villainy,
and each suitor is miraculously reduced to contrition. Abenámar
recognizes Casilda as the arbiter of justice:

> Casilda, tus cosas trata,
> Quieres, dispón, manda, ordena,
> que yo no lo contradigo
> ni de tu virtud creyera
> que me mandaras matar,
> y el alma, que estuvo ciega
> ya desengañada vive.
>
> (584 a)

> [Casilda, dispense your terms,
> order, command, decree,
> for I will not contradict them;
> neither did I believe, because
> of your virtue, that you would
> sentense me to death, and
> my soul which was blind,
> now lives undeceived.]

Tarfe makes a similar acknowledgment of Casilda's unassailable
character:

> Yo tambien digo lo mismo,
> y pido, a tus pies, Princesa,
> perdones mi atrevimiento,
> que no es posible que pueda
> caber en tanta humildad
> lo que imaginé en tu ofensa.
>
> (584 b)

> [I likewise say the same,
> and I ask, at your feet, Princess,
> that you pardon my daring act,
> for it is not possible that there can
> be in such humility that which
> I imagined as an offense.]

In much Spanish poetry of the Golden Age, Astraea symbolizes truth accompanied by spiritual rejuvenation as well as a search for inner peace and harmony. Casilda's spirituality and her quest for self-knowledge reflect themes that resemble those surrounding Astraea in the poetry of Fray Luis, Cervantes, and Lope. The development of Casilda's personality as an individual in the pursuit of inner truth and self-affirmation is tightly woven into the dramatic fabric of the play. From the beginning, Casilda confesses to her attendants that she does not understand herself; she seeks solitude and equanimity in order to know herself better:

> Dejadme sola, que quiero
> en este jardín quedarme
> por si puedo sosegarme
> de la pasión con que muero.
>
> (560 a)

> [Leave me alone, for I
> wish to remain in this garden
> to determine if I can recompose
> myself from the passion
> which consumes me.]

Casilda later explains in more detail that since birth she has lacked *joie de vivre:*

> Todo me ha dado pena
> y al paso que he crecido
> más se aumentan mis males
> y muero si los miro.

Y a la vega bajaba
y al Tajo cristalino
que la sirve de espejo
para adornar sus rizos.
Miraba su hermosura,
los jardines floridos,
música de las aves,
hechos arpas los picos;
las flores, los claveles,
jazmines y jacintos
alhelíes, mosquetas
madreselvas, narcisos,
maravillas, retamas
azahar, cárdenos lirios
y todo me cansaba
cuanto era mas florido.

(561b–62a)

[Everything has given me torment
and at the same time I have
grown up, the more my affections
have increased, and I will die
if I look at them.
I went down to the meadows
and to the crystal clear Tagus
which serves these as a mirror
in which to adorn their curls.
I examined their beauty,
the flowering gardens,
the music of the birds,
the mountain peaks become harps;
the flowers, the carnations,
jasmine and hyacinth,
gillyflowers, musk-rose,
honeysuckle, daffodils,
marigolds, broom,
orange flower, purple iris,
and everything was tiresome
the more it was in bloom.]

Through her dream, however, Casilda learns that she has longed
to become Christian. She informs her attendants:

Este es, pues, mi suceso;
amigas, éste ha sido
el tormento del alma;
A Cristo busco y sigo.

(562 a)

[Thus, this is my story;
friends, this has been
the torment of my soul
I am searching for Christ,
and I will follow him.]

Not only does Casilda's health improve as the action unfolds, but she also asserts and affirms her own identity. After having met with the Christian slaves and having learned their precepts, Casilda is a changed person. During Casilda's first meeting with her father, the king, and accompanied by some of the Christian slaves, the Moorish princess exclaims that her health is improved:

Rey: ¡Hija mía!
              Seas bien venida mil veces.
              ¿Cómo te va? Cómo te hallas?

Casilda: Bien, a tu servicio siempre,
              y con más salud, señor,
              De la con que sueles verme.

                                              (568 b)

[*King:*   My daughter!
              A thousand times may you be
              Welcomed. How are you? How
              are you getting on?

Casilda: Well, and always in your service,
              and with more health, sir,
              than that with which you
              customarily see me.]

A rancorous conflict with her father arises during their second meeting as Casilda tells him that angels have instructed her to leave Toledo in order to be baptized in Castile. The king angrily confronts his daughter:

              ¿Qué dices, loca, qué dices?
              ¿Quieres afrentar mis canas?
              Cristiana quieres volverte
              cuando Toledo te aguarda
              por su reina?

                                              (577 b)

              [What are you saying, you insane girl?
              Do you wish to insult my advanced age?

> You desire to become a Christian
> when all Toledo expects you
> as its queen?]

Nevertheless, Casilda vigorously defends her position and unwaveringly proclaims herself a Christian; her father accedes to her pleas and gives his permission for her to go to Castile where the curative lakes of San Vicente are located. Before her departure, the people officially recognize Casilda as their "imperial" ruler and venerate her as queen of Toledo.

The princess's search for the lakes where she will be cured in body and soul mirrors the arduous journey of her existence prior to her dream and the visitation of the angels. Casilda has to leave her home, and she must roam repeatedly over Castile before she reaches her goal. Abenámar rebukes her for this seemingly fruitless trip:

> Desde allí luego partiste
> y las montañas buscaste
> y en todas ellas no hallaste
> estos lagos que dijiste.
> Y otra vez vuelves, señora,
> hacia Burgos a buscar
> lo que no has podido hallar
> en cuanto el sol rubio dora.

(582 a)

> [From there you then left
> and you looked for the
> mountains, and in all them
> you did not find those lakes
> which you mentioned. And,
> again, lady, you return
> towards Burgos to search
> for what you have been
> unable to find in all that
> the golden sun illuminates.]

Although Casilda freely admits the tedious labor she has expended in her journey, she cannot abandon her convictions or the spiritual truth within herself. Her rejoinder to Abenámar is as follows:

> Cuando Dios así lo ordena,
> yo tengo de obedecer,

> que bien tan grande ha de ser
> hallado con much pena.
>
> (582 b)

> [When God orders it thus,
> I have to obey,
> for such a great good
> can only be found through
> considerable difficulty.]

After finding the lakes that heal her body, and as she draws nearer to baptism, Casilda's fulfillment as a human being is underscored in a monologue which exalts her inner tranquillity and wholeness:

> Mira, señor mío,
> que estamos los dos
> desde hoy desposados,
> y que vuestra soy!
> Dadme vuestra gracia
> divino Señor:
> que me abraso de amores
> que muero por Vos!
>
> (590 b)

> [See, my lord,
> that we two
> are bethrothed from today
> and that I am yours.
> Give me your grace,
> divine Master:
> for I am aflame with your love
> and I am dying for you.]

An important facet of *Santa Casilda* that broadens the sphere of the mythical Astraea's influence upon the saint is that of Casilda's imperial role. Since Casilda is a princess who ultimately becomes queen of Toledo, she represents the state and its political power. That she converts to Christianity is a harbinger of the Christian empire, or the *pax Christiana*, which is to flower in Spain centuries later. Frances Yates writes about the historical associations that developed around the concept of Christian empire and the return of Astraea in a new age:

Virgil's *Aeneid*, with its glorification of Augustus, thus became a semi-sacred poem glorifying the historical framework of the Savior's birth.

Moreover, Virgil was believed to have spoken with the inspired voice of a prophet when he proclaimed in the Fourth Eclogue that the golden age was about to return, and with it, the reign of the Virgin Astraea or Justice, and that a child would be born destined to rule a reconciled world. These words were understood to refer to the birth of Christ in the golden age of Augustus. Through such associations, it was possible to use pagan imperial rhetoric concerning periodic renovations of the Empire, or returns of the golden age, of Medieval Christian emperors, thus retaining something of the cyclic view of history, which such expressions imply, though in Christianized form. A *renovatio* of the Empire will imply spiritual renovation, for in a restored world, in a new golden age of peace and justice, Christ can reign. (Yates, 1975, 4)

In a later reference, Yates cites a direct association between this new golden age and Spain:

In the fifteenth canto of the poem [*Orlando furioso*], Astolfo hears the prophecy of the future empire of Charles V. The prophetess foretells that the world will be put under a universal monarchy by one who will succeed to the diadem of Augustus, Trajan, Marcus Aurelius, and Severus. This ruler will spring from the union of the houses of Austria and of Aragon; and by him Astraea, or Justice, will be brought back to earth, together with all banished virtues. (Yates, 23)

Thus, the *pax Christiana* becomes synonymous with a new golden age, and for many writers in Spain during the sixteenth and seventeenth centuries, Spain is the cultural and political leader which oversees an empire far greater than that under the *pax romana*. *Santa Casilda*, like other *comedias de santos*, is both a record and a statement about Spain's empire.[2] Casilda, a prominent link in the historical chain that binds Spain to Christianity, symbolizes Christian imperial power; royal demeanor and spirituality appear to be fused in Zurbarán's painting of Saint Casilda. For Lope de Vega and his school, the hagiographic dramas afford the dramatists an opportunity to chronicle the history of Spain and to instruct the audiences about the Spanish empire, its rules, its important citizens, and its achievements (Sumner, 1979, 7–15).[3] Under the aegis of this Spanish hegemony, a new order in the world emerged, and in *Santa Casilda*, Lope de Vega dramatized a heroine of the *pax Christiana* whose life and actions embodied the highest ideals of the Spanish empire.

NOTES

1. The *comedias de santos* have sometimes unjustifiably received negative criticism. Although Cervantes criticized the *comedias divinas* for their excesses (in

Don Quojote, part 1, 48), he nevertheless wrote an excellent *Comedia de santos: El rufián dichoso*. Menéndez Pelayo bitterly attacks *El cardenal de Belén* (BAE, vol 178, p. LX), but Elisa Aragone Terni (1957, 13–15) convincingly argues against his views in her edition of *El cardenal de Belén* and in her other work (1970, 127–28): *Studio sulle comedias de santos di Lope de Vega*. In their day, the *comedias de santos* were an important literary tradition as I have attempted to demonstrate in my work: *Una bibliografía anotada de las comedias de santos del siglo diez y siete*.

2. For another example of a *comedia de santos* which prophesies Spain's greatness as an empire, see Lope de Vega's *Comedia de San Segundo* (BAE, 178).

3. The hagiographic dramas or *comedias de santos* are not always easily classified as such. Menéndez Pelayo never really established any concrete definition of the *comedias de santos* despite his invaluable bibliographical studies. However, Aragone Terni (1957, 8–9) has attempted to develop a taxonomy, and others, such as Thomas Case (1988, 13) and José Montesinos (1935, 190–95) allude to the myriad problems surrounding the classification of these plays. Very recently, Elma Dassbach has worked on this problem in Lope's plays for her doctoral dissertation.

Constructing a Goddess: Gila's Role in Vélez de Guevara's *La serrana de la Vera*

Darci L. Strother

A primary concern of mythographers and students of mythology is the definition of this elusive term. The expression "It's a myth," as Jaan Puhvel points out, means to the layperson that the matter in question is devoid of any shred of truth (1). William Doty, for his part, provides examples such as "the myth of the upper class," "the myth of youth," and "the myth of psychology" to demonstrate the type of negative or pejorative connotation "myth" has come to have (6). On the other hand, scholars of myth have been reluctant to shackle this term with one narrow and binding definition, promoting instead a wider conception of myth which is able to encompass its many manifestations across cultures and across time.

For David Adams Leeming, the quest to discover whether or not something really happened is not necessarily relevant to the value of a given myth. "In each case we are considering something intangible, perhaps not literally real, that is nevertheless 'true' in some higher sense" (4). As Doty explains, "my understanding is that myth includes primary, foundational materials. It provides information about the structure of the society or its customs in a narrative form; it is experienced at some point in its development as both true and crucial to those who believe in it" (8). The narrative of a myth, according to Doty, "provides a mode of ordering significant events, that is, a plot . . . of experienced or ideal existence" (16). Although the origin of any one particular myth may or may not be historically factual, Puhvel agrees that myths provide "valuable non-material fossils of mankind's recorded history" (2).

Hispanists who have grappled with the issue of defining myth have likewise debated the term's usage. While not debasing its value, Evangelina Rodríguez and Antonio Tordera have referred to myth as "una mentira negociada" (33: "a negotiated lie"). For his part, Juan Antonio Hormigón affirms that "en todos los mitos, existe o es posible rastrear una vinculación originaria entre su espesor cotidiano y una realidad que le sirvió de fundamento a su construcción y existencia histórica" (161: "In every myth, we trace or it is possible to trace a basic link between everyday life affairs and a reality on which its formation and historical existence were founded"). Despite some apparent contradictions, all definitions of myth, those espoused by Hispanists, mythographers, and others, seem to converge on the idea that, whether based on fact, fantasy, or a combination of both, myth has the ability to indicate to us what it is that is important, meaningful, expected, essential to the community in which it operates. Even the labeling of myth as "una mentira negociada" ("a negotiated lie") tells us of the imperative process of cultural negotiation, a process through which a group of people comes to define for itself that which is significant.

Having in mind, then, the potential of myth to shed light on the values and beliefs of a society, we turn now to the case of Luis Vélez de Guevara's *La serrana de la Vera*, which will be the focus of this study, in order to examine the mythical traditions from which the story springs, and the implications that Vélez de Guevara's reconstruction of the myth, and in particular the figure of the *serrana* (mountain woman), have on our understanding of seventeenth-century Spanish society. Moreover, this study will describe the intent of the play's protagonist Gila to create and propagate her own myth, and will discuss the ramifications of this self-mythicizing activity.

Following nearly three centuries of neglect, Menéndez Pidal's 1916 edition of *La serrana de la Vera* made this work once again accessible, and it is here where the historicity of the story is asserted. Julio Caro Baroja's 1946 article, "¿Es de origen mítico la 'leyenda' de la Serrana de la Vera?," posits the following proposition:

El tema de la serrana de la Vera no es un tema histórico; se trata de un tema mítico que ha quedado en el folklore de una región bajo formas especiales, pero se pueden encontrar también vestigios en el folklore de otras partes. Los romances y las comedias basados en él no son sino una elaboración final del tema por un pueblo con tendencias euhemeristas, a través de la cual se ven muchos de los elementos míticos primitivos. (569)

[The theme of the mountain woman of La Vera is not a historical one; rather it is a mythical theme that has remained as part of the folklore of certain regions in a variety of versions, but we can see traces of it as well in the folklore of other regions. The ballads and *comedias* based on this theme, are nothing else but final renditions of the theme in question, realized by folk people with euhemeristic tendencies, a process in which many of the primitive mythical elements can be discerned.]

Caro Baroja mentions that at the time Vélez de Guevara published his play, there were already numerous versions of a popular *romance* (ballad) dealing with the *serrana de la Vera* (mountain woman of La Vera) in circulation. Moreover, this critic reminds us of the presence in general mythology of legends "parecidas a la de la serrana, o por lo menos fragmentos o elementos de ellas. Divinidades o figuras míticas de carácter silvestre, viril, crueles y eróticas son frecuentes" (572: "similar to the one of the mountain woman, or at least fragments or elements of these legends. Cruel and erotic deities or mythical figures of wild and virile character are frequent"). Additionally, Caro Baroja mentions the possible relationship between the *serrana* (mountain woman) and Mari, "numen de las montañas y de las tormentas, residente en cuevas misteriosas," (572: "muse of mountains and storms, resident of mysterious caves") from an ancient Basque myth.

Despite the fact that Enrique Rodríguez Cepeda's edition of *La serrana de la Vera* offers a number of possible sources for the play's principal character and theme, and supports a theory of polygenesis, the study does not consider the world of myth as a source except in a brief reference to Caro Baroja's aforementioned article.[1] Matthew Stroud, however, has highlighted the *serrana's* (mountain woman's) manifest inheritance of traits of the goddess Diana—"she is brave, strong, daring, and free; she hunts, rides horses, and drives mules" (119)—while at the same time reminding us of Gila Giralda's dual nature: "Diana is still a woman, and Gila wants to be more than a woman—she wants to be a man . . . She is not only like Diana, she is like Achilles" (119), a comparison also made within the play by the Alférez Don Garzía (v. 467). While I agree with Stroud's assertion that Gila shares traits with both mythical predecessors, Diana and Achilles, I believe it important to clarify that Gila did not want necessarily to be a man, but rather to be *herself*, a unique hybrid of male and female characteristics, without having to give up either of her two sides.

Although it does not fall within the scope or intent of the present study to have the final word on the origin or origins of the character of this *serrana* (mountain woman), it is clear that by the seventeenth century her story can justifiably be deemed a myth, for in addition to the various versions of the *romance* (ballad) that continued to circulate, the myth of the *serrana* (mountain woman) was brought to stage by a number of playwrights, including Lope de Vega (prior to 1603), Tirso de Molina (*La ninfa del cielo,* circa 1614), and Valdivielso (*La serrana de Plasencia,* 1619), in addition to Vélez's 1613 version. François Delpech's excellent study of the *serrana de la Vera* (mountain woman of La Vera) legend notes that, although each of these Spanish Golden Age playwrights created a distinct denouement for their *serrana* (mountain woman) figures, there exists a "sistema mítico que funciona en la leyenda tradicional de la Serrana" (27: mythic system which functions in the traditional legend of the mountain woman). By comparing this mythic system to the development (and variance) of the Golden Age *serrana* (mountain woman), in this case the *serrana* (mountain woman) by Vélez, it becomes possible to reach a clearer understanding of those aspects of the myth considered important or essential by Vélez and his audiences. According to Delpech, the legend has three levels of signification:

> Primero se trata de un mito sacrificial: eliminación del obstáculo—aquí un monstruo en forma de mujer—que impide el paso de la vida salvaje a la cultura. En segundo lugar se distinguen muy bien las etapas sucesivas de una leyenda iniciática: las pruebas vespertinas y nocturnas impuestas a un joven por una maga antes de una liberación que cobra el aspecto de un triunfo solar. Por fin esta leyenda se relaciona estrechamente con una serie de cuentos matrimoniales que narran la unión agonística de la 'mujer fuerte', o de la 'mujer salvaje' con un hombre al que se pone a prueba por una lucha y unos juegos erótico-deportivos, juegos destinados a despertar o manifestar sus aptitudes para desempeñar el papel carismático de paredro de la diosa grande. A cada uno de estos tres niveles se representa un combate en que se van a decidir el paso de la vida salvaje a la civilización, el dominio de un sexo sobre otro, y, por lo tanto, la elección del tipo de comunicación cultural sobre el que va a fundarse la vida social inaugurada por este combate. (27)

[First it begins with a sacrificial myth: the elimination of an obstacle—in this case a monster in the shape of a woman—which impedes the passage from wild life into cultured society. Secondly, the successive stages of an initiating legend can be distinguished very easily: the evening and nighttime trials imposed on a young man by an enchantress prior to a liberation which takes on the semblance of a solar triumph. Finally, this legend is closely related to a series of stories of marriage, which recount the agonizing union of the strong woman or the wild woman with a man who is put to the test by means of combat, and some erotically sportive games which are destined to awaken or manifest his aptitude for carrying out the charismatic role of the male companion of the great goddess. At each one of these three levels, a combat is represented in which the following will be decided: the passage from wild life into civilization, the domination of one sex over the other, and, as a result, the selection of the type of cultural communication upon which the social life, inaugurated through this combat, will be founded.]

Vélez de Guevara does stray from the paradigm of the legend in many ways, but the conflict between the sexes and the combat which ensues, as described by Delpech, continues to be one of the centerpieces of Vélez's rendition of this myth. Conflict, in fact, is introduced from the play's inception, as Gila's father Giraldo in the opening lines both greets the captain Don Lucas and refuses him shelter (vv. 1–8). To Don Lucas's initial amusement, Gila soon steps in, and tries to resolve the conflict on her father's behalf, first by simply stating her mind ("Pues yo no quiero," v. 344: "Well, I don't want to"), next by threatening physical confrontation ("que soy muy onbre," v. 352: "for I am very much a man"), and finally by a rhetorical trick that causes Don Lucas to let his guard down, only to be presented with Gila's shotgun and run out of town. The conflict between the sexes continues as Don Lucas, seeking revenge, returns to Giraldo's house with a new scheme. The captain convinces the *serrana*'s (mountain woman's) father that, overcome by Gila's beauty and deeply in love with her, he has returned to ask for her hand in marriage. Gila at first rejects her father's decision to have her marry:

> Hasta agora
> me imaginaba, padre, por las cosas
> que yo me he visto h(az)er, honbre y mui onbre,
> y agora echo de ber, pues me tratas
> casamiento con este cavallero,
> que soy muger, que para tanto daño
> a sido mi desdicha el desengaño.
> No me quiero casar, padre, que creo
> que mientras no me caso que soy onbre.
> No quiero ver que nadie me sujete,
> no quiero que ninguno se imagine
> dueño de mí; la libertad pretendo.

(vv. 1577–88)

> [Until now
> because of the things I have seen myself do, father,
> I had imagined myself to be a very manly man,
> but now I can see, since you are concerting
> my marriage to this gentleman,
> that I am a woman, and this discovery
> comes to mean for me unhappiness and sorrow.
> I do not want to marry, father, for I believe
> that as long as I remain unmarried, I am a man.
> I do not wish to see anyone subdue me,
> I do not want anyone to imagine himself to be
> my master; I seek freedom.]

She later acquiesces out of her sense of obligation to her father, as well as her hope that marriage to the captain might bring with it an increase in her fame and power, thanks to his elevated social status, a topic that will be discussed subsequently.

The combat stage of the legend is arrived at in this play after Don Lucas, whom by virtue of having promised marriage is given the opportunity to spend the night with his betrothed, abandons Gila before daybreak.[2] Gila, realizing the trick, vows to take revenge by killing every man with whom she comes into contact until she can find and kill Don Lucas himself. She goes to live in a hut up on the mountain, and eventually kills two thousand men before fatefully meeting Don Lucas again, whom she hurls off a cliff to his death. When Gila is finally captured by the authorities, she is tied to a stake and shot to death with arrows, thus bringing to a conclusion the question of which sex reaches final dominance over the other. And, although Vélez did not choose to adopt the type of conflict-resolution strategies present in other versions of the *serrana* (mountain woman) myth (such as the marriage which serves as the outcome for Lope's *serrana*/mountain woman), his version certainly does address the issues of "el paso de la vida salvaje a la civilización, el dominio de un sexo sobre otro, y . . . la elección del tipo de comunicación cultural sobre el que va a fundarse la vida social" ("the passage of wild life into civilization, the domination of one sex over the other, and . . . the selection of the type of cultural communication upon which the social life will be founded"), as Delpech outlined as components of the *serrana* (mountain woman) myth.

The most important aspect of Gila's characterization is her unique and powerful combination of both masculine and feminine traits. She is a remarkably beautiful *woman*, and is extremely attractive to men. Gila is able to behave as a woman when she

chooses to do so; she can allure and seduce men at will by playing
the role of the receptive female lover, which she does frequently
throughout the play:

with Mingo   Sospecho
                         que tomarás una mano
                         agora si te la doy.

                                                          (1270–72)

                         [I suspect
                         that you will take my hand
                         now if I give it to you.]

                                                  …

with a   ¿Parézcote hermosa?
"Caminante"   ¿Estimaras que te hiciera
                         favor?

                         [Do I seem beautiful to you?
                         Would you appreciate it if I
                         did you a favor?]
                         .   .   .   .

                         Tengo una choza en que vivo
                         de encinas y robles hecha,
                         donde quiero que conmigo
                         hasta ver el alba duermas.

                                                          (2243–51)

                         [I have a hut in which I live,
                         made of evergreen and oak trees,
                         where I wish you to sleep with me
                         until dawn.]
                         .   .   .   .

Andrés: ¿Dormís sola, linda cara?
Gila: No hay serrana de la Vera
                         que acudir más libre pueda
                         a lo que fuerdes servido,
                         porque me habéis parezido
                         muy bien.

                                                          (2816–21)

[*Andrés:*   Do you sleep alone, lovely woman?
Gila: There is no other mountain woman in La Vera
                         who could more freely attend
                         to your wishes
                         because I find you
                         very attractive.]

Before her role as a female lover is consummated, however, Gila violently rejects her male suitors by overcoming them physically, and, with all except Mingo, killing them by pushing them off a precipice. Added to this traditionally masculine trait of acting physically violent, she mentions on numerous occasions that she is or wishes to be a man.[3] Again, however, I would like to reiterate that I believe such affirmations to be more metaphoric than actual, and that what Gila truly wants to be is simply herself. As cited earlier, Gila states that she had imagined herself a man "por las cosas / que yo me he visto h(az)er" (vv. 1578–79: "because of the things / that I have seen myself do"). She bases her definition of herself as a man on the things she has already seen herself be able to do, in the past ("he visto"—"I have seen"). She does not fantasize about the different types of things she might like to do if she were a man, because she is already doing them. This is true, of course, up until the time when Don Lucas proposes marriage.

Since Gila lacked neither a male nor a female side, she had no desire or necessity to marry, for she was already a *complete* individual. In her completeness, she had been allowed to integrate herself fully into her society, and the villagers accepted and marveled at this strange and unique individual. Her downfall occurs when outside dominating forces (her father and Don Lucas) pressure her into accepting a marriage which would upset the balance of Gila's male-female equilibrium. Gila enters into something that is against her nature from the beginning, and the result is the explosion of fury that causes her to terrify and murder men. Gila loses both her virginity and her rationality, and comes to act on brutal and vengeful instincts, leading to her demise.

In Vélez de Guevara's departure from the portion of the myth laid out in the *romance* (ballad) which describes the *serrana* (mountain woman) as having been engendered by a human and a mare, the playwright has given this character, rather than an inner struggle between human and beast, an inner struggle between man and woman.[4] In the well-known conversation between Joseph Campbell and Bill Moyers, in *The Power of Myth*, they refer to the presence of both male and female characteristics within all humans, and suggest that one goes through life "honoring or suppressing one or the other" (181). Vélez de Guevara's version of the mythical *serrana* (mountain woman), however, did not go through life honoring or suppressing either of her two sides, until she was required to do so by societal forces.

Vélez's presentation of this type of character serves at least two purposes. Keeping in mind the *comedia*'s enormously diverse audiences, we come to recognize that Vélez de Guevara had to make this play appeal to people of very divergent tastes, orientations, and levels of sophistication in understanding. To the *vulgo* (common folk), Gila's masculine traits may have made her come to symbolize precisely those elements that they would find threatening in women: unruliness, straightforwardness, strength, and lack of dependence on men. Since Gila embodies everything that a woman "should not" be, her death would appeal to those members of the audience who would celebrate the triumph of the male-dominated social forces over a woman who would dare attempt to subvert them.[5]

On a more subtle level, Gila's differences are also used by Vélez to make her a representative and champion of those groups that fell outside the hegemonic majority. The pressure she feels to give up being who she is, and to conform to what society has established as normal forms of behavior, causes her to become a symbol for the experience of many marginal groups in Spanish society. In this way, Vélez could also attack the prevailing social climate and its intolerance of diversity, through his creation of Gila's heroic character.[6] One indication of Vélez de Guevara's sympathetic attitude toward his *serrana* (mountain woman) can be seen in his striking departure from a specific aspect of the original myth—the *serrana*'s (mountain woman's) sexual promiscuity. Gila is not characterized following this model, but rather is portrayed as the chaste Diana. As Delpech points out, "Lope y Vélez se las han arreglado para eliminar este aspecto fundamental de la leyenda" (30: "Lope and Vélez managed to eliminate this fundamental aspect of the legend"). Although Gila, as we have seen, does promise sexual favors to her victims, she kills them without fulfilling her promises. Delpech has referred to the fact that the Golden Age playwrights tend to humanize their *serranas* (mountain women) (27–28), and perhaps by allowing Gila to be depicted as a chaste woman following her deceitful deflowering, Vélez de Guevara could manipulate the myth in a way that would serve his purposes, given the seventeenth-century *comedia* audience's expectations for female characters. If he indeed had wished to portray Gila in a negative, monstrous light, Vélez would have had nothing to gain by departing from the model of Gila's promiscuous mythical predecessor. Rather, he places Gila in a category with which the *comedia* audience was quite familiar—that of a pure woman tricked into surrendering her virginity. By constructing her character thus, Vélez opens the door to multiple judgments of Gila's outcome, from justified to tragic.

In addition to the comparisons of Gila to Diana and Achilles that have been mentioned, she is also compared to several other mythical figures during the course of the play, such as Hercules (v. 355), Semiramis, Evadne, and Pallas (Athena) (vv. 1611–12). However, rather than merely emulate these and other figures of mythical stature, Gila, I believe, sets out to mythicize herself. In the play, she is not only aware of the fame she continues to gain for being the extraordinary person that she is, but she specifically and consciously cultivates her own legend, in an attempt to raise herself to the stature of such figures.

The following passage by Francisco J. Díez de Revenga provides a real life example of how self-mythification could be carried out in seventeenth-century Spain:

> El teatro del Siglo de Oro contiene un importante componente mítico y mitos históricos y literarios pueblan las piezas de nuestra comedia áurea. Pero también la vida estaba presidida por el mito, y la ostentación es el elemento provocador de ese sentido mítico.
>
> Está para nosotros claro que el más ostentoso mito viviente de la España de nuestro Siglo de Oro, o por lo menos de la importante parte que le cupo vivir, es la majestad de Felipe IV, llamado «el grande», cuya figura [aparece] hábilmente ensalzada a través de panfletos, relatos, exaltaciones en verso y relaciones en prosa . . . (197)

> [Golden Age theater contains an important mythical component, and historical and literary myths abound in the dramatic works of our Golden Age. But in addition, myth presided over life, and the triggering element of that mythic sense is ostentation.
>
> It is clear to us that the most ostentatious living myth of Golden Age Spain, or at least of the important part of this time period during which he lived, is the majesty of Phillip IV, known as "the Great," whose image appears skillfully aggrandized by means of pamphlets, tales, exaltations in poetry and reports in prose . . .]

Gila, for her part, did not make use of pamphlets to proclaim her heroism (although who could doubt that, having had such means at her disposal, she would have taken full advantage?); however, her ostentatious displays of strength, bravery, and cockiness are apparent from the start. The stage directions prior to Gila's first entrance in act 1 describe the elaborate entourage of villagers that accompany the *serrana* (mountain woman), and their procession is made all the more spectacular by the flowers, songs, costumes, and exotic animal hides that are included to complete the image crafted by Vélez (+ v. 204). It is clear that for others in the play, Gila has come to be considered a living legend, as is apparent in remarks such as:

> Maestro: Mereze
> corónica este valor,
> braba postura, famoso
> partir cerrado y airoso;
>
> (782–85)

> [Maestro: This valor,
> this valiant stature, this
> renowned way of charging, which is
> intimidating and graceful,
> deserve to be chronicled.]

Both the *copla* (folk song) sung in the first act (vv. 207–44) and the *romances* (ballads) sung in act 2 (vv. 2202–24 and vv. 2656–69) serve to highlight the past and present fame that surrounds the *serrana* (mountain woman). Gila even makes reference to the fact that members of the animal world are aware of her prowess: "Ya saben la fuerza mía / los nobillos de la Vera" (vv. 929–30: "The young vigorous bulls of La Vera / already know about my strength").

More remarkable still, however, are Gila's own attempts to create and propagate her legend. She does this through a combination of ever-braver (or at least gutsier) deeds, and boisterous talk. But for her it is not merely braggadocio, since what she talks about, she truly does achieve. Gila has high aspirations for herself, and when her father informs her that he has a wonderful surprise in store for her, these are the first thoughts that come to her mind:

> ¿Anme elegido
> por general, por rey, obispo o papa?
> ¿He heredado las casas, las haziendas
> de los señores de Castilla?
>
> (1555–58)

> [Have they elected me to be
> general, king, bishop, or pope?
> Have I inherited the mansions, the estates
> of the Lords of Castile?]

When she learns that the surprise is marriage, she again thinks in terms of what this would mean for the preservation and enhancement of her own fame:

> Esa razón me puede obligar sola,
> por imitar a vuestro lado luego
> a la gran Isabel, que al de Fernando
> emprende heroycos hechos; que si vivo,
> y ocasiones me ofreze la fortuna,
> a de quedar contra la edad ligera
> fama de la serrana de la Vera.
>
> (1613–19)

> [That is the only reason that can compel me,
> in order to imitate, by your side,
> the great Isabel, who at Ferdinand's side
> undertakes heroic deeds; for if I live,
> and fortune offers me the chance,
> the fame of the mountain woman of La Vera
> will last in spite of time.]

And, even after Don Lucas's deception and her retreat to her mountain hideout, Gila continues to express concern for her image. She is pleased when a *Caminante* (Wayfarer), who will be her next victim, tells her that:

> Agora
> no solamente en la Vera,
> sino en Castilla, no cantan
> otra cosa, y tu belleza
> y tu fama se aventaxa.
>
> (2236–41)

> [Now
> not only in La Vera,
> but also in Castile,
> they sing of nothing else,
> and your beauty
> and your fame continue to grow.]

Gila keeps count of her victims by placing a cross for each one at the site where she kills them, in order to ensure that she will receive full credit for her deeds. In her auto-mythification, she cannot afford to have any doubt cast on her resolve to carry out her horrific threat, so when Mingo stumbles across her by accident, even her past friendship with him (strengthened, it would seem, by an amicable chat about the current village gossip) is not sufficient for her to agree to pardon his life:

Mingo: ¿No me escusará siquiera
             el hábito de rozín?

Gila: Si fueras rozín sin lengua,
             pudiera ser permitillo;
             pero rozín que habla, muera

(2403–7)

[*Mingo:*   Will not my habit of
              a worn-out horse at least excuse me?

Gila: If you were a worn-out horse with no tongue,
              I might have permitted it;
              but a horse that talks, must die.]

When other visitors from her village arrive, Madalena and Pascuala (whom it is not necessary to kill, since they are women), Gila's first and most urgent question to them is "¿Qué dizen en el lugar / de mí?" (vv. 2696–97: "What do they say about me / back home?"), and her final words as they depart are "Vete, / y a los del lugar les di / que se guarden de mí" (vv. 2756–58: "Go now, / and tell the people back home / to watch out for me").

J. A. Drinkwater has pointed out that Gila goes from being called "exenplo / de mugeres españolas" (vv. 256–57: "an example / to Spanish women") by her father at the beginning of the play, to "exenplo . . . a España" (vv. 3297: "an example . . . to Spain") upon her death, by King Fernando (83). Certainly, the first reference alludes to Gila as a positive role model, and the second, as a warning against committing similar crimes. She has, however, *doubled* her notoriety by the end of the play, by now serving as an example to *all* of Spain, rather than only to the female half of the population. Gila's drive to mythicize herself operates throughout the play, whether it is by acting extraordinarily bravely, as she does in the first two acts, or extraordinarily cruelly, as she does in act 3. Her cruel actions are a response to the circumstances society has thrust upon her, but her underlying goal of becoming a legendary figure remains constant, and is attained in the end despite (or perhaps due to) her death. Although some critics have attributed Gila's downfall precisely to her ambition, or her "*cupiditas* (codicia) de poder" ("*cupiditas* (lust) for power"), Delpech argues that this trait of the *serrana* (mountain woman), which I call her self-mythification, "no . . . parece que sea condenable para Vélez. Este presenta a Gila, en la primera parte de la comedia, como personaje positivo, diosa tutelar de su pueblo, que yerra posteriormente por exceso, en su deseo de matar a *todos* los hombres y no solamente a su burlador" ("does not . . . appear to be condemnable to Vélez. He presents Gila, in the first part of the play, as a positive character, a tutelary goddess to her village, who later errs due to excess, in her desire to kill *all* men and not just her seducer").[7]

According to Marc Vitse, the *comedia* is characterized not only by its reliance on traditional mythical figures for character models, but more importantly by "la creación de nuevas figuras míticas. Este es el interés del mito . . . en el teatro clásico español. Es esta invención que siempre conlleva cosas ya pasadas, pero, nuevas figuras nacen, y creo que es ésta la aportación mayor" ("the creation of new mythical figures. This is why myth happens to be of interest . . . in classical Spanish theater. It is this invention that always carries with it things of the past; however, new figures are born, and I believe that this is its greatest contribution").[8] Without a doubt, Vélez de Guevara's Gila serves as an example of a character both developed by the combination of classical and popular mythical sources, and at the same time capable of creating her own new myth, thanks to her author's skillful ability to weave together both the new and the old to form this unforgettable *serrana* (mountain woman), Gila Giralda.

Notes

1. See Vélez de Guevara, (1967) 19–22, for Rodríguez Cepeda's discussion of sources.

2. It should be noted that scenes of conflict/combat between the sexes are also observed prior to this point in the play's development, such as Gila's sword fights with several men in act 1 (vv. 719–814), and her "iron grip" which overpowers her admirer Mingo early in act 2 (vv. 1270–79). In both of these instances, Gila's victory over her male counterparts informs us of her existing status within her community. The combat with Don Lucas is the first one to truly challenge this status.

3. In particular, see vv. 350–52, vv. 659–61, vv. 781–82, and v. 1833.

4. See Delpech, p. 25, for a discussion of the legendary *serrana*'s (mountain woman's) parentage.

5. Ironically, though, male members of society were not in danger when Gila was free to be Gila, the dual-natured being. It is only when she is wedged into a socially acceptable female role (that of the bride-to-be) that she becomes a danger to the male sex.

6. Differing reactions to Gila's execution among real life audience members

would not be unexpected, since the characters within the play who witness the scene also express varied opinions:

Fernando:	A sido justo castigo

(3284–85)

[*Fernando:*	The punishment has been just]

. . . .

Isabel:	A mí me enterneze el alma

(3287)

[*Isabel:*	It melts my very soul]

7. See the debate following Delpech's article, particularly the comments by M. Vitse (and Delpech), p. 37.

8. Cited from Francisco Ruiz Ramón, pp. 305–6, in the "Debate de la Tercera Jornada."

Part 4
The Gods of Calderón

Astral Myths and Emblems: The Duality of Calderón's *La estatua de Prometeo*

María Esther C. de Moux

In a literary text, mythology can be a metaphor for esoteric knowledge. Such is the case with many writers of the Spanish Golden Age who relied upon sixteenth and seventeenth century handbooks such as Juan Pérez de Moya's *Philosophia secreta* (*Secret Philosophy*) (1585) and Fray Baltasar de Vitoria's *Teatro de los dioses de la gentilidad* (*Theater of the Pagan Gods*) (1620, 1623) to inform their literary creations and elucidate the mythical subtexts they suggest (Egido 1993, 7).[1] The emblematic tradition is another important source for decodifying the underlying moral and esoteric layers of meaning in myths. The emblematic tradition, which was an important element of baroque mythological plays, illustrated fundamental principles of philosophy and occult knowledge which were later interpreted and used as moral and religious means of instruction (Sebastián 1993, 19–20). The discovery and subsequent publication of Horapollo's *Hieroglyphica* (*Hieroglyphics*)[2] was fundamental to the Renaissance humanists who first interpreted these signs in the manner of ancient Egyptian hieroglyphics. According to Peter M. Daly (1979), drama during the sixteenth and seventeenth centuries was the most emblematic of all the literary arts because of its combination of visual experience (character, gesture, silent "tableau," and active scenes) with the verbal experience of the spoken and (occasionally) the written word (134). Spanish drama was also influenced by the widely known books of emblems that circulated among the intellectual elite of writers and painters. Thus the mythological, literary, and historical figures of the *comedia* can be read as symbols of esoteric and astrological principles contained within the conventions of emblematic art and literature. Especially important for our study is Andrea Alciatus's critically acclaimed *Emblems,* considered by many as one of the best-known books in Western culture and a fundamental reference in the study of humanism and the baroque period (Sebastián 1993, 21).[3]

Pedro Calderón de la Barca may have learned about emblematic art and literature early in his life at the Jesuit Imperial College in Madrid where he was a student from 1608 to 1614 (Morón Arroyo 1982, 10). According to Mario Praz (1964), emblems were used by the order throughout Europe as religious propaganda. Jesuits were ". . . theatrical producers, engineers and artificers, specialized in classical pageants . . ." (173) using emblems of all types in the education of princes. Iconomystics was not a useless science. It was part of the public solemnities and royal celebrations that required the encyclopaedic knowledge of the Jesuits (173–76). Víctor Infantes points out that Calderón composed poems referred to as "jeroglíficos" (hieroglyphs) in 1672 for festivities held by the Jesuits in Madrid honoring San Francisco de Borja on his canonization (1981).[4] He also wrote emblematic poetry in the Italian style for the poetic funeral homage to Philip IV held at the University of Oviedo in 1666. The funerary catafalque included numerous emblems or hieroglyphs illustrating God's wisdom. These poems, considered to be prose by some critics, follow the "subscriptio" or epigramatic conventions of emblematic literature (1593–602).

La estatua de Prometeo (*The Statue of Prometheus*) initiates a generative, mythological cycle by exploring a relationship between two brothers, a theme which is taken up later in plays such as *Mujer llora y vencerás* (*Woman, Cry and You Shall Win*) (Voros 1988, 181). Calderón's fascination with fragmentation, polarities, and the dual nature of human beings is well documented. In *La estatua de Prometeo* the relationship between the twins can be explained within the emblematic tradition represented by Alciatus in his series on Concord. Emblem 41, "Vnvm nihil, dvos plvrimvm posse" (One man can do nothing, two a great deal)[5] depicts "Sapientia," or Wisdom, as a learned man dressed in oriental robes. To his left stands "Forteza," or Strength, represented as a man of action—a Roman soldier with spear, sword, and shield. Notice that the spear divides this emblem nearly in half. This graphic representation holds the thematic value of balancing strength with wisdom. In the engraving, these two virtues are at peace. In light of his Jesuit formation and his studies at Alcalá de Henares and Salamanca, it comes as no surprise that Calderón should follow this philosophical practice explained by Fray Baltasar de Vitoria in his *Theatro de los dioses de la gentilidad:* "Doctrina es del Principe de la Philosophia [Aristóteles], que para haver de tratarse de una cosa, conviene mucho hablar de su contrario . . . conocido uno de los opuestos, se viene en conocimiento del otro"

Vnum nihil, duos plurimum poſſe.

EMBLEMA XLI.

Alciatus, Emblem 41.

(It is a precept from the Prince of Philosophy [Aristotle], that to discuss one topic it is important to talk about its opposite . . . if one opposite is known, the other one will be understood) (1738, 491). In *La estatua de Prometeo*, Calderón dramatically develops the opposite concept of Concord by inverting the moral lesson of Emblem 41. When strength is not tempered by wisdom, only discord or war can result.

At a first glance Alciatus's Emblem 102, which shows Prometheus chained to a rock, may appear more relevant to our analysis

CAVCASIA æternùm pendens in rupe Prometheus
Diripitur sacri præpetis vngue iecur.

Alciatus. Emblem 102.

than his Emblem 41. Still, it should be remembered that in Calderón's play Prometheus is never punished for stealing Apollo's fire and that he even marries Pandora in the end. Emblems, like tarot cards, should not be interpreted solely by their face value, but rather as ways to illustrate hidden meanings, the "secret philosophy" of mythical tales and figures. This is communicated via a motto ("inscriptio,") an engraving ("pictura,") and an explanatory epigram called the "suscriptio." The sixteenth-century Sephardic scholar León Hebreo explained that myth has four levels of meaning: a literal or historical meaning, a moral interpretation, an astrological or theological meaning, and a scientific signification, which form the core of a story. This system of interpretation was followed by the two most important mythological treatises from the Golden Age (Juan Pérez de Moya and Fray Baltasar de Vitoria) (Gallego 1991, 72) as well as by other emblem comentators in Spain. Thus, in its historic or literal meaning, Emblem 41 represents the union of the heroes Odysseus and Diomedes in their quest to conquer Troy, like the epigram explicitly indicates (Sebastián 1993, 76–79). This moral image of prudent and brave men, one heart working together for a common cause, is further elaborated by the astrological connotations of the figures: the beneficent union of solar and lunar influences on human enterprises. The emblem teaches us that in an ideal world, Prometheus, the astrologer and man of letters, if prudent, would advance human knowledge and social stability assisted by his twin Epimetheus, the hunter and man of action. In *La estatua de Prometeo*, Prometheus, influenced by Apollo, is inclined towards astrological and philosophical studies: "La escuela de los Caldeos, / en que es prinçipal lectura / la astrología, con más / afecto que otra ninguna / seguí . . ." ("The Chaldean school, in which an important study is / astrology, to which with more / inclination than any other [one] / I followed . . .) (vv 129–32).[6] Epimetheus the hunter is guided by the divine light of the goddess Diana, the twin sister of Apollo and reflection of his solar fire. He accepts the authority of his learned brother because in a well-ordered universe, action follows counsel and strength obeys wisdom, arms are at the service of letters, and the moon is below the sun, reflecting its light.

Emblem 41 can also apply to an individual person. An astrological reading of these figures would relate the Eastern sage to the right side of the body, the solar Apollonian masculine aspect of man, the sun rising from the east. By contrast, the warrior on the left would be the sunset and would represent man's feminine, lunar aspect that illuminates, through reflected solar light, the nocturnal cloak of darkness needed to start the foundation of a new task. Emblem 41 is a "hieroglyphic" of Concord inverted in *La estatua de Prometeo* to its opposite Discord. The main theme of the play is the loss of harmony in an unbalanced cosmos that has fallen into chaos by the opposing forces of duality at war with each other.

William R. Blue has shown that continuous transformation is one of the keys to *La estatua de Prometeo,* a play in which one character becomes its opposite (35). The more the twins emphasize their differences, the more undifferentiated they become. This apparent paradox can be understood through Carl Jung's theory of duality. In his gnostic treatise, *Seven Sermons to the Dead,* Jung explains that we can never escape our opposite because ". . . the foundation of our being is differentiation" (44). Qualities such as "difference and sameness / light and dark / hot and cold / energy and matter / time and space / good and evil / the beautiful and the ugly . . ." (45) coexist in human beings. In the *pleroma,* a higher state of existence, opposites cancel each other out. However, opposites are in continuous action in human beings. Thus, when we want to strive for the good and beautiful, we fall in its opposite, the evil and the ugly. For this reason, Jung argues the futility of trying to differentiate ourselves from our opposite. Only by accepting unity in opposition are we able to find our own true nature (44–48). Emblematic literature transmitted ancient ideas of duality as the source of nature's eternal movement and transformation. According to Heraclitus, in order for natural things to remain the same, they must change. The physicist Fritjof Capra explains that "the concept of change as a dynamic interplay of opposites led Heraclitus, like Lao Tzu, to the discovery that all opposites are polar and thus united . . ." (116). Thus, the union of opposites is not a contradiction but rather a mystic and philosophical conception of the universe shared by ancient Greeks, Indians, and Chinese.[7] One of the most valuable aspects of *La estatua de Prometeo* represents the continuation in Baroque Spain of the European hermetic tradition, directly nurtured, in the peninsula, by Jewish and Moslem philosophic scholarship and religious beliefs.[8]

In the play, the twins Prometheus and Epimetheus seek to differentiate themselves from each other but are locked in a dialectic of attraction and repulsion. Understanding that his creation has brought havoc in the Caucasus, Prometheus deplores his artistic ability and his imagination when he portrayed Minerva's beauty and grace:

> O nunca aquella sombra
> que fantástica vi
> despertara la ydea
> para copiar en ti
> de Minerba el retrato
>
> [Oh that never that shadow
> that fantastically I saw
> woke (in me) the idea
> to copy in thou
> from Minerva, her portrait]

(509–13)

Caught between Apollo's burning fire and his search for Minerva's wisdom, Prometheus must flee from his own "sun," the alchemical light:

> Dígalo el que queriendo
> A Minerba rendir
> sacrifiçios . . . con que me vi
> obligado a bolber
> la espalda para yr
> a nunca ver el sol . . .
>
> [It should be proclaimed by he who wants
> to offer Minerva
> sacrifices . . . I was forced to turn
> my back to leave
> and never see the sun . . .]

(549–57)

Thus, the search for knowledge and letters brings strife and war. Realizing this contradiction, Prometheus rejects his own search for wisdom and beauty.

Epimetheus, on the other hand is a man of action who wishes for his brother's eloquence ("Como yo no sé argüir, / sino lidiar" (Since I do not know [how to] debate, / but [only how to] fight) (III. 154–55)) and falls in love with his brother's statue. Epimetheus should be linked to Diana, since, like her, he is a hunter armed with spears and a box of arrows who must catch his prey hidden in the dark. Even though the name of Diana is never explicitly mentioned in the text, her pale reflected moonlight illuminates Epimetheus' encounter with Pandora:

> Y pues por aquí es la gruta
> de Prometheo, a la escasa,
> trémula luz de la luna
> la busquemos; que al hallarla,
> ya ves cuanto ymportaría
> antes que amanezca el alba

[And since Prometheus's cave is nearby, let's us look for it [illuminated] by the dim, flickering moonlight, and that in finding it, you will see how important it would be [to find it] before dawn rises]

(II. 135–40)

Thus, it is Diana's astral influence that makes him decide not to destroy Prometheus's statue, as Palas has commanded. The brothers follow a basic hermetic principle of heaven/earth correspondences, Epimetheus representing the lunar twin while Prometheus is the solar brother. Opposite characters are bound to bring about changes and as the play progresses, their hidden qualities are revealed while their overt characteristics fall into the shadow. This esoteric principle is supported by Thomas O'Connor's observation on character changes when Epimetheus is able to reason clearly and Prometheus takes weapons to hunt or to fight (1988, 335). The difficulty of reconciling the fragmented portions of the psyche and of society is the basic theme of this play, in which heaven and earth can be construed as symbolic images of royalty and courtiers, a vision that enables the political readings suggested by Sebastian Neumeister[9] and Margaret Greer (1988).

By inverting the emblem on Concord, Calderón has shattered Alciatus's image of peace by revealing "Discordia" in its multiple reflections. From a numerological point of view, the number two, considered in esotericism as the source of human mental errors (Papus 29–30) has become the reigning number.[10] Peace exists in "e pluribus unum" (one from the many) but not in "e unus pluribum" (many from the one). The Renaissance ideal of arms and letters united in a quest has been split into the twin brothers Prometheus and Epimetheus. When Diana, the moon principle, loses Apollo's sunlight, her influence becomes deadly. Everything around her will rot in the flood waters that follow in nature the absence of solar heat. In the absence of the "Sun King," Diana becomes Hecate. The king's fire without the temperance of the moon's water becomes the fire of Mars. Diana stands in the semiotic layering of *La estatua de Prometeo* like a palimpsest underlying the Minerva/Palas character. Although Minerva and Palas are

Apollo's twin sisters, Diana, the daughter of Latona and Jupiter, is the true twin sister of the Sun God (Vitoria 1702, 303), corresponding to the astrological opposites Sun/Moon studied by Prometheus in his search for knowledge

> Aquí no solo del sol
> no sólo aquí de la luna,
> las liçiones repasaba . . .

> [Here, not only of the sun,
> but also of the moon,
> I studied the lessons . . .]
>
> (I. 189–91)

In *La estatua de Prometeo*, Minerva and Palas assume the traditional roles played by the true chaste huntress Diana. Cosmic order has been disturbed and astral correspondence between deity and planet altered, resulting in heavenly chaos that will inevitably be reflected on Earth. The concept of inversion has converted Palas, the "armed" deity, the strength and hand of wisdom, into Belona the war-monger, a transformation that leaves Minerva, all mind, totally helpless. As in Fray Baltasar de Vitoria's *Theatro de los dioses de la Gentilidad*, Calderón too equates Palas with the Roman Belona, the opposite of Minerva. According to Vitoria, Minerva and Palas shared so many key characteristics that many sources have wrongly thought them to be one deity. They were, in fact, two completely different goddesses. Vitoria portrays Minerva as a figure of counsel in times of war and Belona as a warrior in battle, riding Mars's chariot.

Tuvo la Gentilidad a Belona por Diosa de las discordias, de las lides, y de las batallas . . . Algunos quisieron decir, que Minerva, y Belona todo era una misma Diosa; mas dice Cartario, que no solo en las personas, y en los nombres eran diferentes, sino tambien en las imagenes, y en los oficios, porque Minerva, dice, que asistía con los Emperadores, Reyes, y Capitanes a los consejos de Guerra, a la buena providencia, a la sabia administracion, y a todas las demas cosas importantes a la Milicia; pero la Diosa Belona presidia a las batallas, a las guerras, a las muertes, a los incendios y estragos, que suelen exercitarse en las guerras. Y assi los Poetas dixeron, que ella era la que guiaba el Carro del Dios Marte, y le acompañaba, como lo dixo Virgilio.

(pt. I, book VII, Ch. IV, p. 491)

[In Pagan times Belona was considered to be Goddess of Discord, strifes and battles . . . Some [commentators] believed Minerva and Belona to be the same Goddess, but Cartarious says that they were different in person, name, image and occupation. Minerva, he says, helped Emperors, Kings and Captains in War Council, in providing, in wise administration and in all other things important for the Military, but Belona presided in battles, wars, death, fires and catastrophes that acompany wars. According to the Poets, she drove Mars's chariot and was by his side, as Virgil said.]

In the play Palas tell her story in the following verses:

> De Júpiter y Latona
> hermanas del sol, Minerba
> y yo naçimos, gozando
> tan vna la ynfançia nuestra
> que el número no podía
> distinguirnos, de manera
> que ya vbo quien dijo, q[ue] equíbocas eran
> o Minerba o Palas, vna cosa mesma.

(I. 645–52)

[From Jupiter and Leto / sisters of the sun, Minerva / and I were born, in our childhood [we were] so united / that we could not be distinguished by number, thus / it has been said, [that] although opposites / Minerva or Palas, [were] one and the same thing.]

The mythological tradition of assigning multiple names for the same deity allows Calderón to create a fragmented goddess figure, while simultaneously claiming that they are two very different goddesses. The Minerva-Palas character becomes further complicated when qualities normally attributed to Belona, the Roman godess of strife and discord who rode Mars's chariot, are ascribed to Palas. Further proof that in *La estatua de Prometeo* Mars and Palas have the same relationship that exists between Mars and Belona can be seen when Prometheus explains the qualities and sphere of influence given to each deity according to astral myths: "A Marte y Palas las lides;" (To Mars and Pallas [were given] strifes) (v 225). Palas, divided from her better self Minerva, becomes Belona, the goddess of "lides," who sows strife and discord. Fragmentation has produced a twin sister, a hand without a mind, who becomes an ally of "Discord." Thus weakened, the solitary Minerva must face the fury of "Discordia" and Palas/Belona alone.

Calderón insists on these mirror images for elaborating dra-

matic tension and conflict in both the celestial and earthly realms.
Minerva and Palas are split in two in spite of their common origin:

> Pero aunque en deydad, en solio,
> en magestad y grandeza,
> naçimos las dos conformes,
> crezimos las dos opuestas
> en los divididos genios
> de nuestras dos ymfluençias;
> blanda ella lo diga, dígalo seuera
> yo, auxiliando lides, dictando ella zienzias.
>
> (I. 653–60)

[But even though in deity and power, / in majesty and grandeur, / we
were born alike, / we both grew opposite / in divided characters /
from our two influences; / yielding she may speak, sternly I may
speak / I, promoting strifes, she explaining sciences.]

The goddesses in turn project their influence on the twins Pro-
metheus/Epimetheus. These twins, like the fragmented deities
whose power they fall prey to, also share a common origin and
they too have become enemies. Minerva's knowledge and indus-
try make Prometheus an astrologer and sculptor, while Palas/
Diana's influence on Epimetheus brings out in him the hunter-
warrior archtype. Following hermetic principles, Prometheus/Epi-
metheus replicate on a material plane the clash between celestial
entities as Palas explains in the following verses:

> Y siendo así que de vn parto
> visteis las luçes primeras
> Prometeo y tú, ymitando
> nuestra fortuna en la buestra,
> partimos los dos asumptos,
> trabada la competencia
> de cual mayor lustre, mayor exçelençia
> da el vno en las armas, q[ue] el otro en las letras.
>
> (I. 661–68)

[And, thus, from one childbirth / you saw the first light / Prometheus
and you, imitating / our fortune in yours, / we parted company / with
fierce competition [between us] / for more fame, / more excellence /
one given to arms and the other to letters.]

The mysterious difference in astrological influences between
twins is explained by Prometheus himself, who, while in Assyria,

learned the Ptolemaic principle that the speed of solar movement causes the primary and secondary influences to be exerted by the stars. According to traditional astrology, this dual imprint spells out good and evil destinies in twins, who, despite being born together, are inclined to act differently:

> no descansé hasta saber
> cuánto en un ynstante mudan
> al rapto curso del sol,
> veloz siempre y tardo nunca,
> los astros semblante, pues
> entre primera y segunda
> ymfluençia se diuiden,
> no sólo, aunque nazcan juntas,
> las ynclinaçiones, pero
> la desdicha y la bentura.

(I. 135–44)

[I did not rest until I found out / how much in an instant the planets will change / [due] to the swift solar movement / always fast, never slow, / since their influences are primary and secondary, / [as are divided] not only inclinations, even though born together, but also fortune and misfortune.]

Once the unity of creation is split into diversity, each atom itself splits into even smaller particles. Thus, the unity of Prometheus and Epimetheus in the womb is shattered at birth and the multiplicity of Palas's astrological aspects will result in Epimetheus's dual occupation of hunter (Moon/Diana's influence) and warrior (Mars/Palas influence):

> A este efecto, en tanto que
> te asista en altas empresas,
> te yncliné a la caza, bien
> como ymagen de la guerra;
>
> [Thus, as long as
> I am helping you in high endeavors,
> I inclined you to hunting
> as an image of war]

(I. 669–72)

In spite of their fraternal love which united them as children, Prometheus acknowledges his brother's different personality (*genio*), which is the result of his opposite astrological inclinations.

Thus, Epimetheus, as a hunter, is inclined to dwell in the wilderness:

> Opuestos crezimos, no
> en la volumptad que anuda
> nuestros corazones, pero
> en la ynclinazión, que muda
> los genios; de suerte que
> dada a los montes la suia,
> no ay fiera que por la saña,
> no ay bruto que por la fuga,
> la piel redima, o la testa,
> de las açeradas puntas
> de su benablo o su aljaba;

(I. 65–75)

[Opposite we grew, not / in the will that binds / our hearts, but / in the inclination, that transforms / our personalities; so / being inclined to live in the wild / there's no beast that for its fury, / nor brute that in its flight / will save its skin, nor its head / from the sharpened tips / of his dart or quiver.]

The symbolism of fire and its emblematic depiction are important keys for reading Calderón's *La estatua de Prometeo* within its astrological and philosophical context. Philosophers since Heraclitus have recognized the dual nature of fire that kindles both sensual passions and spiritual energy (Cirlot 210).[11] Fire has the dual distinction of being able to both freeze and burn. In the second act, Minerva counsels the inhabitants of the Caucasus to beware of fire's dual powers, as portrayed in "hieroglyphics" or emblems:

> Si ya no es q[ue] el ver mezclados
> horrores y voçes blandas
> geroglífico es que diga
> que paçífica, esta llama
> será alhago, será alibio,
> será gozo, será graçia,
> y colérica, será
> ynçendio, yra, estrago y rabia;
> y así, temed y adorad
> al fuego cuando le exparza,
> o afable, o sañudo, a toda
> la naturaleza humana
> la estatua de Prometeo.

(II. 460–72)

[It is no longer seeing together / horrors and soft voices / [there is a] hieroglyphic that says / that this flame if peaceful, / [it] will be delightful, [it] will be soothing, / [it] will be joyful, [it] will be [a] blessing, / and if coleric, [it] will be / fire, wrath, havoc and fury; / and thus, fear and venerate / that fire when the Statue of Prometheus spreads it / either gentle or cruel, to all / of human nature.]

Fire, in the astro-mythical meaning of the element, is a sign of Apollonian power and wisdom. Its nature is both a source of joy and of destruction.

Minerva/Diana, having lost Apollo's reflected sun, helps Prometheus steal the necessary solar rays to illuminate the "pardas nubes" (gray clouds) that surround the sun ("monarca de los planetas / rey de los signos . . . alma de montes y selbas" (monarch among planets / kings of signs . . . soul of mountains and forests) suggesting in the play a solar eclipse, which, according to ancient beliefs, could only bring misfortune to Earth. In the sun's absence, Prometheus must steal Apollo's fire to illuminate the Caucasus:

> Si yo pudiera llebar
> un rayo suyo, que fuera
> su actibidad aplicada
> a combustible materia
> ençendida lumbre, que
> desmintiendo las tinieblas de la noche,
> en breue llama supliese del sol la ausençia

(I. 843–50)

[If I could take / his ray, that were / activity applied / to combustible matter / glowing light, that / disproving the night dark shadows, / with a small flame provided for the sun's absence]

Prometheus's ascension to heaven and his vision of Apollo's light would correspond alchemically to the transformation of base material into solar energy. Within kundalini yoga, Prometheus's mystical, inner experience would parallel the ascent of man's inner fire, from the lower *chakras*, centers of psychic energy, to the uppermost Crown *chakra*. Then, in the outer world, guided by the sacred light of the gnostic(s), Prometheus descends to the Caucasus with a gift to illuminate the dark recesses of the unconscious mind. Finding out, with Minerva's help, that all celestial bodies have souls of fire, Prometheus attempts to create a human being by using Apollo's light to give life to his statue created in the image of Minerva. According to Juan Pérez de Moya (1585), Aristotle had said: "Sol & homo generant Hominem. El Sol y el hombre engendra el hombre . . ." (Sun and man generate man) (f23v). Man begets man by finding his own inner fire. Prometheus understands the principles of creation and, thus, is able to reproduce an image. For the statue to come to life he must steal the solar fire that will ignite matter and beget a new human being. Tragically, Prometheus does not recognize in Pandora his vision of wisdom, and is unable to love his own creature. By contrast, Epimetheus falls in love with the statue, but he cannot understand the enigma of the fire that burns and, at the same time, freezes his soul. He says to Pandora:

> ¡No la azerques, no la azerques!
> ¡Aparta su ardor, aparta!
> que más que alumbra, deslumbra,
> y tanto pabor me causa,
> que arrojándome de sí,
> me fuerza a que a buscar vaya
> quien me desçifre el enigma
> de una escultura animada,
> un ynanimado fuego,
> que con calidad contraria,
> abrasa como que yela
> y yela como que abrasa.

(II. 269–80)

[Do not bring it near! Do not! / Put away its heat, put it away! / Instead of illuminating, it blinds / and so much fear it allays in me, / that separating me from it, / makes me look for / one who will decipher the enigma / of a living statue, / [and] a lifeless fire, / which with contrary quality, / burns as it freezes / and freezes as it burns.]

Apollo's song underlines the contradictory nature of fire that, like man, dies to be reborn and is born to die:

> No temas, no, pues, adquiere
> nueba luz la luz q[ue] yaçe,
> y tanto a todas prefiere,
> que muere de la que naçe,
> y naçe de la que muere.
> Y así no temas caer
> desde el cenit al nadir,

> pues es tan otro tu ser . . .
> . . . que naçe para morir,
> y muere para naçer."

(I. 897–907)

[Don't be afraid, no, since the light that rests buried becomes a new
light, / and it prefers this one to all others / that it dies from the one
that is being born, / and it is born from one that dies. / And thus fear
no fall / from zenith to nadir, / since your being is such . . . / that it
is born to die, / and dies to be born.]

Thus Calderón creates layer upon layer of meaning dependent on
the audience's ability to recognize metaphors based on analogical
correspondences between heaven and earth, and on the positive
and negative aspects of zodiacal signs, planets, and deities.
Earthly duality, as dramatized in *La estatua de Prometeo,* is a reflection of celestial bipolarity, a Manichean notion that has survived
in the esoteric, hermetic tradition of emblems and mythological
treatises.

In conclusion, *La estatua de Prometeo* can be decodified through
León Hebreo's four levels of meaning present in myths. In its
historical, literal meaning, the play refers to the creation of man
by Prometheus as transmitted through pagan texts and interpreted by Christian humanists. On an astrological level, *La estatua
de Prometeo* explores earthly and celestial duality, developing astral
archtypes that have their counterparts in the psychological com-
position of the human soul, symbolized by the split characters of
Minerva/Palas and Prometheus/Epimetheus. As a philosophical
play, *La estatua de Prometeo* deals with "coniunctio oppositorum"
or the conciliation of opposites as a necessary step towards
achieving peace in society and harmony within the individual,
which in pagan philosophy could be attained by the union of
wisdom and strength. In Calderón's Christian play, this "conuiun-
tio" is a gift of Apollo, symbolizing the pardon of the Saviour.
The learned human being has reason and knowledge, but only if
he is wise can action be effective. Beyond analytic mental powers,
prudence is the key to the highest achievement in human being.
By subordinating reason to prudence, Prometheus is able to recognize his shadow in Pandora, who is a true moon to Prometheus's sun. Concord is achieved and peace restored through the
union of opposites. Success is dependent on the internal transformation of the hero when he balances his inner duality. In society,
concord is achieved through the union of paradoxical principles.
Thus, the union of arms and letters is an emblematic symbol of

the ideal monarch, the ideal hero, the ideal society. Such transformations in esotericism are embodied in the principles of continuous change and differentiation in the world. Change is needed if things are to remain the same. Life is an eternal paradox in which peace becomes war, and war leads to peace, light turns to darkness, and from darkness emerges new light. It is within the context of European esoteric tradition of polarities, centrifugal and centripetal forces in the wheel of life, that Calderón de la Barca's play may be read in order to decodify overlaying levels of esoteric meanings, one meaning hiding and inverting the other.

NOTES

I am most grateful to Prof. Anita Stoll from Cleveland State University and Prof. Sharon Dahlgreen Voros from the U. S. Naval Academy for their useful comments and their kindness in reading this article before publication.

1. It was originally published in Salamanca, the first part in 1620 and the second in 1623. I will be using eighteenth-century editions published in Barcelona and in Madrid. See bibliography.

2. According to Peter M. Daly (1979, 11–21), the manuscript of this collection of hieroglyphs, probably of Alexandrian origin, dating from the fourth century or perhaps fifth century, was discovered in 1419 on the Greek island of Andros by the priest Christophorus De' Buondelmonti and taken to Florence. The Greek version was published in 1505, the Latin translation in 1517. Renaissance humanists, particularly Marsilio Ficino, studied these texts and interpreting them in the light of Platonic philosophy, understood the hieroglyphs to be " . . . reflections of divine ideas in the things themselves." (16) Hieroglyphs influenced the graphic and plastic arts of the Renaissance as well as is an important aspect of the emblematic tradition in both its visual aspects as in its poetic or literary explanations.

3. Also see López Torrijos (1985, 45–48).

4. Infantes quotes from *Días sagrados y geniales, celebrados en la canonización de San Francisco de Borja. Por el Colegio Imperial de la Compañía de Jesús de Madrid y la Academia de los más célebres ingenios de España.* Madrid, Francisco Nieto, 1672.

5. This English version was quoted from Peter M. Daly and Simon Cuttler's translation from the 1621 Padua edition. There are translation problems. The Latin "unum" has been translated as "one man," whereas Latin and Spanish can be more abstract. For example, Pilar Pedraza's translation of the *Emblems* reads: "Que uno no puede nada y dos mucho." This capacity for abstraction allows us to read the "motto" as referring to concord between two different persons, or opposing aspects of the same body, or two elements of the soul that has been fragmented.

6. All quotes from Calderón's *La Estatua de Prometeo* are from Margaret Greer's 1986 edition of the play.

7. We should not be surprised by coincidences of ancient beliefs and traditions when considering Greek cultural contacts with the East during this period of economic and territorial expansion. As indicated by Jewish scholar Z'ev ben

Shimon Halevi: "When the Greeks came into contact with the older and much more advanced civilizations of the East in their campaigns of conquest and trade, there occurred a cultural alchemy in which the rational intelligence of the Greeks was fired and fused with the religious and philosophical experience of the Oriental mind. Besides the contacts with the Persian and Indian civilizations and the connection with the Egyptians, there was also the meeting between the Hellenic and Judaic cultures that produced the groundbed of Christendom and Islam" (Halevi 1992, 1).

8. Frances Yates traces the history of Christian Kabbalah to Ramon Lull's *Ars Magna*. It was also in medieval Spain that Kabbalah reached a high point of development. She also indicates that the Renaissance is related to the expulsion of Jews from Spain in 1492, many fled to Italy and spread an interest in their mystical tradition. This diaspora is tied to Ficino and Pico della Mirandola's Christian Kabbalah (Yates 1979, 9–15).

9. For information on Neumeister's study see Alexander Parker (1988, 332).

10. According to D. Encausse (1865–1916), known as Papus, Number 2 in esoterism is feminine, passive, and the source of human mental errors. This ideology perpetuates hatred of women which is not representative of Calderón's portrayal of Pandora. Calderón explores fragmentation, both in female as in male figures, as the source of human tragedies. The resulting multiplicity is not blamed on women.

11. Cirlot quotes Marius Schneider in his explanation of the nature of fire.

Calderón and Borges: Discovering Infinity in the Labyrinth of Reason

Timothy Ambrose

The image of the labyrinth in *La vida es sueño* (*Life is a Dream*), has been taken by critics to represent the way in which lost reason cannot find its way out of entanglements created by the passions. Gwynne Edwards has examined this meaning of the labyrinth not only as an image of passion, but also as a template for much of the action in six Calderonian tragedies. Although he does not include it as one of his six plays, Edwards does mention *La vida es sueño,* as exemplifying the same principle (1978, xxv). In a subsequent article in which he discusses Calderón's *Los tres mayores prodigios* and *El pintor de su deshonra,* Edwards suggests that the labyrinth, interpreted as a symbol for "man's moral and emotional disorientation through excessive passion," may be a "key symbol" to understanding the entirety of Calderón's dramatic *oeuvre* (1984, 331–32).

A. A. Parker, on the other hand, associates "the awakening of sexual passion and its disorderly consequences," with what he calls the "Tower Myth" (1982b, 251), and avows that the tower, along with its connotations, "may be considered to constitute what Henry James called The Figure in the Carpet, a necessary clue to his [Calderón's] mind and his art" (1982b, 248). The tower has been shown by Margaret S. Maurin to be an integral part of the mythology of the labyrinth in *La vida es sueño* (Maurin 165). Thus, although he discredits Edwards's emphasis on the labyrinth in a review of *The Prison and the Labyrinth*,[1] Parker underscores its importance by his own emphasis on Segismundo's tower.[2]

Parker also asserts the superiority of a Christian interpretation: "It is to this high level of theological Suffering and Guilt that Calderón's dramatic world elevates his myth of Segismundo's Tower" (1982b, 254). Although there can be little doubt that Calderón would have agreed with such an interpretation, in our present attempt to understand the meaning of the labyrinth in *La vida es sueño*, we shall need to return to a period of time which predates the Christian era by some three thousand years. But, a particular moment in Parker's review of Edwards's book will serve as the starting point in our consideration of the ancient mythology of the labyrinth.

Parker's review of *The Prison and the Labyrinth* contains an instructive oversight with regard to the ancient mythological associations of the labyrinth. At one point, he takes Edwards to task for making a connection, in *El pintor de su deshonra,* between labyrinth and dance:

> the carnival dance in the streets of Barcelona is said [by Edwards] to be a "maze" ("the maze-like complications within whose patterns human lives are set"[122]), but nothing is less maze-like than the regular rhythm of a dance with its fixed steps and its predictable starting and stopping. (1982b, 342)

However, ancient mythical accounts of the labyrinth at Knossos in Crete associate it most intimately with dancing. After Theseus had escaped from the labyrinth and abandoned Ariadne on the island of Naxos, he "travelled on with the lads and the maidens to Delos, where he danced with them the Crane Dance, an evolution which imitated the windings of the Labyrinth" (Kerenyi 234). And, in the more ancient ritual ceremonies associated with Osiris in Egypt, "dancing, as a ritual activity, was especially associated with the Labyrinth" (Deedes 24).

Both labyrinth and dance were also an important part of the theater from the time of its inception in ancient Greece, Theseus having taken, according to legend, these elements back with him to Athens after his adventures in Crete:

> We find . . . that the early Greek drama preserved in its form the elements of the ancient pattern of religious belief and ritual associated with the labyrinths of Crete and Egypt, and that the earliest Greek theatre was a circular dancing-ground (Deedes 33).

In its most ancient appearances, those of Egypt, the labyrinth was also associated with drama:

> From the earliest times the myth of Osiris was represented in dramatic form, and the stage was set and the parts played by royal and divine persons and by a body of priests . . . The Labyrinth guarded its secret

well and the mystery remained unknown to any save the participants. (Deedes 24)

Thus, Edwards's interpretation of the labyrinthine connotations of the carnival dance are not at all far-fetched, and his idea that the labyrinth was in some way a key figure in Calderón's dramatic world reiterates an association between drama and labyrinth that dates from the earliest beginnings of ritual theatrical production in the Western world.

The coincidence of labyrinth and drama from the earliest of times suggests that dramatic action, which invariably involved dancing (Deedes 32), may also have originally been thought of as a form of labyrinth. These early ritual dramas were perhaps enactments of the divine labyrinth of life and nature, an interpretation that would agree to some extent with Edwards's discussion of the labyrinth in Calderón. Calderón himself would seem to have expressed an awareness of this connotation by giving the title *El laberinto del mundo* (*The Labyrinth of the World*) to one of his *autos* (sacramental plays).

If ancient Egyptian and Cretan ceremonial drama represented the labyrinth of the world at large, then both dramatic action and the world would have concealed a sacred mystery, the idea of concealment of something sacred being an integral part of the labyrinth mythology from its earliest beginnings (Deedes 13). Would we not also expect to find a parallel concealment of something sacred in Calderón's masterpiece? What might this sacred mystery at the center of the labyrinth be? Let us begin to answer these questions by taking a closer look at a general history of the labyrinth and its mythology to see how *La vida es sueño* fits into the general paradigm.

The most ancient labyrinth known to have existed in the Western world was not, as is commonly believed, that at Knossos, but rather another and even larger and more impressive one in Egypt. Herodotus, Strabo (a great traveler of the ancient world) and Pliny all speak of this stupendous labyrinth.[3] By the time later European travelers came upon the geographic location of this labyrinth, it was completely in ruins (Matthews 11). Herodotus, however, as well as the other ancient authorities mentioned above, indicates that the Egyptian labyrinth was a sacred place associated with structures of palace, temple, and tomb (Matthews 6–10).

These same ancient associations are present to one degree or another in *La vida es sueño*. As we have already stated, Margaret S. Maurin has demonstrated that Segismundo's tower is the center of a labyrinth (164–65). This tower can also be thought of as a palace, since it is the dwelling of a prince, but it is also, as Segismundo himself points out, a tomb or *sepulcro* (*La vida* 93). The templelike quality of the tower is brought out in A. A. Parker's discussion of its appearance at very strategic places in the dramatic action, most notably at the beginning, middle, and end of the play. Parker's words confer upon the tower an almost religious signification, and, as we shall now see, connect it quite clearly to the ancient Egyptian labyrinth/temple:

> This symmetrical spacing of the Tower, with the circular pattern of action whereby the ending inverts the beginning, cannot be an accident. . . . We are impelled to ask what it means. The poetic imagery surrounding it, calling it the *cuna y sepulcro* of the inmate, takes us away from an ordinary prison, to the mystery of life and death . . . (1982b, 248)

Like Segismundo's tower, which lies at the center of a labyrinth, ancient Egyptian temples were associated with the mysteries of death and rebirth, specifically those of the god Osiris:

> The plan and construction of the oldest known temple of Osiris at Abydos is interesting . . . in connection with the original meaning of the Labyrinth . . . This shrine was the centre of the dramatic representation of the death and resurrection of Osiris, which took place yearly, practically throughout the whole of Egyptian history (Deedes 15).

There is ample evidence that the famed labyrinth built by Daedalus for King Minos was an imitation of the more ancient labyrinths of Egypt (Deedes 17–20), and that a number of dramatic rituals, such as the death and rebirth of the king-god, associated with Osiris, were also brought from Egypt to Crete along with the labyrinth design. In both Egypt and Crete, the king-god was ritualistically associated with the bull, and a divine bull was slain in his place. In the Cretan version, the bull becomes the Minotaur, offspring of the goddess Pasiphae, a local version of Isis, and the magnificent white bull of divine origin, given to Minos by Poseidon (Deedes 24–27).

From this summary of the labyrinth myth, we can see that Segismundo would represent not one, but several of the characters in the ancient drama. He may be equated with the Minotaur, as well as with the hero Theseus who slew the monster *and* the king-god who was renewed through the sacrifice of the bull, insofar as he (Segismundo) overcomes his own baser nature and is regenerated, as Edwards, Maurin, and Parker have all pointed out.

Of course, Segismundo's regeneration, his ritual death and rebirth as it were, also express the near-death and renewal of the king-god figure in the person of his father, Basilio. Basilio's life and kingdom are threatened by the rebellion led by Segismundo, and restored or renewed by Segismundo's change of heart. It is this threat of death to Basilio, a threat that actually begins with the reading of Segismundo's horoscope prior to the play's commencement, which initiates and conditions to a great extent the dramatic action. Hence, the ancient myth finds a counterpart in Basilio too.

In the Egyptian and perhaps also in the original Cretan version of this myth, the death and rebirth of the king-god in the form of a sacrificial bull was something of great benefit for the kingdom and therefore a cause for celebration. The Greek version of the myth, however, takes a different view of the bull-cult:

> There is a hatred of it, and finally a breaking loose from it, led by a royal prince [Theseus], who, from his position, should be the last person to rebel. The history of Theseus may give us a clue to the origin of this myth. He was a usurper and an innovator (Deedes 29).

According to Thucydides, Theseus "broke down the old divisions, the ancient Moirai, confusing, doubtless, many an archaic sanctity. . . ." (quoted in Harrison 317).[4]

Segismundo obviously expresses the Greek version of the myth, insofar as the drama revolves around him and his struggle with his personal destiny. At the end of the play, for example, Segismundo is the center of attention, Basilio's role having been relegated to that of a secondary character in the scenario. Nonetheless, the more ancient core of the myth, the death and rebirth of the actual king, Basilio, is to some extent also implicit.

Basilio also expresses another parallel with the Cretan mythology. King Minos had promised to sacrifice to Poseidon the white bull that the god himself has caused to emerge from the sea. But, Minos hid the magnificent creature and sacrificed another instead, thus arousing Poseidon's anger. As a punishment, Poseidon caused Pasiphae to conceive an overpowering desire for the bull. As a result of her coupling with the bull, Pasiphae bore the Minotaur, who proclaimed by its montrous presence Minos's guilt. Minos was thus appropriately shamed. Like Minos, Basilio is the architect of his own undoing, for it is because of his pride in his great learning, and his consequently inappropriate action of imprisoning Segismundo that his misfortunes arise.[5] Thus, Basilio, like Minos, creates the situation that produces the Minotaur, represented in the play by Segismundo (Maurin 165).

An Egyptian element that reappears in the myth of Theseus and the Minotaur is that of a magical, protective dance: "when the plan of the Labyrinth was brought from Egypt a ritual dance was imported with it, apparently of a circular kind, and associated with the god or goddess" (Deedes 28). This circular dance, so intimately a part of the labyrinth mythology in the ancient world, parallels "the circular pattern of action whereby the ending inverts the beginning," to which Parker refers and to which he gives great importance in his interpretation of the "tower myth" (Parker 1982b, 248). Indeed, the circularity of the tower itself may be understood as a restatement of the ancient motif of the protective, circular dance.

The fact that the tower is central to the dramatic action also suggests a parallel with the altar to the god that stood at the center of the dance in both Egypt and Crete. According to the myth, Theseus took the labyrinth dance and ritual drama to Athens, and in the earliest Greek theater, the centerpiece of a sacred altar once again appears:

> In the centre of this dancing-ground stood the statue of the god, round which was performed an intricate dance, probably resembling the ancient ritual dance brought from Crete by Theseus. (Deedes 33)

Thus, at the center of the labyrinth, whether in the form of palace, temple, tomb, dance, drama, or the world at large, we are confronted with the mystery of something divine, something that transcends the relative, profane boundaries of human existence. This is very much akin to the sacred and mysterious quality that Parker intuits in Segismundo's tower.

Fragments of the ritual drama associated with the labyrinth were perhaps kept alive into Medieval and even Renaissance Europe, and it is possible, therefore, to imagine that Calderón absorbed certain of the ancient mythical meanings from such remnants. The design of the labyrinth is to be found, for example, inscribed on the walls and floors of certain Medieval Christian churches, "since a new religion cannot eradicate all the traditional forms and beliefs of an ancient past" (Deedes 42). Deedes further explains that:

The break-up of the archaic civilizations, together with the diffusion and democratization of the ancient pattern of religious belief and ritual, resulted in degradation of ritual, confusion of beliefs . . . the old rituals were converted into dances and games which preserved little of their original form and meaning as life-giving acts. (42)

La vida es sueño may be interpreted as an attempt to restore to its original dignity the ancient meaning of the labyrinth. It may be that Calderón was not fully conscious of such an endeavor, but the elements that we discover in the play testify to an underlying awareness of a timeless or transhistorical mythical dimension.[6]

Unlike the strictly Christian, theological interpretation of Segismundo's tower offered by Parker, and the interpretations by Edwards and Maurin that deal more specifically with labyrinth imagery, the Cretan myth contains meanings connoting intellect or reason, as well as those of strong passion. Passion is certainly present in the story of how Pasiphae was overcome with lust for the white bull. From her union with that creature the Minotaur was born, thus suggesting perhaps the negative results of an overly passionate nature. *But,* it was the cunning or intellectual prowess of the craftsman and architect Daedalus which wrought the edifice where Minos concealed the monster that was half human and half bull.[7]

Although she generally associates the labyrinth with passion, Maurin S. Maurin does at times allude to the labyrinth in a way that draws our attention to its possible connection with reason, not in the sense of reason becoming lost in the labyrinth of passion, but rather of reason itself being the labyrinth, or reason being responsible for the construction of the labyrinth in which it (reason) then becomes lost.

When discussing the opening lines of the play in which the hipogryph carries Rosaura into the "confuso laberinto / destas desnudas peñas," (1992, 6–7 "Confusing labyrinth of these naked rocks") Maurin tells us that,

Rosaura, shortly after, says "Bajaré la aspereza enmarañada / deste monte eminente" (I, 14–15 "I will descend the tangled roughness of this lofty rock"), an inescapable clue which would point immediately to a labyrinth had not Calderón already explicitly named it, for the word "enmarañada" (and its associates "intrincado" [intricate] and "entretejido" [interwoven]) in a number of plays directly precedes or accompanies the word labyrinth itself, and leads ultimately to the monster image or its equivalent. (163–64)

Although the connotations of *enmarañada* (tangled) might be debated, the words *entretejido* (interwoven) and more especially *intrincado* (intricate) suggest more clearly the workings of the intellect or reason than they do those of instinct or the passions.

Edwards too emphasizes the use of the word *intrincado* to express the motif of the labyrinth in Calderón's plays, as well as in Spanish Golden Age literature in general (1984, 333). Of Calderón, he states that, "the intricacy of the stage-action and, at a key moment, the groping of the characters in the darkness of the house evidently brings to mind the Cretan Labyrinth" (1984, 332).

Edwards goes on to cite a passage from Calderón's *Los tres mayores prodigios* (*The Three Greatest Wonders*) where Daedalus is mentioned. This allusion to the architect of the labyrinth, as well as the phrase "intricacy of the stage-action," inevitably call forth the meanings of *cunning, artiface,* and *craft,* characteristics of a highly developed intellect. Indeed, one of the possible meanings of Daedalus is "cunningly wrought" (Graves 1992, 758).

When praising the intricacy of the plot in *El pintor de su deshonra* (*The Painter of his Dishonor*), Edwards states that: "The great complexity of the plot as a whole, described by A. A. Parker as 'strikingly contrived,' reveals quite clearly the extent to which the lives of the various characters become so inextricably intertwined" (1984, 333). The phrase "inextricably intertwined" echoes a reference by Parker to the "tangled skeins of human motives" in Calderón's plays (1982b, 251), as well as Maurin's emphasis on the word *entretejido* (interwoven). These textile metaphors all evoke the intelligence and craft of the maker or builder, rather than blind, uncontrollable passion. Parker and Edwards are not, of course, describing characters in the plays, but rather praising the complex quality of the dramatic action.

Indeed, these textile metaphors evoke the weaving of a labyrinthine tapestry of dramatic action by a superior intellect, Calderón's. J. Hillis Miller has pointed out the likeness between narrative and logical (rational) argumentation in the preface to a book, *Ariadnes's Thread,* in which he uses the metaphor of the labyrinth to denote the maze of present-day intellectual, narrative theory (xi–xii). A similar association between logical discourse and storytelling is found in the Spanish use of the word *argumento,* a word connoting intellect and reason, to signify *plot* in dramatic, as well as fictional, narrative.

The words *textile* and *text* are etymologically connected, and the poet, Calderón, is, etymologically speaking, also a maker or builder, just as Daedalus was. The word *text* originally comes from the past participle of the Latin *texere*, to weave or build, which is the origin of the Spanish *tejer*. The Latin *texere* is etymologically associated with the ancient Greek word *technikos* from *techne*, an art or artifice. The word *architect* has the same root.[8] The myth of the cunningly constructed labyrinth may thus encompass the dramatic poet and writer of fiction, as we know from the work of Jorge Luis Borges, to whom we shall presently return.

The notion of the intellect being the architect or builder of the labyrinth is again elicited, albeit unintentionally, by Maurin. In the character of Rosaura she finds a subversion of reason: the paradox of her being both man and woman makes her monstrous and connects her to the image of the labyrinth (Maurin 168). This paradox is the labyrinth that Clotaldo is unable to thread, "donde no puede / hallar la razón el hilo" (976–77, "where reason cannot find the thread").

But, who or what has constructed this labyrinth? It may be argued that reason or the intellect is the artifacer responsible for constructing that linguistic or ideational labyrinth known as a paradox. In his book *Labyrinths of Reason*, William Poundstone suggests just such a connection between labyrinth and paradox. Poundstone states that in ancient Crete, the land ruled by Minos where Daedalus built the labyrinth, "a labyrinth could mean a mazelike building, a grotto or winding cave (a common feature of the Cretan landscape), or an inescapable dilemma in argument: a paradox" (161).

This interpretation is significant, because of the abundance of paradoxes in the Calderón's play. Maurin ends her essay by mentioning the frequency and importance of paradox in *La vida es sueño*. She also places paradox within the general context of the baroque: "All of the images which we have studied, that of the monster, of light and darkness, of the living-dead, are typically Baroque in that they are antithetical, paradoxical in nature" (178). Segismundo, for example, poses many insoluble problems in the form of paradoxes when he first appears.[9] Other examples are those of Segismundo's reference to his tower as "cuna y sepulcro" (195 "cradle and tomb"), and Clotaldo's "antes de nacer moriste" (321 "before being born you died"). The title of one of Calderón's plays, *En esta vida todo es verdad y todo mentira* (*In this Life all is Truth and all is a Lie*) demonstrates the playwright's predilection for paradoxical formulations, which, as Maurin points out, was common in the Baroque period.

Considering Rosaura's montrous androgyny as paradox, we should recall that E. M. Wilson has commented on Calderón's "fondness for words describing monsters and semi-mythical creatures, which express in their names the confusion of two or more characteristics" (42). The Minotaur, of course, immeditaely comes to mind. A paradox too may be thought of as a monstrous creation of the intellect, a monster that, although created by the intellect, cannot be resolved by means of logical or rational analysis. Forming an impenetrable mystery, the paradox, like the monster, suggests a mysterious, perhaps even divine, phenomenon. Both may therefore be considered as "amazing examples of God's power and wisdom" (de Armas 1986, 113, in reference to the Minotaur/monster motif). The Minotaur was, after all, the offspring resulting from the coupling of divine beings, and represented the divine king-god (Deedes 27; Apollodorus, 1:303–05 quoted in Irwin 218). Paradox may thus be associated with both labyrinth *and* Minotaur. Borges notes the proximity, almost identity, of Minotaur and labyrinth: "la imagen del laberinto conviene a la imagen del minotauro. Queda bien que en el centro de una casa monstruosa haya un habitante monstruoso" (*Seres imaginarios* 142 "the image of the labyrinth goes well with the image of the Minotaur. It is fitting that at the center of a monstrous dwelling there be a monstrous inhabitant").

The Minotaur's name, Asterion, means starry (Irwin 158), thus associating it with the celestial realm, and the labyrinth has been linked to the zodiac (Irwin 253–54). The drama of *La vida es sueño* takes as its starting point, and subsequently unfolds from, the casting of Segismundo's horoscope by Basilio. The dramatic action is precisely related to specific astrological counterparts, as Frederick A. de Armas has demonstrated in extensive detail (de Armas 1986, 88–138). We may thus extend our interpretation of the labyrinth to include not only the images and metaphors surrounding Segismundo and his tower, the dramatic action of the play, narrative texts, and the world at large, but also the labyrinth of the heavens with which human life on earth is intimately interconnected, to the extent that the one is a mirror reflection of the other, (de Armas 1986, 86–87). But, how does paradox, that labyrinth of reason, fit into this greatly expanded, cosmic overview of the parameters of the mythology of the labyrinth?

We have so far suggested a likeness between Daedalus who built the labyrinth and the intellect which constructs a paradox. The primacy of the intellect as constructor or architect of the labyrinth, at least insofar as it is present in Calderón, is supported to some degree by Christopher Soufas who argues that Segismundo suffers at the beginning of the play from an overdeveloped faculty of reason (287). He finds that Segismundo's reasoning is "so meticulously logical" (291), and "that his intellectualizing may be part of the very *razón* that keeps him in chains" (291).

Another key example of an overly developed intellect in Calderón's play is that of King Basilio, whose erudition and "science" lead him to create the conditions that will very nearly be his undoing and that of his kingdom. Of his great intellect and learning, Basilio proclaims: "Ya sabéis que yo en el mundo / por mi ciencia he merecido / el sobrenombre de docto," (604–6 "You already know that because of my knowledge I have merited and the world has given me the title of Learned") and he boasts of his knowledge of "matemáticas sutiles" (614 "subtle mathematics").

The theme of Basilio's cleverness in calculation and interpretation of horoscopes, which leads him into misfortune, and that of Segismundo's intellectualizing, which keeps him in chains (Soufas 291), evoke the notion that one may be the architect of one's own downfall. These examples bring out a further parallel with the master-craftsman Daedalus. Daedalus himself was eventually imprisoned in the labyrinth he had so artfully constructed, when Minos learned that he had helped Pasiphae to have intercourse with the bull. But, according to the myth, the ingenious craftsman *did* find a way out of the labyrinth: "his only way of escape was to prepare wings of feathers and wax and discover the art of flying" (Kerenyi 231). Flying has from time immemorial been associated with the transcendence of boundaries characteristic of thought and the world. Mircea Eliade has documented the universal symbolism of flight: "'Flying up to heaven' is expressed in Chinese as follows: 'by means of feathers he was transformed and ascended as an immortal'" (1972, 450). Images of flight are often linked to transcendence:

> such powers often take on a purely spiritual character: "flight" expresses . . . understanding of secret things or metaphysical truths. "Among all things that fly the mind [*manas*] is swiftest," says the *Rg-Veda*. And the *Pañcavimsa Brahmana* adds: "Those who know have wings." (1972, 479)

The symbolism of flight and, hence, transcendence, as personified in Daedalus, is thus an integral part of the Minoan labyrinth mythology. In *La vida es sueño*, Segismundo suggests his desire for transcendence in his reference to flight early in the play (123–32). This and the other examples he cites in his first soliloquy all end with the implicit desire for freedom: "¿y teniendo yo más

alma, / tengo menos libertad?" (131–32 "And having a greater
soul, I have less freedom?") The word *libertad* in these instances
is directly related to the many evocations of the labyrinth myth
surrounding Segismundo, in that it expresses a desire to escape,
to fly away, as Daedalus did, and hence symbolically, to transcend
the boundaries of thought and the world.

A similar transcendental symbolism is present in the portrayal
of Rosaura as simultaneously man and woman. In commenting
on "divine androgyny," Eliade explains that "what is implied in
such a conception is the idea that perfection, and therefore Being,
ultimately consists of a unity-totality" (1969, 108). When discussing "Ritual Androgynisation," that is to say, ritual cross-
dressing, he points out that it is,

> a transcending of one's own historically controlled situation, and a
> recovering of an original situation . . . a paradoxical situation impos-
> sible to maintain in profane time, in a historical epoch, but which it
> is important to reconstitute periodically in order to restore, if only for
> a brief moment, the initial completeness, the intact source of holiness
> and power. (113)

Eliade's words draw our attention to the way in which the symbolism of *La vida es sueño,* exemplified in Rosaura's androgyny,
gravitates toward paradox. The coincidence of death and life in
the symbolism of the tower, mentioned by Parker (1982b 321),
and in Clotaldo's vision of Segismundo's death in life suggest the
kind of sacred "paradoxical situation," to which Eliade refers.
Such paradoxical utterances in *La vida es sueño* repeat on a verbal
level the most ancient drama identified with the labyrinth, that
of the ritual death and rebirth of Osiris, and its later Grecian
manifestation in the dramatic ritual associated with Dionysus,
"the god who yearly died and rose again for the welfare of the
land and people" (Deedes 31).

With these mythical connotations, the labyrinth becomes an apt
vehicle for dramatizing a "transcending of one's own historically
controlled situation, and a recovering of an original situation,"
thus responding to the human need "to reconstitute periodically"
sacred time or a transcendental state of being. Segismundo's symbolic death and regeneration, aligned with the mythology of the
labyrinth, may be interpreted as a dramatic revelation of this sort
of transcendental moment.

Flight and androgyny both imply a transcendence of or going
beyond the pairs of opposites, opposites such as death and birth,

man and woman, truth and falsehood (reality and illusion), opposites which constitute our thinking and the world in which we live. These same pairs of opposites, when they unite, that is to say, when they cease to be two and become one, constitute a paradox. Paradox, like that of androgyny or that of the death/birth motif, thus connotes, just as magical flight does, a transcendence of the pairs of opposites and the world.[10]

Further corroboration of the association of the labyrinth myth with the themes of both paradox and transcendence comes to us from archaeology and its connection to the etymology of the word *labyrinth*. Sir Arthur Evans's discovery in 1900 of "the frequent occurence of the sign of the double axe, which was obviously an object of great importance in Minoan worship, and the profusion of evidence concerning the cult of the bull" (Matthews 31), at an archaeological site at Knossos led to his conclusion that this was in fact "the true original of the traditional Labyrinth" (Evans quoted in Irwin 247). This discovery revolutionized the accepted etymology of the word. Henceforth, the labyrinth would be taken to be "the House of the Double Axe" (Evans quoted in Matthews 176), *labrys* being, "a word which, in some of the early languages of Asia Minor . . . denoted an axe, the axe being the symbol associated with the god known as Zeus Labrandeus" (Matthews 175).[11]

A paradox, like that of one individual, Rosaura in *La vida es sueño*, for example, being both man and woman, may be interpreted as the double axe of rational thought, in that it takes the intellect simultaneously in two opposing and hence contradictory directions, and therefore cuts both ways at once. This interpretation would connect paradox most intimately to the labyrinth, for Evans's labors revealed the sign of the double axe throughout the place of his excavations at Knossos. Indeed, he found at the very center of the structure of the labyrinth a stone pillar marked all around with the symbol of the double axe (Irwin 247).

Thus, the central mystery of the labyrinth is perhaps in some way related to the phenomenon of paradox. In a sense, we have already found confirmation of this relationship in the fact that the mystery of the labyrinth from earliest times was centered upon the paradoxical motif of death and rebirth, paradoxical in that it combines two antithetical moments, birth and death. The profusion of paradox in *La vida es sueño* would thus be closely allied to that group of elements, the motif of temple, palace and tomb, that of death and (re)birth, the Minotaur, the desire for flight symbolizing transcendence, Daedalus as architect of his

own misfortune, and the androgyny of Rosaura, all of which may
be related to the myth of the labyrinth. Paradox would form the
central mystery of this labyrinth of images, motifs, and symbols,
just as the sign of the double axe was found by Evans, not only
throughout the Cretan labyrinth, but also at its very center.

The relationship between labyrinth and paradox in the context
of *La vida es sueño* may be yet further strengthened if we are able
to connect these two elements to the play's central metaphysical
premise, that of life as a dream, from which the title is derived.
All three motifs, dream, labyrinth, and paradox have been linked
by Jorge Luis Borges, and it is to this integration of them in his
work that we now turn our attention. At the end of Borges's story,
"La muerte y la brújula" ("Death and the Compass,") there is a
precise moment when the protagonist Lönnrot uses a paradox as
an example of a labyrinth (1971b, 162–63). He has been caught in
a labyrinth composed of four lines on a map, marking the points
of four successive murders. This labyrinth, although devised by
his archenemy Red Scharlach, is to a great extent one of his own
making, because it has been constructed by his own infallible
intellect, which has led him deductively to the very place, the
abandoned villa of *Triste-le-Roy*, where Scharlach is waiting for
him.[12] Having learned that he himself is to be the fourth murder
victim, he reflects on the nature of this particular labyrinth, and
of labyrinths in general. Before his impending execution, he tells
Scharlach of a labyrinth formed by a single straight line. This
labyrinth in which the reasoning powers of numerous philosophers have become lost, is the famous paradox of Zeno of Elea,
in which a given distance, a line, is subdivided infinitely, thus
disallowing the possibility of its traversal. This paradox among
others was presumably used by Zeno to demonstrate the unreality or ideality (nonphysical quality) of space, time, and motion
(Kirk 277–79). Borges was intrigued by Zeno's paradoxes, precisely because they suggest the ultimately mental or dreamlike
quality of the world. "Zenón" ("Zeno") he states emphatically in
an essay, "es incontestable, salvo que confesemos la idealidad del
espacio y del tiempo" (1964b, 120 "is incontrovertible, unless we
acknowledge the ideality of space and time"). The ideality of the
world is alluded to by the detective Lönnrot when he suggests
that his imminent death is an illusion, and that he will be reincar-
nated to relive the same or a similarly sordid fate (1971b, 162–63).

Directly related to the association between paradox and the
ideality of the world is the concept of infinity, which also greatly
intrigued Borges.[13] He explores the connection between paradox

and infinity in an essay in which he discusses how the *regressus in infinitum* inherent in Zeno's paradox, among others, calls seriously into question the existence of the world of time and space (1964b, 119–20). Infinity, one of the most frequently recurring motifs in Borges's writing, implies something beyond finite boundaries, an absolute reality that transcends the relative limits of the world as dream, something that rises above, like Daedalus, the walls of the labyrinth, something "not restricted to the conditions and limits of this life," in the words of Immanuel Kant (quoted in Moore xiii).

Profoundly influenced by Shopenhauer's idealism, Borges holds a conception of the world as a dream, but he also affirms, as his fascination with the idea of infinity suggests, the existence of an absolute reality which transcends the illusion of the world. In another essay on Zeno's paradox, he comments on that transcendental reality by way of a quotation taken from Novalis:

> *El mayor hechicero* (escribe memorablemente Novalís) *sería el que se hechizara hasta el punto de tomar sus propias fantasmagorías por apariciones autónomas. ¿No sería ése nuestro caso?* Yo conjeturo que así es. Nosotros (la indivisa divinidad que opera en nosotros) hemos soñado el mundo. Lo hemos soñado resistente, misterioso, visible, ubicuo en el espacio y firme en el tiempo; pero hemos consentido en su arquitectura tenues y eternos intersticios de sinrazón para saber que es falso (1964a, 136).

> [*The greatest sorcerer* (writes Novalis memorably) *would be the one who could cast such a powerful spell upon himself that he would consider his own fantasmagoric creations to be autonomous apparitions. Are we not ourselves examples of such an instance?* I conjecture that indeed this is the case. We (the indivisible divinity that functions within us) have dreamed the world. We have dreamed it as resilient, mysterious, visible, ubiquitous in space and time; but we have permitted in its architecture tenuous and eternal interstices of unreason so that we may know that it is false.]

The word Borges uses to characterize the world as dream is *arquitectura*, a word that, given his famous predilection for the labyrinth motif, cannot help but evoke that association. The world is a labyrinth, he suggests, that we have dreamed. It is an illusion we have created. And who are we? He "conjectures" (*conjeturo*) that our essence is that of an undivided divine nature, and that each of us, as this divine, subjective wholeness "la indivisa divinidad que opera en nosotros" ("the indivisible divinity that functions within us"), have dreamed the world. The world has become a labyrinth of illusion, because we have forgotten that we have dreamed it. *But,* there are signs, paradoxes, "tenues y eternos intersticios de sinrazón" ("tenuous and eternal interstices of unreason") which signal the unreality of this illusion. The fact that they are *eternal* implies a sacred or divine quality inherent in them, like that inherent in the sign of the double axe, associated with the divine creative force of Zeus, which Evans found throughout the labyrinth at Knossos.

Paradox, therefore, partakes of a double nature, in that it is not only a labyrinth of reason in which reason gets lost, but also a sign or marker which signifies that the labyrinth itself, which is to say the world, is an illusion. Paradox thus suggests the liberating idea that ultimate reality lies not in the external world but within our own mind, liberating in the sense that it frees us from an illusion.[14] This is essentially what Borges expresses with his notion of the ideality of the world. The mythology of the labyrinth itself evinces a similar double nature, for while on the one hand it represents a prison or infernal enclosure from which escape is difficult if not impossible, on the other it contains a sacred, life-giving mystery at its center. In *La vida es sueño,* the double aspect of the labyrinth is present in Segismundo's tower which is both the place of his confinement *and* the site of his liberation, in act 3, from the false impressions of the dream of life: "que, desengañado ya, / sé bien que *la vida es sueño*" (2342–43 "that, now free from illusion, I know well that *life is a dream*").

The concept of life as a dream, as well as Borges's philosophical idealism (expressed in his discussion of Zeno's paradoxes and in his commentary on Novalis) that it resembles, comes strikingly close to the idea of *maya,* which we encounter in the Vedic texts of ancient India. Borges's idealism comes largely from his reading of Schopenhauer who often identifies his own philosophical idealism with the ancient Vedic tradition. Schopenhauer esteemed Calderón's plays and speaks of his admiration for *La vida es sueño* in *The World as Will and Representation,* the defintive statement of his philosophical doctrine. He praises Calderón's masterpiece, among other works of literature and philosophy, for its exemplification of the Vedic concept of *maya.* Reflecting on his own arguments in favor of the ideality of the world, he writes that,

> Here indeed the close relationship between life and the dream is brought out for us very clearly. We will not be ashamed to confess it, after it has been recognized and expressed by many great men. The

Vedas and *Puranas* know no better simile for the whole knowledge of the actual world, called by them the web of Maya, than the dream, and they use none more frequently. (I 17)

The Vedic tradition of knowledge referred to by Shopenhauer is explained in the Vedic Science of Maharishi Mahesh Yogi. Maharishi's Vedic Science is the science of consciousness, and it considers consciousness as the most fundamental element of existence.[15] Pure consciousness is, according to Vedic Science, transcendental, and, furthermore, it is nothing other than our own consciousness in its simplest form. This most simple, fundamental state of consciousness is simultaneously three and one, because it contains within itself the knower, the known, and the object of knowledge.[16]

At the most primordial level of creation, then, we encounter the paradox of being one while being three. Vedic Science states that pure consciousness, with its three-in-one structure, is infinite and unbounded. In the *Bhagavad Gita*, a basic text of Vedic Science, Krishna explains to Arjuna the infinite reality of pure consciousness:

> Know That to be indeed indestructible
> by which all this is pervaded. None
> can work the destruction of this
> immutable Being.
> These bodies are known to have an end;
> the dweller in the body is eternal,
> imperishable, infinite.
>
> (Maharishi 1969, 96–97)

The entire material universe arises by means of the self-referral process that takes place within this infinite state of Being or consciousness. Pure consciousness "emerges from within its own self-referral performance, which is going on eternally at the unmanifest basis of all creation," and this is how "creation comes out . . . consciousness becomes matter," and "expresses itself in innumerable, divergent ways" (Maharishi 1986, 26).

The phrase "innumerable, divergent ways," used to describe the universe that comes out of consciousness, cannot help but recall the labyrinth motif. Schopenhauer declares that the material universe *is* a "labyrinth" of "beginningless and endless causal series, inscrutable fundamental forces, endless space, beginningless time, infinite divisibility of matter" (II 177). Like the symbol of the double axe at the center of the labyrinth at Knossos, and like the paradoxes that are central to *La vida es sueño*, consciousness is the eternal center and origin of the ever-changing phenomenal world.

The phenomenal or material world, according to Vedic Science, is not substantial, but rather an appearance which arises through the principle of *maya*.[17] In the *Gita*, Krishna expounds this idea:

> The unreal has no being; the real
> never ceases to be. The final truth
> about them both has thus been perceived
> by the seers of ultimate Reality.
>
> (Maharishi 1969, 95)

The concept of *maya* closely parallels the notion of life as a dream and the labyrinth of illusion that we find in *La vida es sueño*. At the center of this labyrinth of illusion, we discover the never-changing reality of pure consciousness, the "ultimate Reality," with its three-in-one structure, other names for which are Being or the Self.

The paradoxes found in *La vida es sueño* may be interpreted as exemplifying the primordial paradox of consciousness that is both three and one, a paradox which lies at the very center[18] of the universe, that labyrinth of illusion created by the principle of *maya*. It is for this reason that paradox may be taken as a sign of the infinite subjective wholeness of life, consciousness, as Borges does in the passage on Novalis. Like Segismundo, one may forget the unbounded and infinite wholeness of the Self and become lost in the labyrinth, which is perhaps what the mind's bewilderment when confronted with any paradox expresses.

The individual who has forgotten his or her unbounded status can, according to Vedic Science, remember it by means of specific techniques.[19] In *La vida es sueño*, Segismundo comes to a point where such a realization, although perhaps not actually achieved, is clearly desired "acudamos a lo eterno" (2982 "Let us reach for that which is eternal").

The changing, phenomenal world to which Segismundo alludes (2973–81) before referring to the eternal is the field of *maya* in which the mind becomes lost, like Daedalus in his own labyrinth. The way out of the labyrinth, a way alluded to by Segismundo, is to transcend the finite boundaries of time and space. Like Daedalus, whose flight symbolizes a transcendence of the pairs of opposites in order to attain a wholeness that is more than the sum of its parts, Segismundo desires to transcend the finite boundaries of creation in order to recover his eternal and infinite wholeness. He may then enjoy the boundaries of life while simultaneously living the infinite reality of the Self. The fulfillment of the desire to live this reality, a desire expressed by Segismundo, is the principal aim and purpose of Vedic knowledge.[20]

The double axe, as we have noted, has been associated with the god Zeus. The axe was in general a divine image in the ancient world. John T. Irwin speculates that the sacred axe was linked to Zeus because of its association with lightning: "an ancient image of the lightning bolt, derived no doubt from the splitting of trees by lightning during thunderstorms, was that of a fiery celestial axe, Zeus's axe" (260). The axe also "evokes Zeus in his role of originator of the human race" (Irwin 267). Irwin suggests a connection between Zeus as the wielder of the axe and Plato's account of how the god split in half an original hermaphroditic race of spherical beings, with the result that the two sexes thus formed long to fuse themselves back into the primordial unity from which they came (261–62).

The motif of paradox as a sacred double axe inscribed throughout the labyrinth, when linked to Plato's account of the androgynous origins of the human race, finds a resonance in *La vida es sueño*. Rosaura assumes, as we have said, an androgynous quality which symbolizes transcendence of the pairs of opposites and a restoration of "the initial completeness, the intact source of holiness and power" (Eliade 1969, 113). De Armas has demonstrated that Rosaura represents Astraea, the goddess who heralds the coming of a Golden Age (1986, 100), a mythical time such as that evoked by the image of Daedalus's invention of flight: "the power of flight extended to all men in the mythical age; all could reach heaven" (Eliade 1972, 479). (In terms of the mythology of the labyrinth, we would associate Rosaura with Ariadne, the daughter of Minos, a very important character in the story, for it was she who gave Theseus the clew, or ball of thread, which allowed him to find his way out of the labyrinth.) The name of the Minotaur, Asterion, and that of Astraea, come from the same root as the Spanish *astro*, or star, thus indicating a common heavenly or divine origin. Their common source evokes the same unified wholeness represented by Rosaura's androgyny and echoes Plato's account of the primordial hermaphroditic unity of the human race, a primordial state that also represents an original Golden Age. Segismundo in this particular mythical scenario, stands for the god Zeus/Jupiter (de Armas 1986, 98), who, according to Plato, split apart the original wholeness. As we have noted, Segismundo already has a double identity as Theseus *and* the Minotaur, representing both the usurping hero and the bull/ king-god, who was ritually slain and reborn periodically in order to restore the primordial or mythical time of beginnings.

Throughout this mythical labyrinth of correspondences, we find the sign of the paradox, just as throughout the labyrinth at Knossos, Evans discovered the sign of the double axe. Segismundo is both father (Zeus) and son (Minotaur). As Zeus, he is both creator of the human race and destroyer of the primordial wholeness of the Golden Age. He is both hero (Theseus) and monster. Rosaura is both man and woman, and the paradox of androgyny is repeated in the identity of Asterion/Astrea (Segismundo/Rosaura). If our interpretation of paradox, suggested by Borges and Maharishi's Vedic Science, is correct, these paradoxes and numerous others in *La vida es sueño* are marks signaling the unbounded wholeness of an infinite subjective reality that contains the primordial paradox of being three while being one. From this original unity-totality of consciousness emerges the illusory labyrinth of the world, as well as that of the dramatic text, a world and a text in which the paradoxes are inscribed. Like Daedalus, who escaped from the labyrinth by flying, the paradoxes in *La vida es sueño*, paradoxes that unify opposing, relative values, imply the possibility of transcendence, that is to say, the possibility of escape from the labyrinth.

Notes

1. In his review of *The Prison and the Labyrinth*, Parker criticizes Edwards for the latter's overly imaginative interpretations of the plays, as well as for what Parker deems Edwards's mistaken reference to the labyrinth as a symbol, rather than as a metaphor or an image (1982a 340–43). Parker's remarks do, however, fully support the idea of the centrality and importance of the theme of the "wildness of human passion unrestrained by reason or civilization" (1982a 342).

2. Another way in which Parker alludes to the mythology of the labyrinth is that he calls the "Tower Myth" a *clue*, a word that derives from Cretan mythology, the *clew* being the ball of thread Ariadne gave to Theseus to enable him to successfully escape from the Labyrinth after he had slain the Minotaur. And, later in his article, Parker speaks of how Calderón "sought to unravel the tangled skeins of human motives, above all the problem of guilt and responsibility, with the wider problem of free-will" (1982b, 251), thus repeating, albeit subconsciously, an image, that of the *clew* or *skein*, closely connected to the mythology of the labyrinth, but also simultaneously suggesting his own predominantly Christian viewpoint.

3. Herodotus, although known for his poetical embellishments, provides a description that agrees in essence with that of other ancient sources:

"I found it," he says, "greater than words could tell, for although the temple at Ephesus and that at Samos are celebrated works, yet all of the works and buildings of the Greeks put together would certainly be inferior to this labyrinth as regards labour and expense." Even the pyramids, he tells us, were surpassed by the Labyrinth. (Matthews 7)

4. Deedes speculates that Theseus's,

object in slaying the Cretan Minotaur may not have been altogether altruistic. Besides freeing Athens from its grim tribute to Crete, he, as the usurper of the throne, performed the act of the ritual killing of the king. But, according to the myth, he preserved the goddess [Ariadne] and her dance. By so doing he would gain her support, and by marriage with her would confirm his title to the throne. (29–30)

In *La vida es sueño,* Ariadne would seem to correspond most closely to Rosaura.

5. De Armas notes this parallel: "King Minos had the labyrinth built to hide his offspring just as in Poland, Basilio incarcerates his son in a tower" (113).

6. It is just such a universal, mythical significance that Parker explicitly states he is seeking to reveal in the play by means of his Christian interpretation of Segismundo's tower (Parker 249). Parker's intuition that such an exalted mythical level of meaning is present in the play was undoubtedly correct, but his almost exclusive reliance on Christian mythology limits the possible extent of that meaning. Indeed, Daniel L. Heiple makes an excellent case for disassociating the play almost entirely from Christianity: "Although a number of critics in the past have assumed the play is a religious work, there are in fact few references to the deity (mostly in oaths). The other references to Christianity are minimal . . ." (1993a, 123).

7. In Calderón's time too, there was an established tradition of associating the labyrinth with both the irrational element of life (the passions) *and* with the intellect (Matthews 177–78).

8. All etymologies are from *Webster's New World Dictionary,* unless otherwise noted.

9. See, for example, verses 143–52.

10. Within the context of the topic of transcendence, it is of interest to note a possible interpretation of the meaning of the word *paradox.* One of the meanings of *para* in ancient Greek was *beyond,* and one of the meanings of *doxos* was *thought. Paradox,* therefore, could be construed as *a going beyond or transcending of thought* (I would like to thank Dr. John Flodstrom of the University of Louisville Department of Philosophy for providing me with the foregoing etymological information).

11. Borges, well versed in matters concerning the labyrinth, alludes to the association of the sacred double axe and the Minotaur in his story, "La casa de Asterión," ("The House of Asterion") where he twice mentions "el templo de las Hachas" ("The temple of the [double] axe)" (1971a, 70,71). And, in the section on the Minotaur in his *Libro de los seres imaginarios (The Book of Imaginary Beings),* he also refers to the double axe and its connection with the etymology of the word *labyrinth* (143).

12. J. Hillis Miller refers to "Death and the Compass," as "this narrative of the dectective's self-destruction through his own perspicacity" (321).

13. The relationship between paradox and infinity is a well-established fact (Moore 1–13).

14. Because paradox is thus a sign of both confinement *and* liberation, it may be said, although seemingly a tautology, that paradox is a paradox.

15. The parallel between the transcendental idealism of Borges and Schopenhauer and Maharishi's emphasis on pure consciousness as the ultimate constituent of the material universe can be glimpsed in Maharishi's assertion that, "The reality that the universe is the observer himself is the reality of the total disclosure of consciousness; it is the total potential of consciousness; it is the total reality of consciousness" (1994, 54).

16. Maharishi states: "Consciousness is that which is conscious of itself. Being conscious of itself, consciousness is the knower of itself. Being the knower of itself, consciousness is both the knower and the known. Being both knower and known, consciousness is also the process of knowing. Thus consciousness has three qualities within its self-referral singularity—the qualities of knower, knowing, and known—the three qualities of 'subject' (knower), 'object' (known), and the relationship between the subject and object (process of knowing)" (1994, 53).

17. Maharishi explains: "The influence of maya may be understood by the example of sap appearing as a tree. Every fibre of the tree is nothing but the sap. Sap, while remaining sap, appears as the tree. Likewise, through the influence of maya, Brahman [one unbounded ocean of consciousness], remaining Brahman, appears as the manifested world" (Brackets are mine) (1969, 491–92).

18. This *center* is found everywhere. The *Upanishads* say that pure consciousness or Being is all-pervading and omnipresent (Maharishi 1966, 35).

19. Maharishi states: "Vedic Science . . . includes the procedures for gaining this knowledge of the ultimate self-referral unity, which underlies the whole creation . . ." (1986, 26). Maharishi's Transcendental Meditation, which is a fundamental part of his Vedic Science, is a specific technique for transcending thought (Maharishi 1969, 470–71).

20. Maharishi explains: "The omnipresence of eternal Being; Its status as That, even in the manifested diversity of creation; and the possibility of the realization of Being by any man in terms of himself—-these are the great truths of the perennial philosophy of the Vedas" (1969, 9).

Versions of Christian Truth in Calderón's Orpheus *Autos*

Daniel L. Heiple

Undoubtedly the material available for religious allegories was somewhat limited, which explains the practice Lope de Vega developed and Calderón followed of converting popular *comedias* into sacred allegorical *autos sacramentales* (allegorical plays). Curiously, the plays they chose to transform were not only their most popular plays, such as Calderón's *La vida es sueño* (*Life is a Dream*) but also plays that seem rather inappropriate, such as honor plays involving wife murder.[1] On other occasions they chose, in spite of the condemnations by patristic writers, classical mythology as the plot for their allegorical dramas. In a recent article, Barbara Kurz has argued that Calderón presents in his later mythological *autos* the argument that the myths contain hidden Christian truths. In this paper I wish to contrast the intellectual differences concerning the interpretation of mythology in the two Orpheus *autos*, both titled *El divino Orfeo*,[2] by Calderón, showing that the earlier play (written perhaps in the 1630s or 1640s)[3] presents an older type of allegory that is completely superseded by the idea that myth is a type of Christian revelation in the play from 1663.[4]

Even though the rise of Christianity was accompanied by a full-scale diatribe against pagan religious practices and the popular gods of mythology, Christian exegetical traditions achieved a certain degree of syncretism with pagan mythology even among the early patristic writers. Modern scholars recognize that popular elements of religious practices from the myths and pagan art and ritual were incorporated into Christian ritual and iconology,[5] but equally important was an intellectual tradition that saw the pagan myths as veils for hiding elements of Christian revelation. The idea of moralizing the works of the pagan poets and the myths they told, either for didactic purposes as in Lactantius, Boethius, and Marianus Capella, or for Christian didactic purposes as in Isidore of Seville or Rhabanus Maurus, dates from late antiquity.

The full revival of an interest in the stories of the pagan myths, however, does not occur until the fourteenth century when the writings of Pierre Bersuire and Boccaccio set out methods of establishing Christian allegory for the mythological deities. The famous *Ovidius moralizatus* (*Ovid Moralized*)[6] of Pierre Bersuire (Berchorius in Latin, d. 1362), French Benedictine monk and friend of Petrarch, collects the stories of the myths from Ovid and supplies moral allegories that could easily have served as material for preachers. Each myth has several complete allegorical interpretations, and curiously, as in the manner of Biblical exegeses, the moralizations are not interrelated from one allegory to the next, so that the mythical character that is the devil in one allegory can serve as the Christ figure in the next. Bersuire begins his book by explaining the value of myths in moral teaching, quoting St. Paul to the effect that people turn their hearing from truth to fables (Ghisalberti 87). He states that he will limit his allegories to natural or historical truths, but then he defends the practice of extracting other truths from pagan myths:

> Licitum est enim quod homo, si possit, de spinis vuas colligat: mel de petra sugat: oleumque de saxo durissimo sibi sumat sibi: et de thesauris aegyptiorum tabernaculum federis edificet et componat sicut etiam & Ouidius dicit. (Berchorius 1960, 4)

> [It is licit for one, if he can, to gather grapes from the thorns, to take honey from cliffs and to take for oneself oil from hard stone, and to construct and compose from the storehouses of Egypt the tabernacle of faith just as Ovid also says.]

In the last example he refers to the Biblical passage made famous by Saint Augustine who quoted it in his arguments for the necessity of providing allegorical interpretations for certain Biblical passages that contained odious moral implications, in this case thievery, or employing pagan myth in Christian exegesis (See Augustine 1958, xiii and 75).

Bersuire's younger contemporary, Giovanni Boccaccio (1313–1375) first suggests that these myths may have more substance. Books XIV and XV form a kind of appendix to his *Genelogia deorum gentilium* in which he justifies the study of pagan mythology. In Chapter 8 of Book XV titled "The Pagan Poets of Mythology are Theologians," he advances proofs that the poets are not liars and that there is meaning beneath the fictions of the myths. He also claims they are properly called theologians, but he also limits their theological insights to physical and moral truths, and like

Bersuire he specifically denies that they had access to Christian truths.

In fifteenth-century Florence, the great center of Platonic studies and magical mysticism, the study of pagan mythology took on a new significance. The Neoplatonic philosophers began to view the myths as veiled revelations of Christian truth. D. C. Allen and D. P. Walker (1953) have explained how Renaissance thinkers came to argue for a syncretism, claiming that the pagan philosophers had studied in Egypt with Moses and had gained access to knowledge of the forthcoming revelation. Renaissance Neoplatonists labeled these pagan works a *prisca theologia* [ancient theology] and argued that the writers veiled their revelations in fables and myths because they were convinced the pagans would have been blinded by and perhaps despised the full truth had it been presented without the veil of myth (Walker 1953, 105–6).

The Spanish Dominican Juan de Pineda in his *Diálogos familiares de la agricultura cristiana* (1589) made these ideas clear, explaining that the pagans veiled their truths with myths "porque . . . el vulgo no menopreciase la verdadera doctrina hallándola en descubierto y con facilidad" (I, 72b) [so that . . . the common people would not spurn the true doctrine finding it revealed and in easy grasp]. He argued that the myths are "enigmas o símbolos o parábolas escuras, que encubren muy otras cosas de lo que se representa en la corteza de la letra" (I, 72a) [dark enigmas or symbols or parables, which enclose things very different from what is represented by the husk of the letter] and provided a way of veiling the divine truths in fables or myths. He maintained that "los poetas inventaron el lenguaje falso para persuadir la doctrina verdadera" (I, 72b) [the poets invented a false language in order to persuade with it true doctrine]. This syncretism by a Spanish religious shows the widespread diffusion of these ideas during the Renaissance.[7]

The figure of Orpheus in particular as a poet, writer, and prophet, became the focus of renewed interest. He was considered to be vital as the intermediary who transferred Moses's teachings to the Greeks. The series of arcane hymns attributed to him were interpreted as true, but purposefully confused, revelations of Christian truth. Juan de Pineda affirmed that poetry is older than philosophy and therefore

los poetas, por entonces, eran los sabios del mundo: y Homero y Hesíodo deben de ser los más antiguos entre los que han llegado a

nuestros tiempos, y ansí ellos son los mayores teólogos, con Orfeo.
(I, 71b)

[the poets, at that time, were the wise men of the world: and Homero
and Hesiod should be the oldest among those who have arrived to
our times, and so they are the greatest theologians, along with
Orpheus.]

This statement adds support for Walker's research into the Platonic fascination with Orpheus in the Renaissance (See Walker
1953, 105–6).

In a seminal article, Barbara Kurz has argued that Calderón's
mythological *autos* present a syncretist view regarding the validity
myth as Christian revelation. In her conclusion she states:

Given Calderón's oft-expressed attribution of pagan myths to divine
inspiration (in the Christian sense), he presumably regarded God as
the supreme and originary author of the myths, which in this vision
analogously acquire something of the status of Christian parable.
(Kurz 1988, 270a)

She does treat extensively *El divino Orfeo* of 1663 because of the
importance of its arguments, but does not treat the early play
because it contributes nothing to the idea she is describing.

In spite of the diffusion of the ideas of syncretism in Spain as
seen in the writings of Juan de Pineda, Spanish allegorical literature tended to present religious allegory as simple metaphor
without the argument for the myth itself representing a distorted
version of the basic truth of Christian revelation. Calderón's two
autos sacramentales, both titled *El divino Orfeo*, actually form part
of a long tradition of works that construct Christian allegories out
of the Orpheus myth.[8] The association of Orpheus and Christ
dates from the early Christian iconological traditions where Orpheus among the animals represents Christ the good shepherd
(Friedman 1970, 38–85). The plot in both versions of Calderón's
Orpheus plays is remarkably similar. In both plays Orpheus is
Christ, Eurydice is the allegorical figure of Human Nature, and
the shepherd Aristaeus who pursues and corrupts her is the devil
who induces Eve to taste the forbidden fruit. The etymology of
Aristeo as meaning "gran príncipe" [great prince] fits with the
Spanish dramatic tradition in which nobles often seek refuge in
the disguises of shepherds.[9] Both plays treat the creation of the
world by Orpheus's golden voice, the marriage of Orpheus and
Eurydice as the marriage of Christ and Human Nature. The bite

of the serpent that kills Eurydice is the evil that causes the Fall of Human Nature is the serpent who tempts Eve in the garden of Eden. And Orpheus's descent into the underworld is Christ's incarnation and sacrifice to redeem fallen human nature. Just as David's harp in Christian exegetes is a figure for Christ's cross Orpheus's lyre becomes the cross in both plays.

In spite of the similarities of plot, the two plays are actually quite different in their treatment of allegorical mythology, and each approaches mythological exegesis from completely distinct methodological models. The early *El divino Orfeo,* like the allegories of the medieval writer Pierre Bersuire, presents a type of allegory that tends to employ allegory consciously as a metaphor for religious truths. Like the very popular poetry "a lo divino" [in the divine manner], which clearly does not pretend that the metaphor is anything other than a metaphor, the early Orpheus *auto* approaches the myth as an entertaining way to convert the profane and secular into holy truth through simple allegorical transformation of the profane myth into a sacred parable.

The early play tends to concentrate on the essential correspondences between the Orpheus myth and the sacred narrative, such as Orpheus's divine powers and his marriage, loss and redemption of Eurydice as representing the creation, fall, and redemption of human beings by God and Christ. In the early play there are several scenes that Calderón either expanded or suppressed in the later play. Orpheus's creation of the universe in the early play takes about fifty lines, and while the poetry is impressive, the drama of such an undertaking pales in the short descriptive passage. In the 1663 play, each of the days of creation are allegorical figures who awaken at the sound of Orpheus's golden voice. Thus, Calderón's firmer dramatic sense makes the creation achieve a dramatic intensity in the later play that is mostly lacking in the early version. The playwright seems also to have had doubts about the presentation of profane love as sacred mysticism. In the early play, after Orfeo and Eurydice marry, they retire to their pastoral cabin for spiritual lovemaking:

> Sube, a mi cavaña, en ella,
> con las sombras te combida
> la siesta; para el rigor,
> del sol, dulze esposa mia
> en mis brazos.

(III. 1822b)

[Come up to my cabin, in it for the afternoon with its shadows invites you against the rigor of the sun, my sweet wife, in my arms.]

This imagery is typical of the way that the Song of Songs and Spanish mystic poets and playwrights employed allegories of marriage and sensual love to represent divine love in secular terms. This scene is completely suppressed in the later play where the two figures retire to their separate carts. This new sense of propriety and decorum seems to break with the type of allegory favored by Lope de Vega in his *autos*, where profane love always serves as a metaphor for divine love. At the end of the early play, Calderón signs off calling the *auto* "el moralizado Orfeo" (III, 1834b), recalling the title and style of Bersuire's *Ovidius moralizatus*, making the play an allegory for the purpose of edification of the faithful, but having no actual reference to the possible validity of the myth as Christian truth. The plot of the first *El divino Orfeo* employs the Orpheus myth as an allegory of Christian revelation, that is, the myth exists as a story parallel to the Biblical narration of the creation, fall and redemption that makes an interesting method of dramatizing the well-known myth in order to reveal through allegorical references the Christian message of the Fall and Redemption of humankind through Christ's sacrifice.

Calderón's second version of *El divino Orfeo*, however, does argue specifically that pagan myths have a grounding in Christian revelation. Calderón begins the defense of mythology in the *loa* where the same arguments concerning mythology that are dramatized in the *auto* are presented in a symbolic fashion. The *loa* is a competition between divine and human letters, a distinction refers to the division of ancient writings into Christian writings, the Church fathers, and pagan writings, the human letters. In the *loa*, eleven characters (five women, "damas," five young men, "galanes," and one old man, "un viejo venerable")[10] enter carrying placards with letters on them in a jumbled order, spelling the nonsense word EAVICTHSAIR. The characters then dance, and when they stop their letters spell the word EUCHARISTIA [eucharist], the key element in the celebrations of Corpus Christi. They dance again, and when they stop the letters spell CITHARA IESU [the lyre of Jesus], resulting in the symbolic transference of Orpheus's mythical lyre to a figure of Christian redemption.

Calderón has Dama 4ª, whose letter S stands for sabiduría [wisdom], explain the meaning of the conjunction of the divine and human letters:

> Y así, el Asunto del Auto
> hallado en Humanas Letras
> es la *Fábula de Orpheo*,
> alegorizado a esta
> universal Redención,
> atento a la consecuencia
> de que en ella su Papel
> también la *Cíthara* tenga,
> pues *Cíthara de Jesús*
> es la Cruz.
>
> (1839a)

[And so, the plot[11] of the *Auto* found in Human Letters is the *Fable of Orpheus*, allegorized to this universal Redemption, paying attention to the consequences that in it the *Lyre* also has its role, for the *Lyre of Jesús* is the Cross.]

Orpheus's lyre is a type or figure foreshadowing the appearance of the cross, just as David's lyre was interpreted as a figure of the cross. In the second version of *El divino Orfeo* Calderón carries association much further than in the first version. The *clavijas* [frets] of the lyre become the *clavos* of the crucifixion, and the strings become the whips with which Christ was beaten (1852a). In spite of the fact Juan de Pineda drew the line at typology, claiming it was a figure reserved to God alone: "y para siempre nunca usó del tipo o figura, por ser éste reservado a solo Dios, que como El solo sabe los futuros contingentes, ansí El solo lo puede debujar antes que venga" (I,73a) [and he never, never made use of the type or figure, because this is reserved only to God, for as He alone knows future contingencies, so He alone can draw it before it comes]. Typology, in which persons and things in the Old Testament are figures or types that foreshadow events in the New Testament, was the most important type of textual figure that Christians adapted from the Jewish exegesis (Grant 28–38).

The *auto* proper also incorporates important arguments concerning the correspondences of myth and scripture. When the devil figure, El Príncipe de las Tinieblas [the Prince of Darkness], and his handmaiden Envidia [Envy] arrive on the island of Thrace, El Placer [pleasure] decides to entertain them with a fable describing Orpheus's creation of Eurydice (1846b). After he has finished the fable, Envidia asks why El Príncipe has remained preoccupied, and he replies "De que este villano crea / que con la verdad me engaña" (1847b) [that this rustic believes he can deceive me with the truth]. Envidia is surprised this fable could be true, but El Príncipe explains to her:

> La Gentilidad, Envidia,
> idolatramente ciega,
> teniendo de las verdades
> lejanas noticias, piensa
> que [a] falsos dioses y ninfas
> atribuya las Inmensas
> Obras de un Dios solo; y como
> sin Luz de fe andan a ciegas,
> hará con las ignorancias
> sospechosas las creencias.
> ¡Cuántas veces se verán
> los Poetas y Profetas
> acordes, donde se rocen
> verdades en Sombra envueltas[!]
>
> (1847b)

[The Gentiles, Envy, idolatrously blind, having distant news of truths, believe they can attribute to false gods and nymphs the Immense Works of one single God; and since they go blindly without the light of Faith, they will with their ignorance make the true beliefs suspicious. How many times will the Poets and Prophets be seen in accordance, where truths enclosed in shadow rub together[!]

He supplies a brief example of how the fall of Phaeton represents a veiled version of his own fall from grace. He argues that the possibilities of such interpretations are endless:

> Y de esta misma manera
> habrá infinitos Lugares
> que por repetidos deja
> mi voz, en que se confronten
> Divinas y Humanas Letras
> en la consonancia amigas
> y en la Religión opuestas.
>
> (1847b)

[And in this way there will be infinite passages, which I will not repeat, in which Human and Divine Letters are confronted, friends in consonance and opposite in Religion.]

El Príncipe also provides further examples of the veiled truths found in pagan literature. He explains that God should be thought of as a musician, making the Orpheus story a veiling of the truth that God is the musical consonance of the world, and the fable related by El Placer makes Orpheus's wife human nature loved by Christ and his descent to the underworld to save her from condemnation Christ's incarnation and crucifixion to save unredeemed humanity. In this way the Orpheus story, having its source in pagan literature, comes to be a veiled fable or parable of the divine plan for the redemption of humanity exiled from paradise because of original sin.

The writings conflating mythology and theology by the early syncretists and their Renaissance followers provided an original and interesting conception of mythology that Calderón came to understand and exploit in his allegorical religious dramas, where the pagan myths take on new meanings of Christian revelation that has been purposely veiled and garbled to protect the divine truths from easy access to an unprepared population.[12]

NOTES

1. Lope's *La locura por la honra* (*Madness Due to Honor*) and Calderón's *El pintor de su deshonra* (*The Painter of his Dishonor*) are both examples of honor plays involving wife murder.

2. Most critics are in agreement that both *autos* are by Calderón. Professor Parker pointed out to me that there are significant parallels between the early *El divino Orfeo* and Calderón's *El veneno y la triaca* (*Poison and Remedy*) which he believed clinched the argument for Calderón's authorship.

3. Pedro León gives the tentative date of ca. 1634. (See León 1982 and 1983, and Calderón 1990). Since the devil figure is not accompanied in this *auto*, this date would not conflict with Parker's observation that the devil in Calderón's later *autos* is always accompanied by a sin. He placed the change around 1638 (Parker 1958, 9).

4. I first wrote a version of this paper that Professor Parker read and commented in 1976 and I presented a version of this paper at the Congreso Internacional en Honor a Don Pedro Calderón de la Barca in Lincoln, Nebraska, on October 16, 1981.

5. In chapter 3, "Orpheus-Christus in the Art of Late Antiquity," Friedman (1970 38–85) summarizes the use of Orpheus iconology to represent Christ as the Good Shepherd in the art of the catacombs and the subsequent identification of the two figures.

6. This work should not be confused with *Ovide Moralisé* (*Ovid Moralized*) a long poem in French that Bersuire came to know and use in the third and final revision of his own work (Friedman 1970, 126–32).

7. Don Cameron Allen (1970) fully documents the Renaissance reading habits that were accustomed to find Christian truths in all pagan myth.

8. "Desta suerte el sapientísimo Clemente Alejandrino, basta decir que fue maestro de Orígenes, acomoda, a Cristo Señor Nuestro en la Cruz, la antigua fábula de Orfeo, aquel que con la armonía de su lira atraía los montes, paraba los ríos, arrancaba los árboles, suspendía las fieras y todo lo atraía a sí. El

verdadero Orfeo es aquel señor, que teniendo estirados sus sagrados miembros en la lira de la cruz, con aquellas clavijas de los duros clavos, hizo tan dulce y suave armonía que atrajo a sí todas las cosas: *Si exaltatus fuero a terra omnia traham ad me ipsum"* (Gracián 493b).

9. The etymology of Aristaeus's name always allowed medieval writers to support their misogyny by claiming that Eurydice was the cause of Orpheus's failure. Boethius first offered an interpretation of the Orpheus myth that approaches moralizing and presents Eurydice in this light. In meter XII of the Third Book of his *Consolation of Philosophy* he presents Orpheus as the Platonic seeker of divine truth whose love for Eurydice impedes his progress and his final backward glance is fatal to his philosophic pursuit (Friedman 107). For William of Conches, Orpheus is the highest voice and Eurydice is natural concupiscence (Friedman 107).

10. I argue in a recent study (Heiple, 1997) that the placement of these figures and the meaning of the letters they carry present a visual effect that has theological significance.

11. Usually "asunto" is considered to be the theme and "argumento" the plot, following Calderón's distinction in the prologue to the 1677 edition of his *autos*. See Parker (1968), pp. 59–60.

12. Parker was of the opinion that *El divino Orfeo* of 1663 was extremely beautiful, but offered no profundity of thought:

> Much later Calderón was to produce a still more lovely allegory in *El divino Orfeo* (1663), an *auto* poetically so lovely that after the first reading one is tempted to rank it as the finest of all. But when analyzed, its appeal is seen to reside only in the poignant delicacy with which Calderón is able to exploit the charm of the myth. Here too the allegory is acceptable as a pleasing analogy of the dogmas, but it is little more; dogma is presented in terms of a myth and no new or special significance is extracted." (Parker 1968, 200)

One could argue that the interpretation of the validity of pagan mythology might consititute the type of "new or special significance" that he was searching for.

Works Cited

Albrecht, Jane White. 1994. *Irony and Theatricality in Tirso de Molina*. Ottawa: Dovehouse Editions.

Alciati, Andreae. 1577. *Omnia emblemata*. Antwerp: C. Plantini.

Allen, Don Cameron. 1970. *Mysteriously Meant. The Rediscovery of Pagan Symbolism and Allegorical Interpretation in the Renaissance*. Baltimore: Johns Hopkins Press.

Ames, Debra C. 1989. "Phaethon's Second Fall: Lope's Burlesque Treatment of the Myth in *La villana de Getafe*." *Romance Languages Annual* 1: 361–65.

Aragone Terni, Elisa. 1970. *Studio sulle comedias de santos di Lope de Vega*. Florence: Cassa Editrice d'Anna.

Augustine. 1854 rpt. *De Genesi ad litteram*, in vol. 28 of *Corpus Scriptorum Ecclesiasticorum Latinorum*, edited by Josephus Sicla. Prague: F. Tempske.

———. 1958. *On Christian Doctrine*. Translated by D. W. Robertson. New York: Bobbs-Merrill.

Austin, Norman. 1990. *Meaning and Being in Myth*. University Park: Pennsylvania State University Press.

Barkan, Leonard. 1975. *Nature's Work of Art: The Human Body as Image of the World*. New Haven: Yale University Press.

———. 1980. "Diana and Actaeon: The Myth as Synthesis." *English Literary Renaissance* 10.1 (Winter 1980): 317–59.

———. 1986. *The Gods Made Flesh: Metamorphosis and the Pursuit of Paganism*. New Haven: Yale University Press.

Barnard, Mary E. 1984. "Myth in Quevedo: The Serious and the Burlesque in the Apollo and Daphne Poems." *Hispanic Review* 52: 499–522.

———. 1987. *The Myth of Apollo and Daphne from Ovid to Quevedo: Love, Agon, and the Grotesque*. Durham, NC: Duke University Press.

Barrera, Cayetano de la. 1860. *Catálogo bibliográfico y biográfico del teatro antiguo español*, Madrid: Rivadeneyra, Facsimile Ed. 1969. Madrid: Gredos.

Bate, Jonathan. 1993. *Shakespeare and Ovid*. Oxford: Clarendon.

Bentley, Eric (Editor), and Roy Campbell (Translator). 1959. *Life is a Dream and Other Spanish Classics*. New York: Applause Theatre Book Publishers.

Berchorius, Petrus [Pierre Bersuire]. 1960. *De formis figurisque Deorum*. Utrecht: Institut voor Laat Latijn der Rijkunstversiteit.

Blue, William R. 1990. "Desire and the Supplement in *La Estatua de Prometeo*." *Bulletin of the Comediantes* 42. 35–52.

Boccaccio, [Giovanni]. 1956. *Boccaccio on Poetry*. Translated by Charles Osgood. New York: Bobbs-Merrill.

Borges, Jorge Luis. 1964a. "Avatares de la tortuga," in *Discusión*, 129–136. Buenos Aires: Emecé.

———. 1964b. "La perpetua carrera de Aquiles y la tortuga," in *Discusión*, 113–20. Buenos Aires: Emecé.

———. 1971a. "La casa de Asterión," in *El Aleph*, 69–72. Madrid: Alianza Editorial.

———. 1971b. "La muerte y la brújula," in *Ficciones*, 147–63. Madrid: Alianza Editorial.

Borges, Jorge Luis, with Margarita Guerrero. 1978. *El libro de los seres imaginarios.* Buenos Aires: Emecé.

Bulfinch's Mythology. 1979. New York: Gramercy Books.

Bullough, Vern L., and Bonnie Bullough. 1993. *Crossdressing, Sex and Gender.* Philadelphia: University of Pennsylvania Press.

Bourassé, Jean Jacques. 1866. *Summa aurea de laudibus Beatissimae Virginis Mariae,* Paris: Migne.

Bravo Villasante, Carmen. 1955. *La mujer vestida de hombre en el teatro español.* Madrid: Revista de Occidente.

Burke, James. 1974. "The *Estrella de Sevilla* and the Tradition of Saturnine Melancholy," *Bulletin of Hispanic Studies* 51: 137–56.

———. 1975. "Dramatic Resolution in *La verdad sospechosa.*" *Renaissance and Reformation* 11: 52–59.

———. 1986. "The 'Banquet of Sense' in *La verdad sospechosa,*" in *Hispanic Studies in Honor of Alan D. Deyermond. A North American Tribute,* 51–56. Edited by John S. Miletich. Madison: University of Wisconsin Press.

Burrow, J. A. 1988. *The Ages of Man. A Study of Medieval Writing and Thought.* Oxford: Clarendon Press.

Butler, Bill. 1975. *Dictionary of the Tarot.* New York: Schocken Books.

Calderón de la Barca, Pedro. 1957. *Obras completas.* : Dramas vol. I. Edited by Ángel Valbuena Briones. Madrid: Aguilar. 2nd ed.

———. 1967. *Obras completas. Autos sacramentales.* Vol. III. Edited by Angel Valbuena Prat. Madrid: Aguilar.

———. 1969. *Obras completas: Dramas.* Vol. I. Edited by Ángel Valbuena Briones. Madrid: Aguilar. 5th ed.

———. 1981. *Celos aun del aire matan.* Edited with translation and notes by Matthew D. Stroud. San Antonio, TX: Trinity University Press.

———. 1984. *El alcalde de Zalamea.* Edited by Ángel Valbuena Briones. Madrid: Ediciones Cátedra, S. A.

———. 1986. *La estatua de Prometeo.* Edited by Margaret Greer. Kassel: Edition Reichenberger.

———. 1990. *Three Mythological Plays of Calderón.* Translated by Pedro León and John Warden. Toronto: University of Toronto.

———. 1992. *La vida es sueño.* Edited by Ciriaco Morón. Madrid: Cátedra.

Calvino, Italo. 1988. *Six Memos for the Next Millennium.* Cambridge: Harvard University Press.

Campbell, Joseph, with Bill Moyers. 1988. *The Power of Myth.* New York: Doubleday.

Canavaggio, Jean. 1987. *Cervantes.* Madrid: Espasa Calpe.

Capra, Fitjof. 1991. *The Tao of Physics*. Boston: Shambhala.

Caro Baroja, Julio. 1946. "¿Es de origen mítico la 'leyenda' de la Serrana de la Vera?" *Revista de dialectología y tradiciones populares* 2: 568–572.

Cervantes, Miguel de. 1983. *El ingenioso hidalgo Don Quijote de la Mancha*. Edited by John J. Allen. 5th ed. Madrid: Cátedra.

————. 1987. *Teatro completo*. Barcelona: Planeta.

Cirlot, J. E. 1962. *A Dictionary of Symbols*. Translated by Jack Sage. New York: Philosophical Library.

————. 1982. *Diccionario de símbolos*. Barcelona: Editorial Labor.

Cohen, Walter. 1985. *Drama of a Nation. Public Theater in Renaissance England and Spain*. Ithaca: Cornell University Press.

Conlon, Raymond. 1990. "The Burlador and the Burlados: A Sinister Connection." *Bulletin of the Comediantes* 42.1: 5–22.

Conti, Natale. 1988. *Mitología*. Edited and translated by Rosa María Iglesias Montiel and María Consuelo Alvarez Morán. Murcia: Universidad de Murcia.

Cossío, José María de. 1952. *Fábulas mitológicas en España*. Madrid: Espasa Calpe.

Covarrubias y Horozco, Sebastián de. 1987. *Tesoro de la lengua castellana o española*. Edited by Martín de Riquer. Barcelona: Alta Fulla.

Curtius, Ernst Robert. 1953. *European Literature and the Latin Middle Ages*. Translated by Willard R. Trask. Bollingen Series XXXVI. 1990; reprint, Princeton: Princeton University Press.

Daly, Peter M. 1979. *Literature in the Light of the Emblem. Structural Parallels between the Emblem and Literature in the 16th and 17th centuries*. Toronto: University of Toronto Press.

De Armas, Frederick A. 1982. "The Four Elements: Key to an Interpretation of Villamediana's Sonnets." *Hispanic Journal* 4.1: 61–79.

————. 1986. *The Return of Astraea. An Astral-Imperial Myth in Calderón*. Lexington: Kentucky University Press.

————. 1993. "El sol sale a media noche': amor y astrología en *Las paredes oyen*." *Criticón* 59: 119–26.

————. 1995. "Splitting Gemini: Plato, Girard and *La Estrella de Sevilla*." *Hispanófila* 37: 17–34.

————. 1996a. "The Burning at Ephesus: Cervantes and Ruiz de Alarcón's *La verdad sospechosa*," in *Studies in Honor of Gilberto Paolini*, 41–56. Edited by Mercedes Vidal Tibbits. Newark, DE: Juan de la Cuesta.

————. 1996b. "The Hermetic Raphael: Ekphrasis in Cervantes' *Don Quijote* and John Crowley's *Aegypt*." Seventeenth International Conference on the Fantastic in the Arts.

————. *Cervantes, Raphael and the Classics*. Cambridge: Cambridge University Press, 1998.

Deedes, C. N. 1935. "The Labyrinth," in *The Labyrinth. Further Studies in the Relation between Myth and Ritual in the Ancient World*, 1–42. Edited by S. H. Hooke. London: Society for Promoting Christian Knowledge.

Defourneaux, Marcelin. 1979. *Daily Life in Spain in the Golden Age*. Translated by Newton Branch. Stanford, CA: Stanford University Press.

Delpech, François. 1978. "La leyenda de la Serrana de la Vera: Las adaptaciones teatrales," in *La mujer en el teatro y la novela del siglo XVII*, 23–38. Toulouse: Institut D'Etudes Hispaniques et Hispano-Américaines.

Derrida, Jacques. 1981. *Dissemination.* Chicago: University of Chicago Press.

Deveraux, G. 1973. "The Self-Blinding of Oidipous in Sophokles' *Oidipous Tyrannus.*" *Journal of Hellenic Studies* 103: 36–49.

Dietz, Donald. T. 1973. *The Auto Sacramental and the Parable in Spanish Golden Age Literature.* North Carolina Studies in the Romance Languages and Literatures, No. 132. Chapel Hill: University of North Carolina.

Diez comedias del siglo de oro. 1939. Edited by José Martel and Hymen Alpern and revised by Leonard Mades. 1985; reprint, Prospect Heights, IL: Waveland Press.

Díez de Revenga, Francisco J. 1988. "Monarquía y mito en la España del Siglo de Oro: el anfiteatro de Felipe el Grande." In *El mito en el teatro clásico español.* Edited by Francisco Ruiz Ramón and César Oliva, 196–202, Madrid: Taurus.

DiLillo, Leonard M. 1973. "Moral Purpose in Ruiz de Alarcón's *La verdad sospechosa.*" *Hispania* 56: 254–59.

Doña Beatriz de Silva. Seventeenth century manuscript attributed to Tirso de Molina, number 16402 in the Biblioteca Nacional.

Doty, William G. 1986. *Mythography. The Study of Myths and Rituals.* University: University of Alabama Press.

Drinkwater, J. A. 1992. "*La serrana de la Vera* and the 'Mystifying Charms of Fiction'." *Forum for Modern Language Studies* 28:1, 75–85.

Ebersole, Alva V. 1966. *Juan Ruiz de Alarcón y Mendoza, Primera y segunda partes de las obras completas.* Madrid: Castalia.

Edwards, Gwynne. 1978. *The Prison and the Labyrinth: Studies in Calderonian Tragedy.* Cardiff: University of Wales Press.

———. 1984. "Calderón's *Los tres mayores prodigios* and *El pintor de su deshonra:* The Modernization of Ancient Myth." *Bulletin of Hispanic Studies* 61: 326–34.

Egido, Aurora. 1993. "Prólogo," in Alciato, *Emblemas.* Edited by Santiago Sebastián. Madrid: Akal: 7–17.

El mito en el teatro clásico español. 1988. Edited by Francisco Ruiz Ramón and César Oliva. Madrid: Taurus.

Eliade, Mircea. 1969. *The Two and the One.* Translated by J. M. Cohen. New York: Harper and Row.

———. 1972. *Shamanism, Archaic Techniques of Ecstasy.* Translated by Willard R. Trask. Princeton: Princeton University Press.

Eliot, T. S. 1950. "Hamlet and His Problems" in *The Sacred Wood: Essays on Poetry and Criticism.* London: Butler and Tanner Ltd. 7th ed. 95–103.

Elliot, J. H. 1970. *Imperial Spain: 1469–1716.* London: Penguin Books.

Else, Gerald F. 1986. *Plato and Aristotle on Poetry.* Chapel Hill: University of North Carolina Press.

Espantoso Foley, Augusta. 1972. *Occult Arts and Doctrine in the Theater of Juan Ruiz de Alarcón.* Geneva: Librairie Droz.

Espasa diccionario de la mitología griega y romana. 1996. Edited by René Martin. Madrid: Espasa Calpe.

Étienvre, Jean-Pierre. 1982. "Le Symbolisme de la Carte a Jouer Dans L'Espagne des XVI et XVII Siecles." in *Les jeux à la Renaissance.* Aries, Phillipe and Jean Claude Margolin, (Editors). Paris: Vrin.

———. 1990. *Márgenes literarios del juego: Una poética del naipe, siglos XVI–XVIII.* London: Tamesis Books Limited.

Exum, Frances. 1986. *Essays on Comedy and the "Gracioso" in Plays by Agustín Moreto*. York, SC: Spanish Literature Publications.

Feal Deibe, Carlos. 1984. "El *burlador* de Tirso: Demonio y víctima expiatoria," in *En nombre de don Juan: (Estructura de un mito literario)*, 9–34. Amsterdam-Philadelphia: John Benjamins.

Fernández de Mesa, Blas, 1996. *La fundadora de la Santa Concepción*. Edited by Nancy K. Mayberry. Ibérica 16. New York: Peter Lang.

Fiore, Robert L. 1977. "The Interaction of Motives and Mores in *La verdad sospechosa*." *Hispanófila* 61: 513–27.

Fothergill-Payne, Louise. 1971. "La justicia poética de *La verdad sospechosa*." *Romanische Forchungen* 83: 588–95.

Freccero, John. 1986. "The Fig Tree and the Laurel: Petrarch's Poetics," in *Literary Theory/Renaissance Texts*, 20–32. Edited by Patricia Parker and David Quint. Baltimore: Johns Hopkins University Press.

Friedman, John Block. 1970. *Orpheus in the Middle Ages*. Cambridge: Harvard University.

Gallego, Julián. 1991. *Visión y símbolos en la pintura española del Siglo de Oro*. Madrid: Cátedra.

Garcilaso de la Vega. 1981. *Obras completas con comentarios*. Edited by Elias L. Rivers. Madrid: Castalia.

Gaylord, Mary Malcolm. 1988. "The Telling Lies of *La verdad sospechosa*." *Modern Language Notes* 103.2: 223–28.

Ghisalberti, Fausto. 1933. *L'«Ovidius Moralizatus» di Pierre Bersuire*. Rome: Giuggiani.

Giles, Cynthia. 1992. *The Tarot: History, Mystery and Lore*. New York: Paragon House.

Góngora, Luis de. 1986. "Soledad primera," in *Antología poética*. Edited by Antonio Carreira. 203–44.

Gracián, Baltasar. 1967. *Agudeza y arte de ingenio. Obras completas*. Edited by Arturo de Hoyos. Madrid: Aguilar.

Grant, Robert M., and David Tracy. 1984. *A Short History of the Interpretation of the Bible*. Philadelphia: Fortress Press.

Graves, Robert. 1959. *The Larousse Encyclopedia of Mythology*. Paris: Librairie Larousse. Translated by Richard Arlington and Delano Ames. New York: Barnes and Noble, 1994.

———. 1992. *The Greek Myths*. London: Penguin Books.

Greer, Margaret. 1988. "The Play of Power: Calderón's *Fieras Afemina Amor* and *La estatua de Prometeo*." *Hispanic Review* 56: 319–41.

Gutiérrez, Enrique. 1988. *Santa Beatriz de Silva e Historia de la Orden de la Concepción en Toledo en sus primeros años (1484–1511)*. 3d ed. Burgos: Aldecoa.

Halevy, Z'ev ben Shimon. 1992. *Psychology and Kabbalah*. York Beach, MA: Samuel Weiser, Inc.

Halkhoree, P. R. K. 1989. *Social and Literary Satire in the Comedies of Tirso de Molina*. Edited by José M. Ruano de la Haza and Henry W. Sullivan. Ottawa: Dovehouse Editions.

Halstead, Frank G. 1943. "The Optics of Love: Notes on a Concept of Atomistic Philosophy in the Theater of Tirso de Molina." *PMLA* 58: 108–21.

Hamilton, Elizabeth. 1940. *Mythology. Timeless Tales of Gods and Heroes.* 1969; reprint, New York: New American.

Harrison, Jane Ellen. 1912. *Themis, A Study of the Social Origins of Greek Religion.* Cambridge: Cambridge University Press.

Hathorn, Richmond Y. 1977. *Greek Mythology.* Beirut: The American University of Beirut.

Haverbeck O., Erwin. 1975. *El tema mitológico en el teatro de Calderón.* Anejos de *Estudios Filológicos:* 6. Valdivia: Universidad Austral de Chile.

Heiple, Daniel L. 1989. "Profeminist Reaction to Huarte's Misogyny in Lope de Vega's *La prueba de los ingenios* (The Test of Wit) and María de Zayas's *Novelas amorosas y ejemplares.*" In *The Perception of Women in Spanish Theater of the Golden Age,* 121–34. Edited by Anita K. Stoll and Dawn L. Smith. Lewisburg, PA.: Bucknell University Press.

———. 1993a. "Life as Dream and the Philosophy of Disillusionment," in *The Prince in the Tower. Perceptions of La vida es sueño,* 118–31. Edited by Frederick A. De Armas. Lewisburg, PA.: Bucknell University Press.

———. 1993b. "The Two of Coins: An Unheeded Omen in El Buscón." *Crítica Hispánica* 15: 105–15.

———. 1997. "Staging Theology in a Calderonian *Loa*" in *The Calderonian Stage. Body and Soul,* 154–62. Edited by Manuel Delgado Morales. Lewisburg: Bucknell University Press.

Heninger, S. K. 1974. *Touches of Sweet Harmony.* San Marino, CA: The Huntington Library.

Hesse, Everett A., 1981a. "Sexual Problems in the Achilles Plays of Tirso and Calderón." *Kentucky Romance Quarterly* 28:2: 177–87.

———. 1981b. "Calderón's *El monstruo de los jardines:* Sex, Sexuality, and Sexual Fulfillment." *Revista Canadiense de Estudios Hispánicos* 5: 311–19.

Hesse, Everett A., and William C. McCrary. 1956 "The Mars-Venus Struggle in Tirso's *El aquiles.*" *Bulletin of Hispanic Studies* 33: 138–51.

Hicks, Margaret Ruth. 1989. "Lope's Other *dama boba:* The Strategy of Incompetence," in *The Perception of Women in Spanish Theater of the Golden Age,* 135–56. Edited by Anita K. Stoll and Dawn L. Smith. Lewisburg, PA.: Bucknell University Press.

Horapollo. 1993. *The Hieroglyphics of Horapollo.* Translated by George Boas. Princeton: Princeton University Press.

Hormigón, Juan Antonio. 1988. "Los mitos en el espejo cóncavo: transgresiones de la norma en el personaje del Rey," in *El mito en el teatro clásico español,* 158–181. Edited by Francisco Ruiz Ramón and César Oliva. Madrid: Taurus.

Horowitz, Maryanne Cline. 1991. "Playing with Gender." "Introduction" to *Playing with Gender: A Renaissance Pursuit,* ix–xxiv. Edited by Jean R. Brink, Maryanne C. Horowitz, and Allison P. Coudert. Urbana and Chicago: University of Illinois Press.

Howard, Jean E. 1993. "Cross-dressing, Theater, and Gender Struggle in Early Modern England," in *Crossing the Stage.* Edited by Lesley Ferris. London and New York: Routledge.

Infantes, Víctor. 1981. "Calderón y la literatura jeroglífica." In *Calderón: Actas del Congreso Internacional sobre Calderón y el Teatro Español del Siglo de Oro.* Edited by Luciano García Lorenzo, 3: 1593–602.

Irwin, John T. 1994. *The Mystery to a Solution. Poe, Borges, and the Analytic Detective Story.* Baltimore: Johns Hopkins University Press.

James, E. O. 1935. "The Sources of Christian Ritual and its Relation to the Culture Pattern of the Ancient East," in *The Labyrinth. Further Studies in the Relation between Myth and Ritual in the Ancient World,* 235–60. Edited by S. H. Hooke. London: Society for Promoting Christian Knowledge.

Johnson, Carroll B. 1967. "*A propos* of Lope de Rueda's *Las aceitunas.*" *Bulletin of the Comediantes* 19: 7–9.

Jung, Carl G. 1959. *Aion: Researches into the Phenomenology of the Self.* Translated by R. F. C. Hull. Princeton: Princeton University Press.

———. 1989. *Seven Sermons to the Dead.* Translated by Stephan A. Hoeller. In Stephan A. Hoeller, *The Gnostic Jung and the Seven Sermons to the Dead.* London: The Teosophical Publishing House.

Kennedy, Ruth Lee. 1974. *Studies in Tirso, I.* Chapel Hill: North Carolina University Press.

———. 1981. "La perspectiva política de Tirso en *Privar contra su gusto,* de 1621, y la de sus comedias políticas posteriores," in *Homenaje a Tirso,* 199–238. Madrid: *Revista Estudios.*

Kerényi, C. 1974. *The Heroes of the Greeks.* London: Thames and Hudson.

King, Katherine Callen. 1987. *Achilles: Paradigms of the War Hero from Homer to the Middle Ages.* Berkeley: University of California Press.

Kirk, G. S., J. E. Raven, and M. Shofield. 1983. *The Presocratic Philosophers.* Cambridge: Cambridge University Press.

Klibansky, Raymond, Erwin Panofsky, and Fritz Saxl. 1964. *Saturn and Melancholy. Studies in the History of Natural Philosophy, Religion and Art.* 1979; reprint. Liechtenstein: Thomas Nelson and Sons.

Kromayor, Astrid. 1987. "Tirso de Molina's *El Aquiles* and Monroy Y Silva's *El caballero dama: A Comparison.*" In *Tirso de Molina: Vida y Obra,* 167–74. Edited by Josep M. Solà-Solé and Luis Vásquez Fernández. Madrid: *Revista Estudios.*

Kurtz, Barbara E. 1988. "'No Word Without Mystery': Allegories of Sacred Truth in the *Autos Sacramentales* of Pedro Calderón de la Barca." *PMLA* 103: 262.

———. 1991. *The Play of Allegory in the Autos Sacramentales of Pedro Calderón de la Barca.* Washington, DC: Catholic University of America.

Lacan, Jacques. 1966. *Ecrits: A Selection.* Translated by Alan Sheridan. New York: W. W. Norton.

———. 1973. *Le seminaire de Jacques Lacan, Livre XI: Les quatre concepts fondamentaux de la pschanalyse.* Texte établi par Jacques-Alain Miller. Paris: Seuil. Translated by Alan Sheridan as *The Four Fundamental Concepts of Psychoanalysis.* New York: W. W. Norton, 1981.

Laroque, François. 1991. *The Age of Shakespeare.* New York: H. N. Abrams.

Larson, Catherine. 1986. "Labels and Lies: Names and Don García's World in *La verdad sospechosa.*" *Revista de estudios hispánicos* 20.2: 95–112.

Lasagabáster, Jesús M. 1988. "La recepción del mito: ¿desmitificación o transmitificación?" In *El mito en el teatro clásico español,* 223–34. Edited by Francisco Ruiz Ramón and César Oliva. Madrid: Taurus.

Leach, Maria and Jerome Fried. 1972. *Standard Dictionary of Folklore, Mythology and Legend.* New York: Funk and Wagnalls.

Leeming, David Adams. 1990. *The World of Myth*. New York: Oxford University Press.

León, Pedro. 1981. "Sobre el manuscrito autógrafo de *El divino Orfeo* de Calderon." *Revista Canadiense de Estudios Hispánicos* 5: 321–37.

———. 1982. "Orpheus and the Devil in Calderón's *El divino Orfeo* c. 1634." Edited by John Warden. *Orpheus: The Metamorphosis of a Myth*, 183–206. Toronto: University of Toronto.

———. 1983. "*El divino Orfeo* ca. 1634: Paradoja teológico-poética." *Calderón: Actas del Congreso internacional sobre Calderón y el teatro español del Siglo de Oro*, 687–99. Edited by Luciano García Lorenzo. Madrid: CSIC.

———. 1985. "Un manuscrito de la loa para *El divino Orfeo*, 1663, de Calderón." *Revista Canadiense de Estudios Hispánicos* 9: 228–50.

López Torrijos, Rosa. 1985. *La mitología en la pintura española del Siglo de Oro*. Madrid: Cátedra.

Lubac, Henri de. 1958. *Exégèse médiévale: Les quatre sens del'écriture*, 4 vols. Lyon: Aubier.

Lundelius, Ruth. 1975. "Tirso's View of Women in *El burlador de Sevilla*." *Bulletin of the Comediantes* 21:5–13.

MacCurdy, Raymond R. 1959. "The Bathing Nude in Golden Age Drama." *Romance Notes* 1.1: 36–39.

———. 1982. "The Bathing Nude Revisited in Golden Age Poetry." *Res Publica Litterarum* 5.2: 159–67.

Madrigal, José A. 1983. "La transmutación de Aquiles: De salvaje a héroe (Tirso de Molina, *El aquiles*)." *Hispanófila* 77: 15–26.

———. 1988. "*La verdad sospechosa* y su falsa soteriología." *Círculo* 17: 129–32.

Maharishi Mahesh Yogi. 1966. *The Science of Being and Art of Living*. Fairfield, IA: Maharishi University Press.

———. 1969. *Maharishi Mahesh Yogi on the Bhagavad-Gita. A New Translation and Commentary, Chapters 1–6*. Baltimore: Penguin Books.

———. 1986. *Life Supported by Natural Law*. Washington, DC: Age of Enlightenment Press.

———. 1994. *Vedic Knowledge for Everyone. Maharishi Vedic University, Introduction*. Holland: Maharishi Vedic University Press.

Mariana, Juan de. 1601. *Historia general de España*. Reedited by Cayetano Rosell, 1923 en *BAE* 31, Madrid: Real Academia.

Mariscal, George. 1990. "Symbolic Capital in the Spanish Comedia." *Renaissance Drama* 21: 143–69.

Matthews, W. H. 1970. *Mazes and Labyrinths. Their History and Development*. New York: Dover Publications.

Maurin, Margaret S. 1967. "The Monster, the Sepulcher and the Dark: Related Patterns of Imagery in *La vida es sueño*." *Hispanic Review* 35: 161–70.

Mayberry, Nancy K. 1982. "Blas Fernández de Mesa: Author of *El Milagro por los celos*" *Journal of Hispanic Philology* 7: 33–46.

———. 1984. "The Relationship between Tirso's *Doña Beatriz de Silva* and *El milagro por los celos*", *La Chispa, '82: Selected Proceedings of the Third Louisiana Conference on Hispanic Languages and Literatures, 1982*, 191–200. Edited by Harry Kirby, Baton Rouge: Louisiana State University Press.

————. 1986. "The Fallen-Favorite Theme in the *Refundición* of *El milagro por los celos*", in *Studies in Honor of William C. McCrary*, 157–64. Edited by Robert Fiore et al. Lincoln, Nebraska: Society of Spanish and Spanish American Studies.

————. 1993. "Two Unpublished Ballads on Don Alvaro de Luna" *La Chispa, 93: Selected Proceedings*, 141–57. Edited by Gilbert Paolini. New Orleans: Tulane University Press.

McElderry Jr., B. R. 1957. "Santayana and Eliot's 'Objective Correlative.'" *Boston University Studies in English* 3: 179–81.

McKendrick, Melveena. 1989. *Theatre in Spain: 1490–1700*. Cambridge: Cambridge University Press.

Miller, J. Hillis. 1992. *Ariadne's Thread. Story Lines*. New Haven: Yale University Press.

Miras, Domingo. 1988. "El mito agrario y la génesis del teatro," in *El mito en el teatro clásico español*. Edited by Francisco Ruiz Ramón and César Oliva. Madrid: Taurus.

Molina, Tirso de. See Tellez, Gabriel.

Monroy y Silva, Cristóbal. *El caballero dama*. Philadelphia: University of Pennsylvania Microfilm.

————. *Héctor y Aquiles*. Philadelphia: University of Pennsylvania Microfilm.

Moore, A. W. 1991. *The Infinite*. London: Routledge.

Moreto, Agustín. 1950. *No puede ser* in *Comedias escogidas de D. Agustín Moreto y Cabaña*. Edited by Luis Fernández-Guerra y Orbe, in *BAE* 39, Madrid: Atlas.

————. 1971. *El desdén con el desdén*. Edited by Francisco Rico. Madrid: Castalia; 2d ed.

Morford, Mark P. O. and Robert J. Lenardon. 1977. *Classical Mythology*. 2d. ed. New York: McKay.

Morón Arroyo, Ciriaco. 1982. *Calderón: Pensamiento y Teatro*. Santander: Sociedad Menéndez Pelayo.

Morreale, Margherita. 1983. "Apuntaciones para el estudio del tema de la serrana en dos comedias de Vélez de Guevara." In *Antigüedad y actualidad de Luis Vélez de Guevara: Estudios críticos*, 104–10. Edited by C. George Peale. Amsterdam: John Benjamins.

Muñoz Peña, Pedro. 1889. *El teatro del maestro Tirso de Molina*. Valladolid: Hijos de Rodríguez.

Murray, Alexander S. 1993. *The Manual of Mythology*. North Hollywood, CA: Newcastle Publishing.

Nadeau, Carolyn A. "Sweetmeats and Preserves: Food Imagery in Lope de Rueda's *Pasos*." In *1995 Symposium on Golden Age Theater* (forthcoming).

Neumeister, Sebastian. 1978. *Mythos und Repräsentation. Die mythologischen Fetspiele Calderón*. Munich: Wilhelm Fink Verlag.

Nichols, Sallie. 1980. *Jung and Tarot: An Archetypal Journey*. New York: Samuel Weiser.

O'Connor, Edward. 1958. *The Dogma of the Immaculate Conception*. South Bend, IN: University of Notre Dame.

O'Connor, Thomas A. 1983. "Sexual Aberration and Comedy in Monroy Y Silva's *El caballero dama*." *Hispanófila* 80: 17–39.

————. 1988. *Myth and Mythology in the Theater of Pedro Calderón de la Barca*. San Antonio, Tex.: Trinity University Press.

————. 1989. "The Harmony/Dissonance of Calderón's *El monstruo de los jardines*." *Texto y espectáculo*: Selected Proceedings of the Symposium on Spanish Golden Age Theater (March 11, 12, 13, 1987). Edited by Barbara Mujica. Lanham, MD: University Press of America.

————. 1991. "The Politics of Rape and *Fineza* in Calderonian Myth Plays." *The Perception of Women in Spanish Theater of the Golden Age*. Edited by Anita K. Stoll and Dawn L. Smith. Lewisburg, PA: Bucknell University Press.

Omaechevarría, Ignacio. 1976. *Origines de La Concepción de Toledo. Documentos primitivos sobre Santa Beatriz de Silva y la orden de la Inmaculada*. Burgos: Aldecoa.

Ovid. 1946. *Metamorphoses*. Translated by Frank Justus Miller. 2 vol. Cambridge: Harvard University Press.

————. 1955. *The Metamorphoses of Ovid*. Translated by Mary M. Innes, Baltimore: Penguin Books.

————. 1965. *Tristia*. In *Tristia & Ex Ponto*, 2–261. Translated by Arthur Leslie Wheeler. Cambridge: Harvard University Press.

————. 1986. *The Metamorphoses*. Translated by A. D. Melville. Oxford and New York: Oxford University Press.

Papus. 1991. *La Ciencia de los Números*. Barcelona: Editorial Humanitas.

Parker Alexander A. 1958. *The Theology of the Devil in the Drama of Calderón*. Aquinas Paper. No. 32. London: The Aquinas Society.

————. 1968. *The Allegorical Drama of Calderón*. Oxford: Dolphin.

————. 1979. "*El monstruo de los jardines* y el concepto calderoniano del destino," in *Hacia Calderón, Cuarto coloquio Anglogermano*, 92–101. Edited by H. Flasche, K-H Korner, and H. Mattauch. Berlin-New York: Walter de Gruyter.

————. 1982a. Review of Gwynne Edwards. *The Prison and the Labyrinth. Studies in Calderonian Tragedy*. In *Bulletin of Hispanic Studies* 59: 340–43.

————. 1982b. "Segismundo's Tower: A Calderonian Myth." *Bulletin of Hispanic Studies* 59: 247–56.

————. 1988. *The Mind and Art of Calderón. Essays on the Comedias*. Edited by Deborah Kong. Cambridge: Cambridge University Press.

Pasto, David. 1988. "The Independent Heroines in Ruiz de Alarcón's Major Comedias." *Bulletin of the Comediantes* 40.2: 227–35.

Paterson, Alan K. 1984. "Reversal and Multiple Role-Playing in Alarcón's *La verdad sospechosa*." *Bulletin of Hispanic Studies* 61: 361–68.

Pérez, Louis C. 1974. "La fábula de Ícaro y *El perro del hortelano*," in *Estudios literarios de hispanistas norteamericanos dedicados a Helmut Hatzfeld con motivo de su 80 aniversario*, 287–96. Compiled and edited by Josep M. Sola-Solé, Alessandro Crisafulli, and Bruno Damiani. Madrid: Ediciones Hispam.

————. 1981. "Con relación a los naipes en el teatro del XVII." *Bulletin of the Comediantes*. 33:2 (Fall): 139–47.

Pérez de Moya, Juan. 1585. *Philosofia Secreta. Donde debaxo de historias fabulosas, se contiene mucha doctrina, prouechosa a todos estudios. Con el origen de los idolos, o dioses de la gentilidad. Es materia muy necesaria para entender poetas, e historiadores*. Madrid: Francisco Sánchez Impressor.

————. 1588. *Philosophia secreta*. 2 vols. 1928 reprint. Madrid: Compañía Iberoamericano Publicaciones.

Pigman, G. W. III. 1980. "Versions of Imitation in the Renaissance." *Renaissance Quarterly* 33: 1–32.

Pineda, Juan de. 1964. *Diálogos familiares de la agricultura cristiana*. Edited by Juan Meseguer Fernández. 5 vols. *Biblioteca de Autores Españoles*, vols. 161, 162, 163, 169, 170. Madrid: Ediciones Atlas.

Poesse, Walter. 1939. *Juan de Ruiz de Alarcón*. Mexico: El libro español.

Pollin, Alice M. 1972. "'Cithara Iesu': La apoteosis de la música en *El divino Orfeo* de Calderón." Edited by Rizel Pincus Sigele and Gonzalo Sobejano. *Homenaje a Casalduero: Crítica y poesía ofrecido por sus amigos y discípulos*. Madrid: Gredos.

Poundstone, William. 1990. *Labyrinths of Reason. Paradox, Puzzles, and the Frailty of Knowledge*. New York: Doubleday.

Praz, Mario. 1964. *Studies in 17th Century Imagery*. Roma: Edizioni Di Storia e Letteratura.

Puhvel, Jaan. 1988. *Comparative Mythology*. Baltimore: The Johns Hopkins University Press.

Ribbans, Geoffrey. 1973. "Living in the Structure of *La verdad sospechosa*," in *Studies in Spanish Literature of the Golden Age Presented to Edward M. Wilson*, 193–216. Edited by R. C. Jones. London: Tamesis Books.

Rice, Philip Blair. 1991. "The Philosopher as Poet and Critic" in *The Philosophy of George Santayana*, 265–91. Edited by Paul Arthur Schilpp. La Salle, IL: Open Court; 2d ed.

Rico, Francisco. 1970. *El pequeño mundo del hombre*. Madrid: Castalia.

Rivers, Elias L. 1980. "The Shame of Writing in *La Estrella de Sevilla*." *Folio* 12: 105–17.

Rodríguez, Evangelina and Antonio Tordera. 1988. "Oficio y mito del personaje en el Siglo de Oro," in *El mito en el teatro clásico español*, 26–54. Edited by Francisco Ruiz Ramón and César Oliva. Madrid: Taurus.

Rodríguez del Padrón, Juan. 1986. *Siervo libre de amor*. Edited by Antonio Prieto. Madrid: Castalia.

Rodríguez Sánchez de León, María José. 1990. "La Academia Literaria como fiesta barroca en tres ejemplos andaluces (1661, 1664 y 1672)" 2, 915–26 in *La edición de textos: Actas del primer congreso internacional de Hispanistas del Siglo de Oro*. Edited by Pablo Jaural, Dolores Noguera y Alfonso Rey. London: Tamesis.

Rowan, Mary M. 1993. "Pallas Athena, Warrior and Worker: Sign of Action and Repose in *Essais* I:38–42," in *Montaigne and the Gods. The Mythological Key to the Essays*, 214–28. Edited by Daniel Martin. Amherst, MA: Hestia Press.

Rueda, Lope de. 1988. *The Interludes*. Edited and translated by Randall W. Listerman. Ottawa: Dovehouse Editions.

———. 1992. *Pasos*. Edited by José Luis Canet Vallés. Madrid: Castalia.

———. 1992. *Pasos*. Edited by Fernando González Ollé and Vicente Tusón. Madrid: Cátedra.

Ruiz Ramón, Francisco, and César Oliva. 1988. *El mito en el teatro clásico español*. Madrid: Taurus.

San Antonio, Sor Catalina de. 1661. *La Margarita escondida*. Reprinted 1903. Madrid: las Madres Concepcionistas.

Santayana, George. 1900. *Interpretation of Poetry and Religion*. New York: Charles Scribner's Sons.

Schevill, Rudolph. 1913. *Ovid and the Renascence in Spain*. University of California

Publications in Modern Philology 4.1. Berkeley and Los Angeles: University of California Press.

Schopenhauer, Arthur. 1969. *The World as Will and Representation. Volumes I and II.* Translated by E. F. J. Payne. New York: Dover.

Schneider, Marius. 1946. *El origen musical de los animales-símbolos en la mitología y la escultura antiguas.* Barcelona: S.N.

Sebastián, Santiago. 1993. "El comentario de Alciato," in Alciato *Emblemas.* Edited by Santiago Sebastián. Madrid: Ediciones Akal.

Silverman, Joseph. 1951. "Oí . . . astrología." *Nueva revista de filología hispánica* 5.4: 417–18.

Simon, Sylvie. 1986. *The Tarot: Art, Mysticism, Divination.* Rochester, VT: Inner Traditions International.

Singer, Armand E. 1981. "Don Juan's Women in *El burlador de Sevilla.*" *Bulletin of the Comediantes* 33: 67–71.

Singleton, Charles. 1954. *Journey to Beatrice.* Baltimore: Johns Hopkins University Press.

Sirera, Josep Lluís. 1991. "Los santos en sus comedias: hacia una tipología de los protagonistas del teatro hagiográfico", 55–75 in *Comedias y Comediantes: Estudios sobre el teatro clásico español.* Edited by Manuel V. Diago y Teresa Ferrer. Valencia: Universitat de València.

Smith, William. 1977. *Smith's Bible Dictionary.* New York: Jove Publications.

———. 1958. *Smaller Classical Dictionary.* Edited by E. H. Blakeny and John Warrington. New York: E.P. Dutton.

Soufas, C. Christopher Jr. 1985. "Thinking in *La vida es sueño.*" *PMLA* 100: 287–99.

Statius. 1928. *Achilleid.* Translated by J. H. Mozley. New York: G. P. Putnam's Sons.

Stoll, Anita K. "Cross-dressing in the Theater of Tirso de Molina." In *Identity, Gender and Representation in the Comedia* (forthcoming).

Stroud, Matthew D. 1983. "The Resocialization of the *Mujer Varonil* in Three Plays by Vélez." In *Antigüedad y actualidad de Luis Vélez de Guevara: Estudios críticos,* 111–26. Edited by C. George Peale. Amsterdam: John Benjamins Publishing Company.

Sullivan, Henry W. 1990. "Lacan and Calderón: Spanish Classical Drama in the Light of Psychoanalytical Theory." *Gestos* 5. 10: 39–55.

———. 1994. "Law, Desire, and the Double Plot: Toward a Psychoanalytic Poetics of the *Comedia,*" in *The Golden Age Comedia: Text, Theory and Perfomance,* 222–35. Edited by Charles Ganelin and Howard Mancing. West Lafayette, IN: Purdue University Press.

Sumner, Gordon H. 1979. *Una bibliografía anotada de las comedias de santos del siglo diez y siete.* Dissertation, Florida State University. Ann Arbor: UMI [800117].

Téllez, Gabriel. 1635 *Doña Beatriz de Silva.* Rpt. 1962 in *Obras dramáticas completas de Tirso de Molina* II, 853–910. Edited by Blanca de los Ríos. Madrid: Aguilar.

———. 1946. *Obras dramáticas completas* vols. 1 & 2. edited by Doña Blanca de los Ríos. Madrid: Aguilar.

———. 1959. *Privar contra su gusto.* In *Obras dramáticas completas,* Vol. 3, 1069–116. Edited by Blanca de los Ríos. Madrid: Aguilar.

————. 1971. *Privar contra su gusto*. Edited by Battista J. Galassi. Madrid: Plaza Mayor.

————. 1990. *El burlador de Sevilla*. Edited by Alfredo Rodríguez López-Vázquez. Madrid: Cátedra.

The Penguin Dictionary of Classical Mythology. 1990. Edited by Pierre Grimal. London: Penguin Books.

Valbuena Prat, Angel. 1968. *Historia de la literatura española*. Barcelona: Gustavo Gili. 4 vols.

Veeser, Harold. 1986. "'That Dangerous Supplement': *La verdad sospechosa* and the Literary Speech Situation," in *Things Done With Words. Speech Acts in Hispanic Drama. Proceedings of the 1984 Stony Brook Seminar*, 51–71. Edited by Elias L. Rivers. Newark, DE: Juan de la Cuesta.

Velázquez de la Cadena, Mariano, Edward Gray, and Juan L. Ribas. 1960. *New Revised Velázquez Spanish and English Dictionary*. Chicago: Follett.

Vega Carpio, Lope de. *El milagro por los celos*, Seventeenth century manuscript attributed to Lope de Vega. Number 16435 in the Biblioteca Nacional.

————. 1733 Madrid and 1770 Barcelona. *El milagro por los celos y D. Alvaro de Luna*, edición suelta. Reedited by Menéndez y Pelayo in *Obras de Lope de Vega publicadas por la Real Academia*, Madrid, 1899, X, 189–212. Rept. 1968. 329–71 in *Obras de Lope de Vega XXII* in *BAE* 213 Madrid: Atlas with the title *El milagro de* [sic] *los celos y Don Alvaro de Luna*.

————. 1856. *El Laurel de Apolo* in *Colección de obras no dramáticas de Frey Lope Felix de Vega Carpio*. Edited by Cayetano Rosell, in *BAE* 38, rept. 1950, Madrid: Atlas.

————. 1916. *Santa Casilda*. Edited by E. Cotarelo y Mori in *Obras de Lope de Vega* (Nueva edición), Tomo II. Madrid: Real Academia Española.

————. 1935. *Barlán y Josafá*. Edited by José F. Montesinos in *Teatro antiguo español*, VIII. Madrid: Centro de estudios históricos.

————. 1957. *El cardenal de Belén*. Edited by Elisa Aragone Terni. Zaragoza: Biblioteca Clásica Ebro.

————. 1966. *El castigo sin venganza*. Edited by Alfredo Rodríguez. Zaragoza: Editorial Ebro.

————. 1970. *El perro del hortelano*. Edited with introduction and notes by A. David Kossof. Madrid: Editorial Castalia, S. A.

————. 1988. *San Diego de Alcalá*. Edited by Thomas Case. Kassel: Edition Reichenberger.

————. 1990. *El perro del hortelano*. Translated as *The Dog in the Manger* by Victor Dixon. Ottawa: Dovehouse Editions Canada.

Vélez de Guevara, Luis. 1916. *La Serrana de la Vera*. (*Teatro antiguo español*, vol. I). Edited by R. Menéndez Pidal and M. Goyri. Madrid: Centro Est. His.

————. 1967. *La serrana de la Vera*. Edited by Enrique Rodríguez Cepeda. Madrid: Ediciones Alcalá.

Virgil. 1978. *Eclogues. Georgics. Aeneid. The Minor Poems*. Edited and translated by H. R. Fairclough. Cambridge: Harvard University Press. 2 vols.

Vitoria, Fray Baltasar de. 1702, 1738. *Theatro de los Dioses de la Gentilidad*. Primera Parte. Barcelona: Imprenta de Juan Pablo Marti, por Francisco Barnola Impressor. 1702. Segunda Parte. Madrid: Juan de Ariztia, 1738.

————. 1722. *Segunda parte del teatro de los dioses de la gentilidad*. Barcelona: Juan Piferrer.

Vivas, Eliseo. 1944. "The Objective Correlative of T. S. Eliot," *The American Bookman.* 1: 7–18.

Voros, Sharon Dahlgreen. 1988. "La semiótica de los gemelos en Calderón: *Mujer, llora y vencerás." Dispositio* 13: 33–35.

Wade, Gerald E. 1970. "Tirso's *Privar contra su gusto." Kentucky Romance Quarterly* 17: 93–107.

Waite, Edward Arthur. 1991. *The Pictorial Key to the Tarot.* York Beach, ME: Samuel Weiser Inc.

Walker, D. P. 1953. "Orpheus the Theologian and Renaissance Platonists." *Journal of the Warburg and Courtauld Institutes* 16: 100–120.

———. 1954. "The *Prisca Theologia* in France." *Journal of the Warburg and Courtauld Institutes* 17: 204–59.

Wardropper, Bruce W. 1967. "Comic Illusion: Lope de Vega's *El perro del hortelano." Kentucky Romance Quarterly* 14: 101–11.

Watterson, Barbara. 1984. *The Gods of Ancient Egypt.* Bicester, U.K.: Facts on File Publications.

Webster's New World Dictionary of the American Language. Second College Edition. 1980. David B Guralnik, Editor in Chief. New York: Simon and Schuster.

Weiner, Jack. 1984. "La reina Ester en el teatro del Siglo de Oro español; dos puntos de vista," 1–38 in *En busca de la justicia social: Estudio sobre el teatro español del siglo de oro.* Potomac, MD: Scripta Humanistica.

Welles, Marcia L. 1986. *Arachne's Tapestry: The Transformation of Myth in Seventeenth-Century Spain.* San Antonio, TX: Trinity University Press.

Wilson, E. M. 1936. "The Four Elements in the Imagery of Calderón." *Modern Language Review* 31: 34–47.

Wilson, William E. 1943. "Tirso's *Privar contra su gusto:* A Defense of the Duke of Osuna." *Modern Language Quarterly* 43: 161–66.

Wittkower, Rudolf. 1977. "Transformations of Minerva in Renaissance Imagery," in *Allegory and the Migration of Symbols,* 129–42. London: Thames and Hudson.

Woods, M. J. 1978. *The Poet and the Natural World in the Age of Góngora.* Oxford: Oxford University Press.

Yates, Frances. 1975. *Astraea: The Imperial Theme in the Sixteenth Century.* London: Routledge and Kegan Paul.

———. 1979. *The Occult Philosophy in the Elizabethan Age.* London, Boston and Henley: Routledge and Kegan Paul.

Zabaleta, Juan de. 1972. *Errores celebrados.* Edited by David Hershberg. Madrid: Espasa-Calpe.

Index